Indo-Pak Conflict
Threat to South Asian Security

Indo-Pak Conflict
Threat to South Asian Security

Ajoy Ghosh

Reference Press

4831/24, Ansari Road
Darya Ganj
New Delhi-110 002
Phone: 3260807
Fax: 3274173
E-mail: essess@del3.vsnl.net.in

First Published 2003

ISBN: 81-88583-06-5

Price: Rs.725/-

Published by:
Reference Press
4831/24, Ansari Road,
Darya Ganj,
New Delhi-110 002.
Phone: 3260807
Fax: 3274173
E-mail: essess@del3.vsnl.net.in

Printed in India by:
Mehra Offset Press

CONTENTS

Preface

India and Pakistan are two nations that have experienced war with each other—in 1947 over Kashmir, the Punjab area in 1965, and the Multan-Sind-Kutch region in 1971. With an ever increasing spread of weapons of mass destruction (WMD), the South Asian region does not escape this trend. The increase of nuclear proliferation is evident in the nuclear programs of both India and Pakistan. Both countries are known to be accumulating relatively large stockpiles of nuclear explosive materials-plutonium and highly enriched uranium. Such programs have furthered fears by the West of an escalation of nuclear weapons to counter and maintain a semblance of balance within South Asia.

Both India and Pakistan continue to be plagued by an array of political crises and internal security problems, some explosive proportions, as in the case of the conflicts in Kashmir and Indian Punjab. Both are facing economic crisis, aggravated by the effects of the September 11 attack and US-Afghan war. Each is afflicted by government and or regime instability, internal political violence, and secessionist movements. The internal politics of each nation-state reflects the external political policy that each nation-state pursues. The economic conditions that each nation endures is a factor that comes into the analysis if a conflict arises. A state's willingness to maintain its interests by extending a conflict to the point of war may be hampered by economic difficulties. For India and Pakistan, the future of economic development will be a decisive factor to policy determination in a case of conflict. The consolidation of the state through territorial integration and the establishment of effective political institutions were perceived by the leaders as preconditions for steady economic growth.

This book will address and outline the following issues India and Pakistan face that have increased the tension and proliferation of nuclear weapons on the South Asian continent: territory, religious diversity, economic conditions, Indian leadership, Pakistani leadership, and the nuclear issue.

1

Introduction

India and Pakistan are two nations that have experienced war with each other—in 1947 over Kashmir, the Punjab area in 1965, and the Multan-Sind-Kutch region in 1971. With an ever increasing spread of weapons of mass destruction (WMD), the South Asian region does not escape this trend. The increase of nuclear proliferation is evident in the nuclear programs of both India and Pakistan. "Both countries are known to be accumulating relatively large stockpiles of nuclear explosive materials-plutonium and highly enriched uranium (uranium concentrated to over 20 percent uranium 235". Such programs have furthered fears by the West of an escalation of nuclear weapons to counter and maintain a semblance of balance within South Asia. Dramatic as the external changes are, they have done nothing to reduce the rivalry between India and Pakistan. Those countries are no less adversaries today than before. If anything, the events of the last decade deepened their hostility. Each alleges it has been the victim of "low- intensity war" and "subversion" by the other.

Both continue to be plagued by an array of political crises and internal security problems, some explosive proportions, as in the case of the conflicts in Kashmir and Indian Punjab. Both are facing economic crisis, aggravated in both India and Pakistan by the effects of the Iran-Iraq and Gulf wars, and in Pakistan also by the loss of foreign aid. Each is afflicted by government and or regime instability, internal political violence, and secessionist movements. The internal politics of each nation-state reflects the external political policy that each nation-state pursues. This book will address and outline the following issues India and Pakistan face that have increased the tension and proliferation of nuclear weapons on the South Asian continent: territory, religious diversity, economic conditions, Indian leadership, Pakistani leadership, and the nuclear issue.

The issue of territory is one factor that has lead to conflict between India and Pakistan. The region of Kashmir has brought heated tension to both nations that has resulted in war. In Dr. S.P. Shulka's book, India and Pakistan: The Origins of Armed Conflict, it cites Michael Breecher's book The Struggle for Kashmir, that "between 1947 and 1955, there were several ups and downs marked by many events. The problem of Kashmir arose because Maharaja Hari Singh was unable to make up his mind to which Dominion the State of Kashmir should accede to or whether to accede at all". "If Partition itself has been the subject of much anguished and rhetorical writings, so too has been the drama of the Kashmiri Maharaja's indecision about whether to join the Dominion of India, become an independent Kashmiri state, or become part of Muslim Pakistan".

The indecision by the Maharaja furthered the interest of territorial gains by both nations. To establish control over the Kashmir would bring territorial power to either state in the region. The religious demography also had an influence to the natural alliance of one of the states. "At the time of partition the State of Jammu and Kashmir, popularly called simply Kashmir, had an overall Muslim majority of 78 percent. In the most desirable part, the Vale of Kashmir, the Muslims numbered 93 per cent".

Yet the exclusive majority of Muslims did not change the outcome of events in Kashmir. "Having a Hindu leader over a Muslim majority state, Pakistan's claim to the kingdom seemed to be justified on the basis of the two-nation theory. Moreover Kashmir's proximity to Pakistan also favored the Ratcliffe principle of grouping together contiguous Muslim majority areas. Following implicit Pakistani support for the tribal invasion into the valley to help their fellow Muslims, the Maharaja signed up to join India and received immediate military help. This led to outrage in Karachi and an immediate conflict between the two dominions".

With a Muslim religious majority and the geography of the Kashmir close to Pakistan, the natural assumption would be close ties Kashmir would have to Pakistan. But, the Indian position was quite different, "Indian spokesman single out two events as the "basic facts" in the Kashmir dispute and wish the rest of the world to infer from them that Pakistan has been the "aggressor" in Kashmir.

The first is the tribal invasion of Kashmir, which began on 22 October 1947, and the second is the intervention of the Pakistani army inside Kashmir in the week of May 1948". This correlation does not take into account that, "they completely ignore India's provocations that led to these developments and also that, first, the United Nations never pronounced Pakistan the aggressor and, second, these occurrences notwithstanding, India agreed in the United Nations that the people of Kashmir should decide their own future by plebiscite, thus making the holding of a plebiscite the central issue in the dispute". With such a plebiscite the Kashmiri would decide their political fate. Ultimately, both states, India and Pakistan desired the Kashmir is to improve their geographic and political standing. The settlement of the dispute was best left to the parties in the conflict. "The handling of the Kashmir issue by the international community goes a long way to explaining India's antipathy to the role of "external" mediation in regional affairs.

Following the United Nations fiasco, India was determined to solve the Kashmir crisis on the basis of bilateral relations with Pakistan". Kashmir is still the most puzzling subject, if only because the Indian polity shows no desire to devise any policy addressing the clear message from the Kashmir valley and from its four million Muslim Kashmiri inhabitants, a message of near total isolation from India. "Over the years Kashmir has become for all sections of national opinion in India, a test of Delhi's resolve to preserve India intact. After the 1947 Partition, Delhi hoped that the Muslim majority in Jammu and Kashmir would give the lie to Pakistan's religious foundation for nationhood. Kashmir would become living proof that secularism "worked." The disputed territory, which has caused two wars between India and Pakistan since 1947, entered a new phase after December 1989 with a situation of civil disobedience and wide popular support for various separatist groups". Religious and political sensibilities in the Kashmir lent to uncertainty as to the political extension, ie. territory, of India or Pakistan. Both states vied for the position of influence to the Kashmiri issue. In a pattern of asserting political interest, India and Pakistan judged the territory issue as the geopolitical relationship in the South Asian region. Whether it be hostile or peaceful intentions, the issue of Kashmir's self determination is of interest to India and Pakistan that may result in the escalation of tensions or compromise.

The Hindu view of the world as other worldly and "the religious teachings of Hinduism and its belief system deeply influence the social behavior and political attitudes of its followers". "Hindus have often been described as other-worldly and fatalistic because Hinduism teaches that an individual is bound in the cycle of birth and death. It is the karma (the action in one's life) that determines the nature of one's following life.". The dominance of religion in politics has generally been negative. The association of theocratic states such as Iran, perpetuates an uncertainty to political decisions based on religious dogma. This is not to say that India and Pakistan are theocratic in governing, but the distinction of religious demography plays an important role in understanding a potential conflict between both nations. And yet, as S.M. Burke points out in Pakistan's Foreign Policy, "as a result of the unbridgeable gulf between Hinduism and Islam, their followers existed together in the same land for hundreds of years like two streams, which continue to run parallel to each other indefinitely, without ever becoming one body of water". The following extended passage by S.M. Burke is worth quoting to illustrate this central theme:

Indeed, it is difficult to think of any two religions more anti-thetical to each other than Islam and Hinduism. Islam is the youngest of the universal religions. Its basic doctrine of belief is brief and explicit: belief in one all- powerful God, in Muhammad as his messenger, and in the Quran as the message. Hinduism, on the other hand, is an ancient religion and has no central dogma or agreed scripture: "Hinduism, as a faith, is vague, amorphous, many-sided, all things to all men". It is hardly possible to define it, or indeed to say definitely whether it is religion or not, in the usual sense of the word. Mahatma Gandi defined the Hindu creed simply as "search after the truth through non-violent means". Many Hindus, however do not consider non-violence as an essential part of Hinduism.

That of course is no definition at all. While belief in one supreme God is the central theme in Islam, the Hindu pantheon comprises some 330 million gods and Radhakrishnan explains that all the gods stand for some aspect of the Supreme. Hinduism is also heavily caste-ridden. For a person to belong to a caste in the Hindu society he must be born in it. Islam, too, sets up a strong barrier of its own. It divides all humanity into two watertight compartments, Muslims and non-Muslims. All the Muslims, according to the Quran, belong to one brotherhood. It follows, to use poet philosopher Muhammad Iqbal's words, that "there is only one millant [community] confronting the Muslim community, that of the non-Muslims taken collectively. Quaid-i-Azam Muhammad Ali Jinnah pointed out that Islam imposes a duty on its followers not to merge their identity and individuality in any alien society. In an attempt to build bridges to the Hindu community, "the four most august sages in Hinduism are the shankaracharya who head famous monasteries. Prime Minister, P.V. Narasimha Rao, has persuaded the four to preside over a new religious trust to build a temple to the warrior god Ram at Ayodhya, at the site of the disputed mosque that was demolished by Hindu fanatics in December 1992".

The economic conditions that each nation endures is a factor that comes into the analysis if a conflict arises. A state's willingness to maintain its interests by extending a conflict to the point of war may be hampered by economic difficulties. For India and Pakistan, the future of economic development will be a decisive factor to policy determinations in a case of conflict. The consolidation of the state through territorial integration and the establishment of effective political institutions were perceived by the leaders as preconditions for steady economic growth. India's leaders also realized that the country need industrial and agricultural revolutions if it was to enter the twentieth century. In particular, the key to the removal of the mass poverty existing in India was believed to be the application of science and technology to the utilization of the material and human resources of the country.

The process of development in the South Asian region has been gradually slow. "India's planned economic development as Asian region has been slow paced. "India's planned economic development has been directed toward

1) achieving a high economic growth rate,
2) building the country's industrial and technological self-reliance,
3) creating full employment, and
4) achieving social justice by removing the gross inequalities existing in society.

Yet the necessity for external support is evident in India's economy. The large population has affected the development process as well. Perhaps it is time to promote this notion again, this time more robustly. After all, a large share of India's external financing is provided by official creditors—the bilateral and multilateral aid donors. With the deepening external payment crisis, the importance of aid from the Paris Club grows accordingly. Even with the usual devices such as informal currency depreciation to keep exports competitive, India's chronic and structural imbalance in trade flows portends a constant need in the coming five years for external financing of the country's deficit. The case for Pakistan is not wholly different. Much of its external aid has been limited because of the perception of an increasing nuclear weapons program that would match that of India's. Then the United States abruptly cut off almost all aid to Pakistan.

The occasion was the annual presidential certification to Congress under the Presler amendment, due in October 1990. President George Bush was unable in this case to certify that Pakistan did not 'possess' a nuclear explosive device. An automatic aid suspension shut off all U.S. assistance not already in the pipeline. The cutoff preceded the election and installation of the new Pakistani government of Prime Minister Nawaz Sharif and thus deprived Sharif of the opportunity to try to head off the rapture.

The impact of economic improvement is relevant to the expenditure of military programs. For instance, the estimate of The World Bank in their World Development Report, 1989 cites the Gross Domestic Product (GDP) for India as 220,830 (million in US$) and for Pakistan 31,650 (million in US$). The added benefit of population and

GDP supports India's effort to increase military expenditures to counter the Pakistani military threat. This is not to say that these factors are exclusive in assuring success in an armed conflict, but a stronger economy lends to a solid base in military readiness on either side.

"One of the most important components of national security for the states in South Asia involves the need to create continued economic growth and industrial development. Each South Asian state in turn has attempted to carry through an industrial revolution to end poverty, create gainful employment, and to increase trade. The process of political and economic change collectively referred to as development--keeps the positions of elites within the state precariously balanced even as it legitimates their right to rule.

The perception that development would bring stability to a state may be realized through external assistance. Yet, it is not a guarantor of stability. Development strategies generate instability by either failing to meet popular expectations of material advancement, or by failing to distribute the benefits of development equally.

India has always afced a national security threat not only from Pakistan but China as well. China has become an important player in the South Asian struggle for power. In addressing these threats the former Prime Minister P.V. Narasimha Rao has assumed many leadership roles. According to the U.S. Central Intelligence Agency's publication from the Directorate of Intelligence, its Chiefs of State and Cabinet Members of Foreign Governments outlines the following positions filled by Rao: "Minister of Atomic Energy, Minister of Chemicals and Fertilizers, Minister of Defense, Minister of Industry Minister of Law, Justice and Company Affairs, Minister of Non-Conventional Energy Sources, Minister of Personnel, Public Grievances and Pensions, Minister of Rural Development, Minister of Science and Technology, and Minister of Space.

The numerous titles that Rao has indicates a 'hands-on' approach with detail to government structure and control. In key positions such as Minister of Defense, Minister of Atomic Energy, and Minister of Science and Technology it would seem that the leadership is invested in one individual and little else for external advice. This may fashion policy decisions on one focus rather from a diverse corps of advisors.

The political structure of India's government might be characterized by a strong cohesion. Along with political institutions and political parties, bureaucracy is an important element in that it helps ensure stability and administrative continuity. The bureaucracy of India consists of tenured civil servants who remain in their administrative posts even when their bosses lose their elective positions. The members of a bureaucracy are expected to make decisions on a rational rather than a political basis.

The government of India is a complex network of departments, bureaus, regulatory agencies, boards, and a host of commissions and autonomous organizations. Politicians head the departments; bureaucrats assist them in the administration of these departments. Key policy decisions are made by the members of the cabinet, which is also responsible for the coordination of the works of the various departments of the government. This structural order has brought a semblance of democratic stability to India. External threats have furthered the readiness by the Indian government to counter issues of security. The development of nuclear weapons establishes a base of regional security from the Indian point of view. Yet, if one takes the realist perspective of international relations, the state is in constant struggle for power with other states in an anarchic system. Criticism of the realist paradigm points out, "realism fails to conceptualize the ways in which internal politics shapes and directs the foreign policy agenda".

And Caroline Thomas notes that, "the state-centric geopolitical approach to international relations is inadequate for conceptualizing the third world security environment". To approach the international security issue in the third world, it must address a fundamental paradigm, the self-interest of the state. Indian military growth and developed nuclear capability provide the leadership ample political tools to address the threat to the Indian state. To provide for security, Indian leadership must believe in a self-preservation paradigm if it is to provide stability of the state from external factors that would ultimately affect the domestic politics of the state which critics of the realist paradigm believe is lacking in realist analysis.

The growing violence in Karachi is one example of an increasing proliferation of arms in Pakistan. As a result of arming the Mujahidin in Afghanistan, Pakistan faces an internal crises with leftover arms from the Afghani war. Thus, Pakistan's future domestic tranquility remains hostage in special ways to the continuation of the warfare in Afghanistan. As spillover within Pakistan, drug running, arms smuggling, and the predatory attacks of armed gangs in the big cities and, in Sind, along the north-south road axis of communications, are persisting manifestations of the intra-Afghanistan conflict.

War Clouds Over India-Pakistan

Nuclear testing and weapons in both Pakistan and India have escalated tensions between the countries. As soon as the borders were officially announced, over 10 million people decided to move to new homes. Hindus, Muslims, and Sikhs had to flee from their familiar homes to the countries they felt offered the best opportunity for them to practice their religion.

This mass exodus of people proved to be one of the bloodiest in history. About one million people were slaughtered as they tried to reach their new homes. Refugees were murdered, raped, and robbed. Sometimes, an entire train would arrive in a station with nothing but corpses on board. Hardest hit were the Sikhs. They had hoped to have a third country — a Sikh country — formed during partition. Instead, they found their homelands in Punjab divided by the newly drawn border. Today, some Sikhs still call for an independent country. They have proven their willingness to fight for it. In 1984, Prime Minister Indira Gandhi was assassinated by some of her own bodyguards, militant Sikhs, angry at her unwillingness to work for an independent Sikh country.

The Indian-Pakistan War of 1971 began when Pakistane forces struck an Indian Air Force base. India and Pakistan still have great difficulties. In 1971, India intervened in a dispute between East Pakistan and West Pakistan. As a result, East Pakistan became the independent nation of Bangladesh. Border disputes, especially in the Kashmir region, constantly threaten to erupt into new hostilities. In 1998, India tested its first nuclear bomb. Within weeks, Pakistan responded with a successful test of its own. The bitter divide between the two nations now has horrific stakes. Sixteenth century disputes between villages have evolved into a potential 21st-century nuclear holocaust – if cooler heads do not prevail.

The question of War Clouds is dominating the minds of everyone. At one level there are at least two wars already going on: the one being waged by the US-led international coalition against international terrorism and the core of that in the shape of Taliban regime and the Al Qaeda group of terrorists, and the other war being waged through terrorism by Pakistan against India for a decade and a half now.

The events of recent past and, with the attacks on Jammu & Kashmir (J&K) legislature on October I, 2001 and on the Parliament of India on December 13, 2001, the marked escalation in the nature of cross-border terrorism have raised serious concerns and interest in whether India and Pakistan would go to war again. Given the nature of adversarial relations between the two countries for more than five decades this does not come as something totally new except that there are new apprehensions since both countries possess nuclear weapons. This makes it necessary to look at the issues as objectively as possible and evaluate likely trends.

Pakistan has been insisting that Kashmir is the "core issue" and it remains the "unfinished agenda of partition" (of India in 1947). The argument is built up that the subcontinent was divided along communal lines into two independent sovereign states, and Pakistan was created out of what constituted the Muslim majority areas of India.

Jammu and Kashmir was a Muslim majority state. According to this logic, therefore, the state should have formed part of Pakistan. But, the argument continues that Indian perfidy resulted in forcible occupation of the state, and that India refused to honour the UN resolutions requiring a plebiscite to be held in the state.

On the face of it, the argument looks plausible enough, and leaves a large number of people across the world confused, and in Pakistan, angry. This is the basic rationalisation of Pakistan's claim to J&K and international support at the same time. But this also inevitably wards off any queries about the legitimacy of Pakistan's aggression and de facto annexation of nearly one-third of J&K. But this was not the only logic that dictated Pakistan's attempts to acquire Jammu & Kashmir immediately after partition of the subcontinent. The core rationale that keeps peeping out of the literature and articulation by responsible Pakistanis is that accession of Jammu & Kashmir to Pakistan was a critical need from the geo-economic strategic point of view.

This was perceived to be necessary because four out of the five rivers in West Pakistan, that is, the Indus, Jehlum, Chenab and Ravi, originate in the mountain reaches of Jammu & Kashmir, and, the fifth (the Satluj and Beas combined) flow through the state of Himachal Pradesh bordering Jammu & Kashmir on its southern flank. It needs to be, recalled that the primary economic activity in West Pakistan's in 1947 was agriculture and canal irrigation had brought prosperity to Punjab. And equally important, it created the landed gentry which formed the core of the feudal system in west Punjab. This elite, which also, provided most of the civil and military officer class of the newly created state of Pakistan, had a natural stake in what they believed to be the new vulnerability. At the same time it was clear Kashmir's economy was also dependent on Pakistan since the primary route of access into the valley now would be from the new country.

The importance of the geo-economic logic is perhaps best understood from the writing of the man who claims to have planned the invasion of Kashmir in 1947. Even 23 years after the event (and ten years after the Indus Waters Treaty assured water supply from the rivers of Punjab to Pakistani Major General Akbar Khan wrote: "From the economic point of view the position was equally clear. Our agricultural economy was dependent particularly upon rivers coming out of Kashmir. The Mangla Headworks were actually in Kashmir and the Marala Headworks were within a mile or so of tree border. What then would be our position if Kashmir was to be in Indian hands?"

Similarly the military-strategic logic of the new officer class was, also built upon the perceived, geo-strategic compulsions. Once again, the writing of Major General Akbar Khan, writing provide a clear indication: negotiate agreements with Pakistan or Hindustan as considerations of contiguity or their own self-interest may dictate, or they may choose to assume complete and separate sovereign status themselves. According to Mr. Jinnah the Indian States were sovereign states for every purpose except in so far as they had entered into treaties with the Crown. In a statement issued on June 18, 1947 he unequivocally declared that constitutionally and legally the States would be independent sovereign states on the termination of Paramountcy and they would be free to adopt any course they liked. behalf of the BJP in the foreign policy arena. Gujral told the media that he had told Talbott that U.S. policies had pushed the Indian people towards the "bomb direction" and that the U.S. administration should not pressure India into signing the CTBT.

Gujral is now in favour of India signing the CTBT but wants the Government to be given more time to build a consensus among the people. As External Affairs Minister and later as Prime Minister, Gujral was one of the most articulate opponents of the CTBT. The United Front government was opposed to the idea of signing the CTBT on the principled ground that the treaty did not address the question of elimination of nuclear weapons at the global level and that being a signatory to it would foreclose India's option of nuclear testing in the future.

The first point still remains valid. But Gujral and the BJP think that the strategic environment has changed radically since then. Senior Ministers and officials have in recent months suddenly made the discovery that the country is surrounded by hostile powers, with additional threats coming from Diego Garcia and Myanmar. The alleged threats from Pakistan and China were articulated more openly and strongly. Talbott tried to sell the CTBT idea to Sonia Gandhi. But although Sonia Gandhi has not been forthcoming about her views on the CTBT, some of her advisers such as Manmohan Singh, who are greatly concerned over·the economic impact of the sanctions, are said to be pragmatic" about signing the CTBT.

Interestingly, after the Sonia-Talbott meeting, a Congress (I) spokesman said that the national interest should dictate foreign policy; he, however, added that the CTBT should not be signed in its present form. India, he also said, should not sign the "discriminatory" treaty under U.S. pressure. Leader of the Opposition and former Defence Minister Sharad Pawar echoed this view. "There is a consensus within the country and within Parliament that India should not be a signatory to the CTBT because the treaty does not give equal terms to all," Pawar said.

India, he said, was committed to total nuclear disarmament Former Defence Minister and Samajwadi Party leader Mulayam Singh Yadav said that there was "no question of, signing the CTBT." Prakash Karat, Polit Bureau member of the CPI(M) told *Frontline* that there should be no question of India striking, a "deal" on the CTBT with the Clinton administration. "The only deal," he said, would be a surrender. India will not get anything substantial by signing the CTBT."

Maj. Gen. Dipankar Bannerjee of the Institute of Peace and Conflict Studies is of the view that the time for bargaining with Washington is over. The BJP-led Government is only posturing and it has no coherent policy to deal with the after-math of Pokhran, says Bannerjee. Many independent analysts feel that the BJP I's now paying the price for the "aggressive image of itself that it cultivated over the years.

It was evident that Talbott did nor come to Delhi with any "package". Instead, there are indications that Talbott's major goal is to make a "deal" with Pakistan. A bailout package from the International Monetary Fund-World Bank seems to be ready for Islamabad. In return, Pakistan is likely to sign the CTBT.

The powerful U.S, farm lobby has already wangled a concession from the Clinton administration to sell wheat to Pakistan. Given the precarious state of the country's economy the Pakistan. Government is getting ready to live a "ship to mouth" existence. (U.S. ships could be soon bringing food aid, a fate India faced in the 1960s during the PL480 days.) India will have no problems paying its debts but a sluggish growth rate as a result of the sanctions seems to be inevitable.

The security scenario for India has worsened in the last three months. China, according to Bannerjee, has again got its missiles arrayed after the worsening of relations. China has a deployed weapons capability that will be difficult for India to match. The next round of the meeting of the Joint Working Group JWG) of the two countries stands postponed indefinitely.

The Clinton administration, meanwhile, continues to insist that India sign the CTBT. When Talbott was still in Delhi, State Department spokesman James Rubin reiterated that India and Pakistan should sign the CTBT "one way or the other".

The hand of peace

When President General Pervez Musharraf extended his hand of friendship to Indian Prime Minister Atal Behari Vajpayee at the last SAARC Summit in Kathmandu, he was really reviving and living up to an old Islamic and Pakistani tradition. The Islamic tradition of human fraternity was laid by no one else but the Holy Prophet Muhammad (PBUH) himself, in his life-time, with his magnanimously magnificent interaction with friends and foes, alike, and in his diplomatic dealings and international relations. The supremely sublime and spiritual role model for the Quaid-i-Azam, according to his own speeches and statements, was the Holy Prophet (PBUH). Indeed, he remains so for all Muslims. The Pakistani tradition of friendship was firmed up by the Quaid-i-Azam Muhammad Ali Jinnah. President Pervez

Musharraf has declared more than once publicly that his hero and role model is the Quaid-i-Azam. Quaid's concurrent membership for years as an active leader of both the Hindu Indian National Congress, and the Muslim All-India Muslim League and his creative and peaceful role as the Ambassador of Hindu-Muslim unity was most impressive. Late Aziz Beg, in his book "Jinnah and his Times" writes: When in 1912, "Gokhale called Jinnah the Ambassador of Hindu-Muslim unity, she (Sarojini Naidu) 'improved upon it and called him the finest ambassador of Hindu-Muslim unity;'" (p 273 Jinnah: a biography: Babur and Amer Publications, Islamabad; 1986). The sources of Aziz Beg Sahib's information on the subject are significant: Padmini Sengupta's biography, Sarojini Naidu (India; 1966); and AN Dwivedi's Sarojini Naidu and her poetry (Allahabad; 1981).

In the opinion of Mr Aziz Beg: "In fact, Sarojini loved Jinnah and always held him in profound regard. Hindu-Muslim political unity was a passion for Jinnah, and it was also part of Sarojini's life. She was visibly perturbed at the periodic tremors of communal disunity in India. In June 1913, she wrote to Mr G Natesan, Editor of Indian Review, before she sailed for England:

"You have realised that the Musalmans have definitely held out their hand to the Hindus. Be gracious, be wise, be brave when the Hindus hold out their hand to the Musalmans at the next Congress. Do not analyse motives too closely, but take the proffered hand and hold it fast, and so represent truly the Indian world as far as your influence reaches;. This sound advice is as much applicable to India today, nearly 89 years later. It applies to India, both internally in regard to its relations with its

Muslim minority (which is 16-20 per cent of the total Indian population) and other minorities, as well as to its present Cold War with Pakistan. Bharat needs to hold the hand of friendship already proffered to it by President Pervez Musharraf, in order to enable the two countries to explore the possibilities of peace between them in the days ahead. To be able to do so, India would need a pragmatic visionary futuristic leader of the calibre, status and stature of Jinnah and Sarojini Naidu. Can Sonia Gandhi fit herself into the role of Sarojini Naidu? That would be for her a challenge, a chance and an onerous responsibility, which can turn the tide of events and history of Indo-Pak relations. Aziz Beg also reported of Sarojini Naidu that:

"In fact, she admired Muslim culture and even the Muslim way of life" (p 276). That is one sure way for India to create peace at home: by protecting, promoting and respecting Islam and the Islamic ideology, values and lifestyle, including the Islamic culture and language like Urdu, Persian and Arabic. That would also be the best means of building bridges of friendship with the Muslim world. Pakistan and Bangladesh, being geopolitical closest to India, could become the recipients of abiding good neighbourliness from New Delhi. But for that, Bharat would have to truly turn over a new leaf. It might begin by curbing its own extremists and obscurantists, fanatics and militants, the way Pakistan has done recently. Interestingly, the current global debate on the alleged and actual "extremists" and "moderates," in relation to terrorism and war, has its echoes in British Indian history, as under.

"Jinnah threw his weight with the Moderates who emerged as victors and succeeded in expelling" (from the

Congress) the (extremist) group led by Tilak in the next decade (1907-1919). What were the qualifications and credentials of the so-called 'moderates' and those labelled as 'extremists'?. Aziz Beg answers this critical question (on p 2480 of his book under reference) by quoting SR Malhotra, from his book: towards India's freedom and partition, as reproduced below:"Generally speaking, moderates were upper middle class men, elderly, well-to-do, liberally educated, anglicised, 'secular' in outlook, conservative in political matters, influenced by British constitutionalism, apathetic and cautious.

In the same manner, extremists may be described as lower middle class men, younger in age, not very well-to-do, not so liberally educated, less anglicised, less secular in outlook, radical in political matters, influenced by European revolutionary ideas, energetic and bold." (Delhi; 1979 p 10). The above refers primarily to members of the then Indian National Congress of those times (1900 onwards). But it is (equally) applicable to the Muslim League of the same period. What is the position today in India and Pakistan? How many of those aforementioned characteristic still persist and apply? Perhaps several. A comparative study will prove to be most interesting and informative.

The fact is that every age and country has its 'leftists, rightists and centrists; extremists and moderates; secularists, agnostics, atheists, religionists and believers; doves and hawks.' Both a 'secularist' and a religionist' can be a fanatic, extremist and militant—as distinct from 'fundamentalist' in the sense of sticking to the fundamentals of his/her creed. He/she can be so because of their inflexible and uncompromising, close-minded and close-hearted temperament, attitude and behaviour.

2

Indo-Pak Relations

India is the largest democracy in the world. It has the biggest number of people with franchise rights and the largest number of political parties, which take part in election campaign. Many predicted that India, because of diversities in its cultures, religion, languages, castes, manners, local histories, nationalities and identities, would not survive as a single democratic country, but would break up into smaller countries. Since independence, India had many political problems. During independence the most burning issues were the riots between the Hindus and Muslims while the Sikhs were siding with Hindus. Another issue was convincing the Princely states not to declare independence or join Pakistan but to join the Indian Union. India also had a few wars with its neighbors on border issues. India also has many internal problems. Different communities with different identities—regional, language, caste, religion—demanded different rights for their communities. Some communities demanded more autonomy for their cultures within the Indian states. Others demanded autonomous states within the Indian Union, while the others demanded to be independent from India. With all its problems India survives as a single state with democratic character.

A country's foreign policy is largely determined by the intra-societal as well as extra societal factors. The object is always the interest of the nation. The formulation and evaluation of the domestic compulsions and external influences are processed by the ruling elite. The foreign policies of India and Pakistan are no exception to this rule. The geopolitics of Indo-Pakistan sub-continent demanded that they may remain away from power blocs. Both were equally close to international communism by geography and to Western democracies by historical ties. The prepondering factor in the determination of foreign policy goals was their love for newly won independence. Both the countries wanted to guard their freedom which they had obtained after a prolonged struggle. Moreover, the ruling elite that came to power in India and Pakistan had a common history and common cultural and traditional heritage.

They had fought against colonialism, racialism and imperialism during the freedom struggle. The Western democracies have always been associated with imperialistic and colonial tendencies. This factor did not allow either of the countries to accept the membership of the Western blocks initially. British imperial policy contributed a lot towards the origin and growth of Congress Muslim League rivalry. Even after partition Britain had strategic interests in both India and Pakistan. But by the time the two countries were declared independent Britain's ability to play a global role had declined considerably. In its place United States started playing her role against Communist expansion. But the newly emergent states of India and Pakistan found no initial gains in alignment with power blocs i.e. the US or the USSR. Thus the global politics demanded a neutral, independent uncommitted and non-aligned foreign policy. In the bifocal world politics the membership of nations with either bloc would have meant compromise with newly won freedom. Moreover both shared a dislike for the crude manifestation of colonialism and racialism with which the Western bloc had come to be associated. Both India and Pakistan were opposed to Communism because of the annihilation of freedom under its yoke. In this context of global politics and domestic compulsions India put its foreign policy goals as that of co-existence and non-alignment.

This was an unmistakable demonstration of its friendly feelings towards, all. It was a policy of keeping out from power blocs with a desire to decide each issue on merit. Obviously the attempt was to make the foreign policy fully independent. These foreign policy goals defined by India were the culmination of its past history and desire of peace and goodwill towards all. Summarising his idea on Indian Foreign Policy, Nehru made a statement at Columbia University during his visit to US in 1949:

> "The main objectives of that (Indian foreign policy) are: the pursuit of peace, not through alignment with any major power or group of powers, but through an independent approach to each controversial or disputed issue, the liberation of subject people, the maintenance of freedom, both national and individuals, the elemination of racial discrimination, and the elemination of want, disease and ignorance which affect the great part of the world's population".

Perhaps the most characteristic feature of India's foreign policy after independence was the vigorous pursuit of nonalignment. Non-alignment means simply an independent policy involving no political or military commitments to another state or group of states, limiting one's independence of policy and action. Specifically it meant the rejection of political or military alliances—bilateral and multilateral. Positively, it meant the taking of adhoc decisions on international problems, as and when they came up, according to the merits of each case.

The primary and overriding goal of India's foreign policy after independence was maintenance of international peace and security. "Peace to us is not just a fervent hope, it is an emergent necessity", said Nehru. Secondly, promotion of self determination for all peoples was one of the important goal of India's foreign policy. This was necessary because all peoples, irrespective of race, religion and state of economic development or even civilization, were entitled to foreign as a matter of fundamental human rights. Furthermore, suppression of freedom was a threat to international peace. Opposition to racialism and all its manifestations was the third important object of India's foreign policy. Peaceful settlement of disputes was another major goal of India's foreign policy. The fifth goal of India's policy was to secure for the newly independent Asian African countries the voice and influence to which they were entitled in the councils of the world. India also sought international assistance for the economic development of these under-developed or developing countries-an assistance to which India felt they were entitled.

Lastly, both to achieve the above goals and in the broader and long term interests of international society, India became a staunch supporter of international organisation, especially of the United Nations and accepted the membership of the common wealth.

Pakistan's first Prime Minister, Liaquat Ali, believed in and followed a policy of non-commitment. Speaking at Gujranwala he said, "Pakistan was not tied to the apron strings of the Anglo American bloc, nor she is a campfollower of the communist bloc". "Pakistan", he maintained, "had all along been uninfluenced by the international bloc struggle going on in the world". He claimed that it was on this principle that Pakistan had voted in the United Nations sometimes with Western bloc at others with Communist.

Evidently the foreign policy goals were identical with that of India. If Indian foreign policy was the policy of non-alignment, Pakistan foreign policy was one of non-commitment. Both mean an independent foreign policy. Moreover India and Pakistan were equally interested in eradicating colonialism and imperialism and racialism from the world. Both were interested in the independence of Afro-Asian countries, maintenance of international peace and development of underdeveloped countries. It was with these intentions that both India and Pakistan Joined the international forum of United Nations. It was also significant that despite their mutual disputes-Kashmir included—the leaders of both the countries were able to keep their countries outside the power blocs.Pakistan's foreign policy during 1947-54 was one of non-involvement in the inter-bloc rivalary. G.W. Choudhary and S.M. Burke hold the view that in this period Pakistan's foreign policy was a policy of non-alignment.

It is said that till the spring of 1954 her (Pakistan) foreign policy so far she had one—had nominally been unaligned as between the world's two contesting power blocs, communist and non-communist. In this period Pakistan did not make any commitment to either of the two power blocs. Liaquat Ali tried to gain the friendship and goodwill of all nations. Pakistan's internal conditions and world situation at large prompted her to follow such policy.

Soviet invitation in 1950 to Liaquat, the then Pakistan's Prime Minister was hailed in Pakistan, However, the invitation was not availed of and instead Liaquat went to United States. But there is difference between Pakistan's desire for friendly relations with U.S. and her military alliance with the later. Liaquat gave enough indications of earnest desire to foster close and friendly relations with US, but even while in US Liaquat Ali Khan never talked about Pakistan's desire to join either of the Power blocs. That phase of Pakistan's foreign policy was characterised by a spirit of independence. Liaquat Ali had even warned that "Pakistan must not be taken for granted, Pakistan is not a camp follower of the Common wealth". Pakistan's desire to pursue a foreign policy independent of both the power blocs was her effort to forge an Islamic bloc, to resist the "political and economic infiltration of the West" and pursue a "middle path" between Western Capitalism and Communism.

The first Pakistani Prime Minister's foreign policy even enabled a limited development of economic and cultural relations with Soviet Union. His Successer, Khwaja Nazimuddin, pursued the general lines of foreign policy laid down by his predecessor, though within the broad framework of his pro-western attitude.In any case no change in the broad contour of Pakistani foreign policy as laid down by the first Prime Minister, was affected during the tenure of Nazimuddin. As late as 14 September 1952, Dawn in an editorial said "Even those among our leaders who might have laid great store by promise of generous American aid were at no time willing or committed to Anglo-American aid even politically, much less military. The tide of popular opinion in this country has run strongly against such a policy.

Thus Pakistan had no strong conviction about the balance of righteousness between the West and Communist Powers. Economically and culturally her ties were with the West but in political matters, before 1953, she wished to pick and choose.

Colonialism and Racialism

On issues such as colonialism and racialism, both India and Pakistan co-operated inside and outside the United Nations—in championing the cause of colonial people for self-government and of coloured people against white discrimination, both discovered the triple coincidence of national interest, promotion of peace and morality. The Dutch military action in Indonesia evoked widespread resentment in both the countries. Pakistan joined hands with India in the Asian wide conference called by India in January 1949 and condemned Dutch military action. Again on the problem of Libya, Eritrea, Italian Somaliland and Fezzan one finds identical attitude in India-Pakistan foreign policies. On the question of Tunisia, Morocco and Algeria both India and Pakistan have more or less the same stand. Moreover, the policy of racial discrimination pursued by the South African

Government was watched with grave concern by both India and Pakistan. India and Pakistan strongly disapproved the racial discrimination practised by the South African Government. Logically the problem of racial discrimination is intimately related with the problem of human rights.

Naturally, therefore, India and Pakistan rook identical stand on the problems concerning human rights. India and Pakistan took a sustained interest in the question of human rights in the United Nations. When in 1948 the Universal Declaration of Human Rights came before General Assembly, the Pakistan delegation supported it because, in the words of Begum Ikramullah, Pakistan believed in the diginity and worth of man. She said;

> "... it is imperative that the people of the world should recognize the existence of a code of civilised behaviour which would apply not only in international relations but also in domestic affairs".

India was also an ardent supporter in the United Nations of the adoption of draft covenants on human rights as well as the observance of human rights and fundamental freedoms all over the world. In 1948, India and Pakistan supported Yogoslav proposal that rights proclaimed in the Declaration of Human Rights should apply also to the people of non-self governing and trust territories. The 1948 session was also notable for the adoption of the Genocide Convention, India and Pakistan voted for it both in Sixth Committee and in the plenary session in the General Assembly. In the Sixth Committee Pakistan made efforts to have the crime of cultural genocide specifically mentioned in the convention. In the General Assembly's Session in 1951 India and Pakistan co-sponsored a resolution in the Third Committee that two covenants on human rights should include an article in the following terms: "All people shall have the right to self determination". This resolution was carried. It was further provided that the right of self determination was to be promoted in the non-self governing and trust territories by the respective administrative powers.

India and Pakistan were among the twenty countries that asked the Third Committee in 1954 that the right of self-determination be mentioned in the first article and all other relevant articles of the two covenants that were under preparation, respective, on the civil and political rights and economic and social rights.India being a member of the Human Rights Commission, she was closely associated with the preparation of draft covenants. An analysis of the foreign policy attitude of both India and Pakistan on the problem of aparthied, colonialism, imperialism and human rights clearly demonstrates that both the countries adopted not only similar stand but also the independent nature of their respective foreign policies immune of power blocs.

While the issues related with colonialism and imperialism form the subject matter of the next chapter the under mentioned issues demonstrate the policy of non-alignment and non-commitment followed by India and Pakistan. Both India and Pakistan have adopted a similar approach of Isreal twoards Palestine. The Palestine problem was the offspring of two contradictory promises made by Britain. First, a pledge was given to the Arabs during the First world war that, in the event of an allied victory, the Arabs would be granted independence. Secondly and subsequently, the Balfour Declaration said that His Majesty's Government favoured the setting up of a Jewish National Home in Palestine. The question was referred to the United Nations by

Britain, who held Palestine under League of Nations mandate.

In the pre-independence period both the Indian National Congress and Muslim League had opposed the imposition of a "Jewish National Home" on the reluctant Palestinian Arabs. While Gandhi strongly condemned the inhuman treatment meted out to the Jews in Hitler's Germany the Zionist plan to penalise the Arabs for the wrongs done by the Nazis was revolting to his conception of justice and fair play. Nehru on the other hand, saw in Palestine problem a manifestation of the wider problem of colonialism; the British trying to put up Jewish nationalism against Arab nationalism in order to protect their own imperial interests.

From 1942 to 1946, Muslim League continued to express increasing anxiety about the Palestine question. It regretted that Britain was "trying to force Jewish domination over the Arabs against their will, in direct, violation of the pledges made in the last war, and the principles it claims to follow for winning the present war" and assured "its Arab brothers in Palestine that Muslims in India will stand by them in their fight for their rights against the domination of international Jewry. Similarly the Indian National Congress before independence had proclaimed solidarity with the Arabs in opposing the Western plans to colonise Palestine with Jews.

In the General Assembly, India and Pakistan vehemently opposed the partition of Palestine. Zafrullah Khan declared that the Pakistan delegation was utterly and uncompromisingly opposed to the creation of a Jewish state in Palestine. Arguing that the proposed scheme of partition was unfair and impractical and if implemented would lead to strife, Zafrullah urged that the juridical issues involved in the question should be referred to the International Court of Justice. Pakistan, he said, deeply sympathised with the Jews but the proper solution of the problem would be that Jewish refugees should be reintegrated in the European countries from whence they had been driven out. Should this not be possible, Zafrullah Khan pleaded they should be offered facilities for settlement in the never and larger countries which had more space and greater resources than they had in tiny Palestine.

In the United Nations Special Committee, the majority plan recommending partition of Palestine. Instead, it put forward, alongwith Iran and Yugoslavia, the proposal to create an independent federal state of Palestine comprising autonomous Arab and Jewish units. In a separate note, Abdul Rahman, the Indian member of the Committee, pleaded that partition would not lead to a lasting solution and argued that the two states sought to be created would not be politically viable. In the second session of general Assembly in September 1947, the General Assembly finally accepted the recommendations of the majority plan of the 4 power "working committee" (consisting of the representative of the US, the USSR, Canada and Guatemala) appointed by the UN.

Special Committee on Palestine, which provided for "the partition of the country into separate Jewish and Arab States, bound together by a system of economic union, with an international area of Jerusalem. The resolution containing these recommendations was accepted by the General Assembly on November 30, 1947 by a vote of 33 and 13 with 10 abstention. Indian and

Pakistan were among the 13 who were opposed to the partition of Palestine.

Pakistan has continued to take an active interest in all subsequent developments in regard to Palestine and to sponsor resolutions about it on behalf of the Arabs year after year. The state of Israel was created on May 14, 1948. When the issue of Israel's admission to the UN was raised in May 1949, India and Pakistan voted against its admission. M.C. Setalvad pleaded that his government, "could not recognize an Israel which had been achieved through the use of force and not through negotiations". But there was a gradual realisation in India that the new state had come to stay and that it had to be recognised one day.

The Chinese People's Republic was proclaimed in Peking on 1st October 1949, after the final defeat of the Chiang Kai Shek forces by the Chinese communists. The significance of China's emergence as an independent and strong country in Asia could not have gone unnoticed by the foreign policy formulators of India and Pakistan. Being an Asian as well as a neighbouring country it was imperative geo-political compulsion on India and Pakistan to take due cognizance of this fact.

The leadership of India and Pakistan, subscribed to the idea that in so far as Chinese revolution of 1949 was aimed at those who undermined China's sovereignty and territorial integrity, it was part of Asian resurgence. Though India extended her recognition to People's Republic of China on December 30, 1949, yet she continued to have "informal contacts" till then. India was among the first non-communist country to recognise Communist China. Prime Minister Nehru subsequently explained in Lok Sabha:

> "When the revolution came, we discussed this matter with our Ambassador there and others concerned. It was perfectly clear that the revolution was not some kind of palace revolution. It was a basic revolution involving millions and millions of human beings...It produced a perfectly stable government, strongly entrenched and popular.

While according recognition to the People's Republic of China, India was not prejudiced by her pursuit to Communism and her alliance with the Soviet Union. According to Prime Minister Nehru: It was not a question of approving or disapproving it was a question of recognising a major event in history of appreciating it and dealing with it.

Pakistan saw in the emergence of the People's Republic of China "the return of much needed peace to China" and expressed her desire to "establish early diplomatic relations. She welcomed "the inevitable shift in international politics" due to the victory of the communist forces in China. The Dawn commented: "As Asia gains in political importance internationally Pakistan will also share it". On January 4, 1950, Pakistan recognised the People's Republic of China as the de jure Government of China. She was the first Muslim country to accord recognition to Communist China. It also made attempts to persuade other countries to do the same.

The press in Pakistan was very critical of the attitude of some of the countries of the West, particularly the US and UK, in their refusal to recognise the People's Government in China. Their refusal was viewed in Pakistan as a threat to "stability in Asia" and setting up "a process of international tension".

Acting on the same principles which compelled them to accord recognition to Peking, both India and

Pakistan championed the cause of China in the UN. Both India and Pakistan did not share and support the views expressed by the Western countries in the UN over the issue of the substitution of the representative of the Republic of China by the representative of the People's Republic of China. Pakistan voted for the India resolution of September 1950 challenging the credentials of the nationalist Chinese delegation and asking for the seating of the representative of the Peking Government. Zafrullah Khan, while participating in the debate on the issue of Chinese representation in the United Nation regretted that "the General Assembly is unwilling to concede the existence of a fact, not because the fact has not been established, but because the majority regard it as unpleasant".

According to the Pakistani writers, it was the independent, approach of Pakistan to cold war issues between 1950 and 1954 which paved the way for mutual friendship between Pakistan and China.

A serious international crisis broke out during the last week of June 1950, as a result of invasion of South Korea by the forces of North Korea regime in the early hours of June 25.

India's approach to the Korean crisis was based on the following considerations:

(a) The war must be localised.

(b) The whole country must get independence.

(c) The future of Korea must be decided by the people of Korea without any outside interference.

India voted in favour of the Security Council resolution of June 25, 1950, which called for the withdrawal of

North Korean forces to the 38 parallel and requested all members to render every assistance to the UN in the execution of this resolution. But it did not participate in the voting on June 27, when the Security Council adopted a resolution recommending assistance to the Republic of Korea from all member nations. On June 29, 1950, the Government of India issued a press communique accepting both the resolutions. The Communiques stated:

> This decision of the Government of India does not however, involve any modification of their foreign policy...The Government of India earnestly hope that even at this stage it may be possible to put an end to the fighting and to settle the dispute by mediation.

India's stand regarding the Korean war, was clarified by Nehru, at the press conference on July 7, 1950. Denouncing the action of North Koreans, he declared that the invasion had been made on a large scale and that it had been well planned. He said that India had made no offer of mediation and had no intention of doing so unless so requested. 'The best assistance that India can render in this grave crisis' he said, is to help in limiting the area of conflict and ending it.

At the outbreak of war Liaquat Ali Khan was in US. He lost no time in declaring in public statement that his Government 'will back the United Nations to the fullest' in any action it may take in the Korean war. On June 30, 1950 the permanent representative of Pakistan to the UN formally confirmed, in a letter to the Secretary General, that Government in Pakistan "will give their full support to measure proposed in the Security Council to stop hostilities".

In New York, Liaquat said that Pakistan accepted the UN resolution to aid South Korea, "knowing fully, well what its implications are". It was announced in Karachi on July 2, 1950 that Government of Pakistan had informed Jr. Trygre Lie that it regarded the events in Korea as a clear case of aggression on the part of North Korea. India abstained from voting when the Security Council passed its third resolution on July 7, 1950, setting up a unified UN Command. Nehru earnestly tried to find a basis for terminating the conflict.

On July 13, 1950, he addressed identical messages to Marshal Stalin and Dean Acheson, US Secretary of State. He explained that India's purpose was to localize the conflict and to facilitate peaceful settlement by breaking the deadlock in the Security Council so that the Peoples' Republic of China might be admitted to the UN, the USSR resume its place in the Security Council, and these two together with the US find the basis for terminating the hostilities in Korea.

In view of the deteriorating situation in Korea, a special session of the India Parliament was summoned on July 31 1950. In the opening address, the President of India, emphasised the Indian support for the action taken by the UN and insisted that Nehru's initiative had been intended to strengthen the moral force of the UN and in no way to condoneag gression. Initiating the debate on Korean situation on August 3, 1950. Nehru said that the first things were to localize the conflict and to explore ways of stopping the war and of ensuring that the Koreans might decide the future of Korea.

Pakistan, on the other hand, had been one of the co-sponsors of the October 7, 1950 resolution it recommended that steps be taken to ensure conditions of stability throughout Korea and for the establishment of unified Korea, implicitly authorised U.N. command to move into North Korea.

On October 11, 1950, Prime Minister Liaquat Ali Khan said in the Parliament that the 38th parallel had never been recognised by the General Assembly as a permanent boundary and that in any case, North Korea had destroyed the line by crossing it first. When the cease fire proposals were discussed in the UN in November 1952, the Indian delegate B.N. Rau circulated a resolution which called for the establishment of a repatriation Commission. The resolution was accepted by the General Assembly on December 3, 1952, with some amendments, But the Chinese and the North Korean authorities rejected it. All the same the provisions of the final agreement of June 8, 1953, were to a great extent similar to those in Indian resolution.

The preceding review makes it clear that both India and Pakistan were one in their wish to settle the Korean issue through UN were in favour of avoiding war in that area. Consequent on the Korean war, when the US sponsored a draft resolution in 1951 seeking to brand China an aggressor and proposed imposition of selective economic embargo on China and on bombing of China Pakistan abstained from voting. So in the voting behaviours in the UN, particularly on the Korean war, and on the question of Peking's admission to the UN, Pakistan indicated some semblance of her desire for independence.

In the Indo-China Region, the Vietnam Republic Government was established during the world war II. It functioned very efficiently during the interval between Japan's surrender and the arrival of Allied forced. The response of newly constituted Government of France to the growing nationalist sentiment and the establishment of an independent republic in Indo-China was to re-establish French control with the assistance of British troops under Brigadier Gracey. The Vietnamese offered a vary stiff resistance, this was followed by negotiations between Vietnam and France.

The representatives of the two countries met in a conference and signed a preliminary convention. France recognized Vietnam as "Free state with its own Government, Parliament, army and Treasury, forming part of the Indo-Chinese federation and the French Union. But the attitude of French authorities to these negotiations was itself a major obstacle. They seemed to conduct negotiations only to gain time. Peace was not established in Vietnam even after the signing of this agreement.

There were conflicts between the forces of the French and the Nationalists throughout the country. President Ho's protests to France were in vain. Realising their failure from the military standpoint, the French tried to establish puppet Governments. They brought back the ex-Emperor Bao Dai from Hong Kong in order to make him a rival to president Ho.

After it, in order to obtain international support against Ho Chi Minh, France asserted that he was a communist and that his Government was totalitarian in character. Fighting between French and Vietnamese forces continued throughout 1948-1949. An Agreement was reached between ex-Emperor Bao Dai and French Government on March 9, 1949 by which Bao Dai was proclaimed Emperor and Head of the French sponsored 'Central Government of Vietnam'.

All that important newspapers attacked the French Government's policy and characterised Bao Dai as its puppet. Even the Government spokesmen declared their dissatisfaction at the extent to which power was still retained by the French authorities in Indo-China. But the Indian Government had not openly supported Ho Chi Minh against the policy of the Western Powers. They stated that they would not support one Government or the other as it was not policy of Government of India to get involved in other people's quarrels.

Pakistan till 1954, was also critical of French policies in that area. In an interview with Norman Cliff, Foreign Minister Zafrulla Khan declared that:

> "the struggle in Indo-China had taken on the character of a struggle between Western domination and Communism. It is choice between two evils. In my opinion, the opportunity of winning the people to the side of freedom and peaceful development was lost through. French hesitation to grant full freedom, say five years ago. The evil, that has expanded so much, could at that time, have been checked by the people of that country, possibly with the assistance of friendly France."

Both India and Pakistan were represented in the Colombo Conference held in April-May 1954, and through that conference supported the efforts made at Geneva to find a solution to the Indo-Chinese problem. Both the countries were of the view that solution of the problem of Indo-China required that an agreement on a ceasefire should be reached without delay. Both felt that the solution of the problem required direct negotiations between parties principally concerned, namely France, the three-associated states of Indo-China and Vietminh, as well as other parties invited by the agreement.

In the New Delhi Conference held in January 1949 to discuss and condemn Dutch military action in Indonesia, Pakistan also participated in the Conference. The Conference condemned Dutch military cessation of hostilities in Indonesia and suggested number of steps leading to the transfer of sovereignty of the United States of Indonesia.

In the Baguio Conference of 1950, this trend of cooperation was also noticeable. India, Pakistan along with the Phillipines, Indonesia, Thailand, Ceylon and Australia participated in it. The resolution passed in this Conference stated perhaps for the first time, the concept of South and South-East Asian area. It recommended to the participating Governments that they "ensure that in the consideration of the special problems of South and South-East Asia, the point of view of the peoples of this area is prominently kept in mind, by any conference dealing with such problems, so that better understanding and cordial relations may subsist between the countries in the region and other countries of the world". It also recommended to the Governments that they "seek joint action so as to exercise due influence in the United Nations, its specialized agencies and other international organisations.

In the Colombo Conference of April-May 1954, India and Pakistan were the major participants along with Burma, Ceylon and Indonesia. As the final communique stated, they had met "to exchange views and discuss problems of common interest and concern to them all". This conference, which was held at the Prime Ministers level, was the first of its kind. The conference proposed a ceasefire without delay in Indo-China, and suggested direct negotiations between the parties involved in the conflict. The participants also raised their voice against the hydrogen bomb and other weapons of mass destruction.

They condemned colonialism, reaffirmed their faith in democracy and democratic institutions, and declared their "determination to resist interference in the affairs of their countries by external, anti-communist, communist or other agencies". On the question of Red Chinese representation in the UN, the conference supported it on the ground that it would help to promote stability in Asia, ease world tensions and assist in bringing about a more realistic approach to the problems concerning the world, particularly the far east.

The Conferences also stated deep sympathy with the Arabs of Palestine in their sufferings and affirmed desire to see a just and early settlement of Palestine problem. In all this there was no disagreement between India and Pakistan.

In December 1954, Indian and Pakistani Prime Minister met at Bogor along with the Prime Ministers of Burma, Ceylon and Indonesia. The main object of their meetings was to consider matters concerning the proposed Asian-Africa Conference suggested at the Colombo Conference. The Prime Ministers took advantage of the opportunity of their Bogor meeting to review briefly and in general terms problems and issues of common interest and concern to them all.

The Prime Ministers expressed gratification at the results of Geneva Conference on Indo-China and the cessation of hostilities. They expressed hope that the Geneva Agreement would be fully respected and implemented. The Prime Ministers on the West Irian issue supported the position of Indonesia. They also expressed their continued support of the demand of the people of Tunisia and Morocco for their national independence. The Prime Ministers reiterated their grave concern in respect of nuclear and thermonuclear explosions for experimental purposes which threaten not only their countries but the world and their far-reaching and yet unascertained effects which may do permanent damage to human life and civilization. The Prime Minister also considered that cooperation in the economic sphere for the supply of technical personnel and in all other ways should engage the attention of their Governments. In all this there was no disagreement between India and Pakistan.

India and Pakistan were among the five sponsoring countries for the Bandung Conference. They agreed at Bogor to convene an Asian-African Conference under their joint sponsorship with Indonesia, Burma and Ceylon. The sponsors left it to the Conference to decide its own procedure and agenda but indicated that the objects of calling an Asian-African Conference were to consider problems of special interest to Asian and African peoples, e.g. racialism and colonisalism, and to view the position of Asians and Africans in the world and the contribution they could make to world peace and cooperation.

The Conference opened at Bandung, Indonesia, on April 18, 1955 and concluded with a joint communique on April 25. It was attended by representatives of twenty nine nations with an aggregate population of 1.4 billion, more than half of all mankind. Even in this Conference, though Pakistan was aligned with the West there were certain area in which India and Pakistan took the same stand.

In the field of economic cooperation the participating countries recommended the early establishment of the Special United Nations Fund for Economic Development (SUNFED) and the International Finance Corporation, they also agreed to prior consultation of participating countries in international forums with a view to furthering their mutual economic interest.

The Conference also condemned racialism as well as the denial of fundamental rights in the sphere of education and culture in some of the colonial territories in Asia and Africa. In the matter of human rights and self determination, the conference declared its support to them as provided for in the UN Charter and the Universal Declaration of Human Rights; condemned racial segregation and discrimination in large parts of the world, especially in Africa.

On the question of problems of the dependent peoples, the Conference declared that 'colonialism in all its manifestations' was an evil and should be brought to an end, supported in particular the rights of the peoples of Algeria, Morocco and Tunisia to self determination, it also supported the position of Indonesia in the case of West Irian and of Yemen in respect to Aden and other related areas.

The Conference declared its support to the rights of the Arab people of Palestine and called for implementation of UN resolution on Palestine. On the promotion of world peace and cooperation, the Conference, supporting the principle of universality of membership in the UN, urged that Combodia, Ceylon, Japan, Jordan, Libya, Nepal and unified Vietnam should be admitted to membership.

It complained the inadequacy of representation of the countries of the Asian-African region in the Security Council, proclaimed support to disarmament and prohibition of production, experimentation and use of nuclear and thermonuclear weapons, and pending such prohibition, suspension of test explosions. In all this there was no disagreement between the stand taken by India and Pakistan.

Pakistan's Foreign Policy

Pakistan's foreign policy over the years shows that the infant state adopted an independent non-committal foreign policy till 1954. Pakistan's policy of non-commitment was not much different from India's policy of nonalignment. A significant break in Pakistan foreign of non-alignment. A significant break in Pakistan foreign policy came on April 30, 1953 when the new Prime Minister Nizamuddin announced the new orientation.

(i) New approaches to be made for better relations with India and Afghanistan.

(ii) Early revision of Pakistan's relationship with Britain, particularly the former's status within the commonwealth so as to bring it more in conformity with India's status.

(iii) Pakistan, it is said, will be prepared to do everything, short of prejudicing its sovereignty, to foster friendly relations with U.S.A.

(iv) Efforts towards improved relations with West European countries for developing Pakistan's industrial and mineral resources to help the country and tide over her economic crisis.

(v) Developing friendly relations with Japan.

(vi) Renewed efforts to improve friendly relations with countries in West Asia, Turkey and Indonesia.

(vii) Relationship with the communist countries to be left to the latter's initiative, and, meanwhile, restrictions to be imposed upon the movements of Russian and Chinese diplomats in Karachi. Moreover, "Preliminary to entering the first phase of her new foreign policy more Pakistan is also reviewing her foreign trade relations and may reduce her exports of jute and cotton to the Soviet Union.

It becomes obvious, that despite a shift in the foreign policy of Pakistan and her announcement to join US bloc it was declared that the new approach would be made for better relations with India. Very many factors have been given by scholars and statesmen which led Pakistan to give up its policy of noncommitment and join SEATO and CENTO. Khurshid Hasan writes:

> "Pakistan, in view of the inherent weakness and limitations of her position vis-a-vis India, from the outset sought to counter this bid (India's bid "to become the spokesman of the newly independent Asian states") by seeking a "patron" who would support her in her diplomatic disputes with India and guarantee her security against any threats from that quarter. The search for a `patron' first made her turn to commonwealth, then the Muslim states and finally, after being cold-shouldered by both, to the United States".

Keith Callard holds that most people were prepared to be convinced by the argument that they were necessary to strengthen the nation against India. To Norman D. Palmer "Pakistan accepted United States military aid because Mr. Nehru said they should not do so. For them it was part of a pro-Western policy". The underlying factor was also the absence of strong leadership in Pakistan after the death of Jinnah and Liaquat. Coupled with it was the economic crisis and bureaucratic leadership which leaned heavily upon the armed forces. It was at this point that the leadership in favour of a policy of military alliance coincided.

Pakistan forces needed sophisticated armaments and the civilian leadership needed strong army for internal support. The military alliance promised both. The alliance also promised powerful external aid in defence of integrity of the country which came to be threatened from inside due to political vacuum. The intense desire on the part of Pakistan to find allies was also conditioned by her infant nationhood and a small country with limited area and population. India could afford to remain non-aligned because of her bigger size and greater strength. It is natural that a neighbourhood of a strong country compells a weaker country to find allies for survival.

In these circumstances Pakistan changed over from the policy of non-commitment to the policy of alignment. All these factors worked together for this vital change in Pakistan's foreign policy. This was a major break in Pakistan's foreign policy. Henceforth Pakistan's foreign policy was controlled and guided by America. It was virtually bloc politics which is diametrically opposed to the policy of non-alignment. But inspite of this change Pakistan continued to oppose colonialism and racialism in world politics.

Incidentally the view point of India and Pakistan was similar on the Palestinian issues. Both the countries showed a hostile attitude towards Israel and vigorously supported the cause of Palestinian Liberation Organisation. Despite Pakistan's participation in Western sponsor pacts in 1954-1955 and the resultant pressure on it to adhere to the Western view point vis-a-vis the Arabs, Pakistan did not abandon the support of Arab causes. India and Pakistan condemned Israeli attack on Arabs in 1967 and voted together on all issues that came up before the UN General Assembly.

The Middle East crisis demonstrated to what extent Pakistan's foreign policy had become independent of the West. Pakistan's supported U Thant's withdrawal of UNEF despite the fact that US and some Western countries were criticising. The US anti-Arab posture did not deter Pakistan from openly supporting the Arabs. This identify of Indian and Pakistan view point clearly shows that even after joining US bloc there was yet an area of agreement between Indian and Pakistani foreign policy on the Middle Eastern question. This similarly in the foreign policy perception of India and Pakistan continues even to this day.

Apart from it Pakistan like India agreed to demand the withdrawal of foreign troops from Indo-China as evidence from the communique issued by Pakistan and Soviet Union in June, 1970. Another area on which we can see the coincidence of interest between Indian and Pakistani foreign policy is New International Economic order.

By the another resolutions the General Assembly adopted at the same session, a programme of action for the establishment of NIEO, which included the following broad items:

I. Fundamental problems of raw materials and primary commodities as related to trade and development.

II. International monetary system and financing of the development of developing countries.

III. Industrialisation.

IV. Transfer of Technology.

V. Regulation and control over the activities of transnational corporations.

VI. Charter of economic rights and duties of states.

VII. Promotion of cooperation among developing countries.

VIII. Assistance in the exercise of permanent sovereignty of states over natural resources.

IX. Strengthening of the role of United Nations system in the field of economic cooperation.

X. Special programme for the most seriously affected developing nations.

The charter of Economic Rights and Duties, as mentioned in item VI of the Programme of Action was adopted by the General Assembly at its Twenty ninth session in ye same year. Article 8 of the charter of Economic Rights and Duties expressly stated that 'state should cooperate in facilitating more rational and equitable international economic relations and in encouraging structural changes in the context of a balanced world economy in harmony with the needs and interests of all countries, especially developing countries and should take appropriate measures to this end'.

The emerging new order is the result of sustained struggle of developing countries which realised that the existing international institutions were big obstacles in the path of achieving full economic independence without which political independence was neither secure nor meaningful. The developing countries recognised the identity and their interests and fought to protect those by what is known as Group of 77.

The present international economic system has led to a systematic and ruthless exploitation of underdeveloped countries thus widening the gap between the rich and the poor. During the twenty five years after second world war, international relations were dominated by East-West confrontation. Today they are dominated by a conflict between the developed North and developing South. It is an intolerable state of affairs with which poor countries can hardly stay content. How agonising it is that:

> "One quarter of world's people control 80% of its income 90% of its gold reserves and consumes 80% of its protein, 98% of all scientific research and development is directed primarily towards improving the lives of the wealthy quarter rather than those of other three quarter of mankind."

These statistics reveal the division of mankind into two distinct world-one embarrassingly rich and the other desperately poor. To remedy such an intolerable system, inefficient, and unjust system, the developing countries made attempt to solve the problems of poverty, hunger and backwardness through the collective efforts, by organising regional conferences such as Afro-Asian Conference in Bandung and other non-aligned conferences. The issue was also raised at various organs of the united Nations and its special agencies. As a result some significant development emerged. 'First Development decade' was declared in 1960. UNCTAD was set up in 1962. Despite these developments no effective or workable system of economic cooperation could be evolved due to luke warm attitude of the developed nations.

Before the declaration of Second Development Decade in 1970, that there was a great need to increase cooperation among developing countries if their economic condition was to improve. This position was made clear by India in July 1969 Consultative Committee of the non-aligned countries. Moreover in the debate on the Second Development Decade in the UN General Assembly in March, 1970, Indian representative Samar Sen lamenting the very limited success of First Development Decade urged definite commitments on the part of the developed countries. The strategy for Second Development Decade must contain a definite plan of action, with target dates for their implementation and firm commitment for realizing the objectives of the decade.

The acknowledged policy of India from the beginning of 1970's has been to advocate cooperation among nations of Asia and Africa. India regarded the programme for trade development and liberalisation and for monetary cooperation as hard core of integrated strategy for economic cooperation among nations at Asia and Africa. India considered it necessary to secure assistance from international agencies and other sources for investment in multinational industries' development projects. It regarded that programme of trade expansion also needs the development in the field of transformation and communications infrastructure among nations of Asia and Africa.

The rigid attitude of developed nations has always been a matter of concern for India and she has always been expressing her resentment against it. Subsequently India participated in UNIDO's Industrial Development Board on 22 April 1970. The Indian representative advocated a change in the structure of UNIDO so that it might function properly.

India repeatedly expressed her resentment over the working of GATT, World Bank, and IMF and stated that these institutions did not get success in the balanced growth in the world economy. India regarded that security and political stability could not be achieved unless and until there was economic cooperation among the countries of the world. The Indian stand was indicated at the UN General Assembly's 26th session. The General Assembly's resolution on 16th Dec. 1971, criticised the protectionist policies adopted by the developed countries.

The third conference of UNCTAD which was held in Santiago (Chile) in 1972, from 13 April to 21 May adopted a number of resolutions. By this time a consensus had emerged on the principle of full effective participation by all developing countries in the making of international decisions and on issues of vital importance to them. The adoption of 13 principles, which were proposed by developing countries saw the victory of developing countries in UNCTAD.

The year 1974 witnessed remarkable progress for the developing countries. Developing countries rejoiced at the declaration on the establishment of a NIEO and a programme of action to carry it out by UN General Assembly at its VIth session, devoted to raw material and development.

The VI special session of the UN General Assembly started from 19th April to 2 May 1974. It provided an opportunity to make public and clarify its stand on various economic issues. India's Minister of External Affairs, Swaran Singh, while expressing India's stand at VI special session on 19th April 1974 stated that a comprehensive policy for rationalisation of prices of raw materials should be elaborated. He proposed that emergency needs of specially affected countries should be met by timely provisional liquidity. He further said that a scheme of reforming the international monetary system, providing a substantial degree of stability should be formulated and implemented as soon as possible. He stressed on the need for a SDR aid link and more equitable pattern of voting rights of IMF. Swaran Singh supported the sovereign right to states determining the prices of primary products. And he stressed upon cooperation among developing countries.

The leader of Pakistani delegation Hasan while addressing the session said that problem before the session is all embracing one-political, social, economic, biological and ecological. It affects every fact of national and international life. Its implications are awesome and mind-bogging, but for us in the third world or call us the fourth, the fifth or indeed the last world, the essentials of the problem are simple.

Hasan highlighted various questions. The First problem he talked of was transfer of resources from poor to rich nations. He was of the opinion that active mode of this transfer was unequal exchange. The prices of commodities exported by the developing countries are low in international markets due to tariff and non-tariff barrier. The trend of unequal exchange is continually worsening and the magnitude of unequal exchange of hundreds of billion dollars. He also described the reasons for unequal exchange.

Another problem touched by the leader of Pakistan delegation was debt burden under which developing countries are seeking. Most of the third would countries owe huge debts to the developed countries. The financial aid was given and received with the express objective of economic development of poor countries. But the intended objective could not be realised because of various conditions attached with the financial aid by the donor countries. These policies have generally played villain's role in economic development of poor countries. He therefore suggested the bilateral rescheduling of aid and debt by the donor countries.

The statements and suggestions by the leaders of delegation of third world including India and Pakistan created an impact on the thinking of developed nations. After a month long deliberation, on the issues India and Pakistan had consistently exerted, were finally given an important place in the UN Declaration on the establishment of NIEO.

The programmes for the resolution of NIEO set forth by UN General Assembly comprised of following points for which India and Pakistan have always agitated such as promotion of self reliance and cooperation among developing countries, just and equitable relationship between the prices of exports and imports of developing countries, the exercise of sovereignty over natural resources, transfer of financial resources to developing countries and effective participation of developing countries in the decision making procedures of international institutions like IMF and IBRD etc.

The year 1975 was a year of conference devoted mostly to the world economic problems. India tried her best to utilise every forum for explaining its stand on international economic problems. The Dakar Conference of developing countries from 4-8 February 1975 was held specially to discuss the problem of raw materials and economic development. Both India and Pakistan actively participated in this conference. The declaration asked the developed countries to assist developing countries by supplying food and technical aid and credit. It also called upon the developing countries themselves to take joint action which would make them less dependent upon developed ones.

At a preparatory meeting in Paris of Energy and Economic matters conference on 7th April, India reiterated its views like sovereignty over natural resources and restructuring the present international institutions. In the conference of commonwealth Heads of States India advocated the change in prevailing unjust economic order. India called for global response to problems like food, raw materials.

At the nonaligned conference India advocated solidarity among developing countries. India considered the restructuring of present world economic order as a necessary requirement of age.

At the VII Special session of U.N., Y.B. Chavan leader of Indian delegation put forth following suggestions.

(a) Recognition of interdependence of nations.

(b) A more managed approach for promotion of trade of developing countries to the problems of trade which could deal not only with the renewal of trade barriers, both tariff and non-tariff, but also with the question of supply of production marketing and distribution.

(c) A great say for developing countries in the management of monetary system.

(d) Greater regulation on the conduct of transnational cooperation.

So far Pakistan is concerned, Quaiser at the VIII special session elaborated the crucial areas of immediate concern in the context of NIEO and put forth suggestions

(i) An increase in net flow of real resources to the developing countries should be promoted with a view to mitigate the balance of payment difficulties;

(ii) Debt relief in appropriate cases should be provided to prevent the erosion of net transfer of resources;

(iii) Improvement in the volume and terms of their international trade should be brought about;

(iv) The process of industrialisation in the developing countries should be accelerated;

(v) The technological capacities of developing countries should be strengthened and

(vi) IMF and World Bank should be reformed and democratized.

The view point put forward by the Indian and Pakistan delegations reflect the broad strategy on the basis of which third world countries want to bring the transformation in the existing order. Most of the points made by Indian and Pakistani delegations were incorporated in the resolutions passed by the seventh special session of UN General Assembly.

During the IV UNCTAD held at Nairobi 1976, India headed key negotiations group on commodities. She reiterated at UNCTAD IV that cooperative endeavour of both developing and developed countries should be to secure definite and urgent solutions. Most suggestions made by India were incorporated in the resolution adopted at Nairobi in IV UNCTAD 1976.

In 1977 when Janta Party came to power in India, there was no change in Indian foreign policy in respect of demand for NIEO. The realistic approach was maintained by the Janta Party for the quest of NIEO. Morarji Desai at the Common-wealth Conference at London on 14th June 1977 stated that the NIEO about which many pious sentiments have been expressed since the VI special session of UN General Assembly must not be allowed to remain a utopian dream. It is really disappointing that the idea of NIEO would not make any headway despite the fact that the resolution to this effect was adopted by the General Assembly eleven years ago. Since then the problems of developing countries rather than mitigating have been magnified. The developing countries have expressed discontentment with the Tokyo Round Negotiations which came to an end in 1979.

The reason for this sordid state of affairs is that the U.S. leader of the rich nations has been stubbornly resisting the just economic demands of the developing countries. Apart from stiff opposition to the developing countries at UNCTAD V meeting at Manila. UNIDO III at Delhi, at the Eleventh session of UN General Assembly on NIEO the US sought to ignore even the conservative recommendations of Willy Brandt Report entitled, North South: A Programme of Survival.

ECDC/TCDC/and India Pakistan

As dark clouds continued to hover around North-South relations, the non-aligned and group of 77 turned to South-South cooperation as a way to sustain the process of development and maintain to some extent its momentum. The efforts made in late sixties and early seventies had not yet yielded substantial results. The major achievement has been the growth of certain regional groups whose objectives vary from preferential arrangement to custom union and some emphasis on the need for joint investment in industry and infrastructure. Some typical cases are the Latin American Free Trade Association, the Caribbean Common Market and the Association of South East Asian Nations. In the field of finance and payments several regional development banks with clearing payment union were functioning. But what has been achieved so far is short of potential. Economic and Technical Cooperation amongst developing countries can hardly be expected to make up, even partly, for the deficiencies in their commercial, financial and technical relations with the industrial world. There is a however, a growing consciousness of the complimentarities between different economies and several conferences held on ECDC and TCDC.

The strengthening of ECDC/TCDC is primary objective of both NAM and Group of 77. Indian and Pakistan both are now members of NAM and Groups of 77 and because of this reason despite their bilateral clashes in their respective foreign policies both accept that the process of economic cooperation among developing countries occupies an important place in the economic strategies and policies of developing countries.

Both India and Pakistan believe that Economic Cooperation among Developing Countries (ECDC) is the way to engineer change in international economic order. The most methodological examination of ECDC within the group of 77 and NAM has been made at Ministerial Meetings in Manila; Action Programme on Economic Cooperation by V Conference of Head of states on Government of Non-Aligned Countries held in Colombo; The Report of conference on Economic Cooperation Among Developing Countries held in Mexico City; The Buenos Aires Plan of Action, adopted at the UN Technical Cooperation among Developing Countries; the Amsha Programme for Collective Self Reliance adopted at the IV Ministerial Meeting of the Group of 77, and the Careas Programme of Action adopted at High Level Conference on Economic Cooperation among Developing countries in May 1981. What is required is that developing countries should reduce vertical integration and increase horizontal integration and should look inwards rather than away from itself and its own problems.

Developing countries should attempt to build a viable trading bloc by fashioning a new institutional framework for shipping, banking, supplier's credit, exchange rates etc. to promote trade among themselves. UNCTAD can play a constructive role hereby concentrating its energies on the evolving of patterns of intra-developing countries trade.

Speaking at Pakistan Institute of International affairs on 11 June 1981, P.V. Narsimha Rao stated 'that on matters concerning the future of developing countries, both inter-se and vis-a-vis the developed world, as also on the new International Economic order and the Strategies for the Development, India and Pakistan have held almost identical views and worked in close cooperation'.

India has played a leading role in expansion of intra-regional trade. Its cooperation in regional financing and clearing institution is significant. It is making the largest contributions next to Japan to the Asian Development Bank which was established in 1966. She has been the largest contributor of experts to UNIDO to assist other developing countries in accelerating their process of economic development. It contributed a sum of 10,000 million $ to ESCAP in 1975 as contribution to cost of preparation of a feasibility study and a comprehensive project report for the establishment of a Regional Centre for Transfer of Technology of India.

In contrast Pakistan has not shows much enthusiasm in forming regional arrangements. Instead,·She is a member of sub-regional grouping i.e., RC.D. In fact Pakistan's approach toward international relations has been influenced by religious overtones. General Zia call for a Islamic order. The flow of financial resources from OPEC to Pakistan has been due to the fact that they profess the same faith.

Non-aligned movement and India-Pakistan

In the interest of economic development of the country, for maintaining the independence of action in foreign affairs, for safeguarding the security of the nation and for working effectively for world peace, India decided to keep away from the rival power blocs and follows an independent foreign policy.

India has continued to be in the forefront in all the non aligned summits. Indira Gandhi, the late Prime Minister of India was of the following opinion on the subject of genesis of non-alignment:

> 'It was shaped in long years of our national struggle, much before the cold war developed and blocs were formed. The cold war had ended, but has its legacy? Colonial rule has almost gone, but has its consequences? Many of our nations remain politically vulnerable to external pressures...Economic exploitation persists in old and new garbs. So do the technological disparities and psychological complexes bred by colonialism.

Shyam Nandan Mishra, India's Foreign Minister, represented India at the Havana Summit in place of the Caretaker Prime Minister Charan Singh. He emphasized the relevance of non-alignment in the present day world and said:

> 'In the spirit of philosophy of Gandhi and Nehru non-alignment signified respect for the individually and personality of other nations, it recognized the right, like ours, to chose their own social and economic systems, and in this spirit permitted dignified and beneficial cooperation between nations... It (non alignment) enables us to support decolonization and liberation movements and take principled stand on issues which confronted the world'.

After its emergence on world map, Pakistan has been haunted by a crisis of identity. Its ruling elite in their quest for an artificial power parity with India pursued a policy of close alliance with US sponsored military pacts like CENTO and SEATO. Because of Pakistan's pro-

Western stand in general and conceding a military base to the US in particular alienated Pakistan from the Afro-Asian Solidarity as championed by the Non-Aligned Movement (NAM).

In 1970's Pakistani rulers make strenous efforts to bring their country closer to the NAM. Zulfikar Ali Bhutto, in his quest for leadership in the third world and in his pursuance of his policy of positive bilateralism, slowly deviated his country's policy of alliance to a 'relative neutrality'. In November 1978 in an article on 'bilateralism' in the Dawn, Bhutto said: 'If non-alignment is to become a movement of great value, developing countries should not be kept out'. However, he also conceded there was 'nothing repugnant to the values and objectives of the common cause of the third world if an Asian, African or Latin American country enters into and alliances with either East or West. Several explanations have been given both in the Pakistan press and elsewhere about the reasons which motivated Pakistan to join the Non-aligned community.

For instance, it is argued that-'newer forms of hegemonism and imperialist domination' have emerged that require to be politically countered. Besides there is also an awareness of pervasive 'economic imperialism', that provides a common factor for the unity among developing countries. It also believed that Super Powers struggle for influence needs to be countered by strengthening NAM'.

Pakistan was given a guest status at the non-aligned Foreign Ministers Conference in Colombo in 1978. When it was invited to attend Havana Summit by President Fidel Castro of Cuba, the then Chairman of NAM, Dawn wrote in an editorial: "In view of the independent line

Pakistan has been following in its foreign policy for years its contribution to the third world solidarity and its formal withdrawal from CENTO in March 1979 (Islamabad), having quit SEATO in 1972, Pakistan's case for inclusion in the NAM rests on sound considerations. At a time when the movement is under severe strain a result of big powers rivalries smaller countries like Pakistan would be in a better position if they adopt a strict ly neutral line with non-aligned groups". It was a clear indication of Pakistan's future course of action vis-a-vis NAM.

Pakistani President, Mohammad Zia-ul Haq, in his maiden speech at the Non-aligned Summit, underlined the vitality of non-alignment in our strife torn world:

> 'Pakistan perceive the Non-Aligned Movement as an affirmation of independence of opinion and action and a force for peace, justice, equality and progress...It is directed against no bloc or grouping. Nor should it identify itself with any power block. It is a voluntary association of states joined by their common commitment to the liquidation of colonialism, neo-colonialism, imperialism and racialism (including Zionism) and (by their common) opposition hegemony or domination in any guise or form. It is committed to the search for general and complete disarmament, the creation of Universal system of collective security, and the establishment of new and equitable world order'.

He warned against the dangers of neo-colonialism and added: 'It is a matter of deep regret and anxiety that small and weak states, the vast majority of the members of this movement are exposed to threats, aggression, intervention, subversion and pressures of every kind'.

Pakistan took a non-committal attitude on the issue of military bases in the region. However it indirectly supported the idea of establishing nuclear weapon-free zones. President Zia-Ul-Haq as the leader of his country's delegation said at Havana:

> "Measures to enhance the security of non-aligned states can also be considered at the regional level, accompanied whenever possible by regional disarmament arrangements. Pakistan for its part, renew its commitment to renounce the use of force in the conduct of its relations with other nations and is willing to enter into appropriate arrangements for peaceful settlement of disputes at all levels-bilateral, regional or multilateral".

Now let us analyse the response of India and Pakistan on some of the burning global issues at the Havana and New Delhi Summit. Table I of Appendix III briefly notes their almost identical perception on colonialism, racialism and somewhat similar on disarmament.

In the Sixth, Summit held in Havana. India and Pakistan were almost unanimous in their condemnation of colonialism and racialism. They also denounced with equal fervour all forms of imperialism and hegemonism. The liberation movements in Zimbabwe and Namibia received support from both India and Pakistan. They not only inweighed amongst increasing collaboration between racialism and Zionism but also welcomed by and large the world conferences against Racial Discrimination held in Geneva during 1978.

Thus we find that there was broad unanimity in Indo-Pakistan stands for such causes as decolonization, anti-racialism, disarmament at both global and regional levels and the establishment of NIEO, although they differed with one another in their emphasis. The issue of Kampuchean membership of non-aligned block dominated the proceedings of Havana Summit. Both

India and Pakistan were critical of Vietnam's military intervention in Kampuchia. While Pakistan made a sharp attack on Vietnam's role in Kampuchea, India's condemnation was modest.

On the issue of establishment of NIEO India and Pakistan have adopted a similar stand in Havana Summit. They emphasized the need for the South to make a united stand during its negotiations with north. Both India and Pakistan have always held identical views in matters like transfer of technology, corrections of imbalances in the trade between the developed and the developing countries, on ECDC and TCDC, and lastly on South-South cooperation.

New Delhi summit of Non-aligned nations was seventh in the line and it has been acclaimed as one of the largest ever gathering of Heads of the State or Government. In this summit Conference about 100 nations participated and about two dozens countries being given the guest or observer status.

On the eve of the New Delhi Summit, the Foreign Ministers of most of the non-aligned countries briefly met in new Delhi and India's Foreign Minister, Narsimha Rao was formally elected as the Chairman of Non-aligned Coordination Bureau for the next three years. The foreign ministerial meeting also arrived at a consensus on the contentious issue of Kampuchean representation at the summit. In place of allowing a seat to either the Heng Samrin Government or the so called democratic government led by Prince Sihanouk, it was decided to keep it vacant. It was also decided that Kampuchean issue will not be further discussed at the Seventh Summit.

On the morning of 7th March 1983, Prime Minister Indira Gandhi was unanimously elected as Chairperson. In her inaugural speech, the major thrust was on disarmament, the threat of annihilation of human race by nuclear war and the NIEO. However at the outset she did point out on the meaning and content of non-alignment which emerged out of the dangers of colonialism. Indira Gandhi said 'Only 35 years ago, most of our peoples were under foreign thrall...With independence from colonialism, non-alignment came into being. And anti-imperialism still conditions our outlook. While explaining the rationale of non-alignment in the present day world she added:

> "It stands for peace and the avoidance of confrontation. It aims at keeping away from military alliances. It means equality among nations and democratization of international relations, economic and political...It is a strategy for the recognition and preservation of world's diversity".

It is important to highlight the main themes of her inaugural address. First, while emphasizing on the dangerous consequences of mad race of armament, she strongly appealed to the custodians of power in the global theatre to concentrate their efforts for more viable agreement on nuclear disarmament.

Secondly, while linking the process of decolonization with the emergence of the NAM, she reiterated that anti-imperialism still conditions the out look of non-aligned world because as she added 'Technically the colonial age has ended, but the wish to dominate still persists'.

Third, here major emphasis was for strengthening of the movement for a NIEO based on justice and equality. She particularly wanted the conference to outline a common strategy for follow up action by the non-aligned countries on the global forums. Moreover as a matter of caution to the developed North in the starting of more meaningful dialogue with the under developed South she said: In this interdependent world where you cannot stir a flower without troubling a start 'even the most affluent are not immune to such disturbances'.

Finally she expressed her concern for the points of discord within the movement, particularly in the light of conflict areas like the Iran-Iraq war, the Afganistan situation and the Kampuchean issue. She made a frantic plea for unity within the movement at such a difficult and trying moment.

India as the host country was represented at the subcommittees concerned with political and economic declarations India's overall contribution at the New Delhi Summit may be summed up as follows: As a host country in order to ensure, a successful working of the Summit meeting saw to it that its own preferences on global and regional issues did not stand in the way of accommodating other's view points. To cite one instance, in the draft political declaration circulated by India, on the Afganistan issue, a political solution was envisaged on the basis of withdrawal of Soviet forces from Kabul but on Pakistan's insistence, the mediatory and constructive role played by the UN secretary General Parez de Cuellar was especially mentioned.

Indira Gandhi clarified India's view points in her major addresses and press conferences. While on one hand she expressed a major concern on the increasing threats of nuclear disarmament and pathetically slow movement of disarmament talks between two Super Powers, on the other hand she could foresee an independent and constructive role for the non-aligned community without having a naturally or any natural enemy.

In fact in the opinion of Indian Premier NAM's attitude towards the two Super Powers were taken on merits of each case without any consideration of whether some one was friendly with it or not. NAM's main task as outlined by her at the press conference were ' to promote the cause of non alignment, work for peace, freedom, equality, justice for all people in all parts of the world including women who constitute half the population. She expressed optimism for the solution of some intra movements conflicts like the Iran-Iraq war and Palestinian issue etc. She expressed major concern at the further militarization of the Indian ocean and saw only limited and educative role by the non-aligned group in that direction. On the North-South dialogue, India's stand as clarified by her was that it is an interdependent world, the developed countries have equal share as the developing countries in its success'.

Pakistan's contribution to at the New Delhi summit was qually meaningful with the exception of a single aberration of behaving raised an exclusively bilateral issue like Kashmir by General Zia in his plenary address. Other distinguished members of his team like Foreign Minister Shahib Zada Yaqub Khan and a noted economist very richly contributed the deliberation stage especially on the issue of global economic negotiations. The most significant point from Pakistani point of view which emerged out of these talks and discussions are as follows:

For Pakistan it was the second exposure to the non-aligned Summits. It was obvious for Pakistan to contribute modestly in all major decisions taken in New Delhi. No doubt it did not want to project itself as a country with a special relationship with the US. On the other hand by somewhat diluting its earlier stand on Afganistan it wanted to show an olive branch to Moscow. The major thrust of General Zia's speech as expected was focussed on the interference of an external power in the internal affairs of no aligned countries (with reference to Afghanistan and Kampuchea).

Yaqub Khan rationalised Zia's mild reference to Kashmir by stating the 'military dictatorships were as sensitive to public opinion as democracies'. Mehbuba Haq submitted two ambitious proposals including one for institutionalization of the Cancum Summit and another for a regular non-aligned summit devoted entirely to economic issues. Pakistan also favoured the setting up of a third world Secretariat to service the non-aligned summit. Besides, in its view, a committed of top experts of the developing world should being out an authorative annual report on the state of the economy of these countries.

When the economic declaration was finally drafted he expressed his happiness and listed the achievement of Delhi Summit as follows: 'a shift in priorities, emergence of a new realism in a global negotiation strategy and recognition of a need for organising political pressure to strengthen the hands of economic negotiations.

Then it concludes that India and Pakistan were more or less agreed on the major economic problems faced by the developing countries as well as on the proposed solution of regional disputes in West Asia and else where. There were differences on the bilateral matters among them. So far as their attitude to world issues is concerned there were certain differences among them not only at the level of operationalization but also in their perception of certain cold war.

No Two countries in the world perhaps have so much of persistent mutual hatreds ,suspicion, competition and rivalry as do India and Pakistan in the post-Second World War history of international-relations. The two Koreas North Korrea and Korea fought a war-in-early 1950s, signed and armistice agreement in 1953 and are officially at war even now. But they have trot fought any war since then.

And both the sides have an agenda item called unification of the Korean Peninsula. North Vietnam and and South Vietnam fought a war for years, but finally got unified as one nation. China has flexed its military muscle against Taiwan, but these two entities do not consider each other as undiluted enemies. China hopes to unify Taiwan with the mainland someday. And Taiwan considers Mainland China- as part of its territory. The Korean,-Vietnamese;and Chinese. issues were part of tile Cold War, Cold War, Russia (the main Successor State of the former Soviet Union) and the United States do not consider each other as enemies any more.

While Arab-Israeli question is a different kettle of fish, as Arabs do not constitute one stae and Palestine is not a state entity yet, Indo-Pakistani relations have remained a burning example of hate-hate international relations. Since their birth as independent countries, India and Pakistan have fought four rounds of armed conflict - the latest was in the summer of 1999. The character of the conflict between India and Pakistan is indicated by the kind of disputes the two countries are engaged in. For instance, India and Pakistan fought a war over the Rann of Kutch in 1965. The Rann of Kutch is incidentally a marshland, which is neither fit for navigation nor for farming. The dispute is far from over. These two countries have been fighting an undeclared war in the Siachen Glacier for decades, where more casualties take place due to weather conditions than real exchange of fire by the men in uniform. India and Pakistan, moreover, are engaged in a proxy-armed conflict in Kashmir for more than twelve years where Indian soldiers are employed on a combat role to meet the challenge from Pakistan-backed well-armed terrorists.

While the approach of the major powers towards India and Pakistan was deeply complicated during the Cold War, many nations, particularly the major powers, in the post-Cold War context appear to be trying to project a neutral posture towards the subcontinental mini-Cold War. Practically; no single country in the world seems prepared to take sides on Indo-Pak disputes. Simultaneously, the international community is increasingly concerned about the South Asian mini-Cold War in the light of the recent nuclearization of India and Pakistan. Notwithstanding Indian views to the contrary. several nations appear to have been convinced that the Kashmir issue is a potential nuclear flash point. Pakistan, of course, takes advantage of the general fear around the world of the nuclear -exchange by projecting Kashmir as a nuclear. flash point.

The continuing conflict in Kashmir today poses the gravest danger to India and Pakistan. While majority of the countries go by. the Indian view that Indo-Pak disputes and bilateral issues.should be resolved by the two concerned countries on the basis of healthy bilateralism, Indian cannot easure external non-interference in the.case of a major war in South Asia in the light of new realities of the 21st century. Although Pakistan has always sough: to internationalise its disputes with India, Pakistan today cannot. ensure that any- kind. of external role would be beneficial to its self-interest.

In other words, in the changed circumstances, India has to realise that it cannot solve its problems with Pakistan bilaterally~any more. This is particularly related to the ongoing low intensity armed conflict in Kashmir. India has to understand that half of its army is engaged in Kashmir, but no solution is visible in the horizon because the situation does not reflect a conventional-armed conflict. If the US could not fight terrorism its own and had to establish as international coalition, can India do it-alone? Pakistan too has to learn a couple of lessons from the ongoing war against terrorism in Kashmir. The first lesson is that promoting terrorists as an instrument of foreign policy has a boomerang effect. Since terrorists do not understand the language of non-violence and they cannot be as responsible as state actors, they can strike back at their creators. Recent history is replete with such examples. Secondly, the international community has increasingly felt the need for dealing with terrorism in a relatively more cooperative method. As a result, states sponsoring terrorism will have to face international isolation and punishment if they continue to back terrorist elements. Pakistan, in this context, has to learn a lot from its recent experience with the Taliban and Al Qaida.

It appears at the moment that Pakistan is seeking to run with the hare and hunt with the hound by pledging support to the US war against terror and simultaneously promoting terrorism in Kashmir, is understandable that Pakistan could not have antagonised the Americans. And that it has successfully waged a proxy war in Kashmir for more than a decade against Indian interests.

After receiving a severe blow to its policy of encouraging religious extremism in the wake of,US war against the Taliban, the Musharraf regime apparently is. trying to win back the support of local Jihadi groups by not abandoning the Kashmir policy. It has perhaps.found some comfort from the fact that India is not to a position to build a coalition of nations to wage a war against the kind of terrorism it has been facing for years.

However, Pakistan has to realise that it has trot succeeded in achieving its nefarious goal in Kashmir even after twelve years of its proxy war efforts. It is unlikely to win this war in next thousand,years!.Thus, before its policies backfire, the Pakistan Government, military or otherwise, will have to change course as far as the Kashmir policy is concerned.

In other words, India has to quickly draw lesson from the fact that it cannot end terrorism in Kashmir by unilateral measures and Pakistan has to) earn that it cannot achieve its foreign policy objective by using terrorists as an instrument of its policy. And both have to comprehend the mammoth opportunity cost of not coming to terms with the issue in realistic terms. Neither country can afford to delay or postpone resolution of this issue. since opportunity cost would increase in geometrical proportion with each passing day.

There is an element of sentiment involved in this issue both for the secular Indians-and non-secular Pakistanis. After all, Kashmir has come-to symbolise the indo-Pak ideological conflict. However, if sentiments begin to hurt. reason has-to prevail afterall there was no country cal led Pakistan a little over half a century ago. India did not have a current geographical shape around that time! In this age of globalisation, political boundaries are increasingly becoming irrelevant to national prosperity and strength. India and Pakistan thus should look for alternative ways of resolving this issue to avoid missing the bus.

No serious research and study has been, done from either side of the Indo-Pak border on the "opportunity benefit", and not cost, of burying the hatchet and initiating cooperative measures. Some argue-that the first step should be burying the hatchet.

Others point out that efforts towards resolution of the conflict and adoption of confidence building measures, should go. side.by. side. Islamabad seems to be interested "in neither. It is neither prepared to take up standstill approach and just put the differences in the deep freeze nor is in favour of a comprehensive friendship and cooperation treaty with India. What it wants is only dialogue at any place, at any time and any level! But dialogue for what? It is for resolving the issue! In other worlds, Islamabad does not seem to be serious about it states.

However, it does not require extraordinary wisdom to grasp Islamabad's predicament. Its suspicion of India cannot vanish into thin air in the backdrop of half a century of hostility. For that matter, India too is suspicious of Islamabad's motivation. All four rounds of armed conflict Pakistan thrust on India in the past and especially the Kargil misadventure close on the heels of Indian Prime Minister Atal Behari Vajpayee's Lahore Bus Diplomacy cannot make India forget the treachery so soon and begin believing in Islamabad's so-called "peace moves".

Does it mean that the hate-hate relationship between the two countries have become a permanent feature of the 'India sub-continent?Actually fifty years is nothing in the life a nation: If Indo-Pak ties have remained strained for half a century, there is no certainty !hat it would remain so. .for an indefinite period in the future. We have heard about "hundred years of war" in Europe. We have more recently witnessed eight-years of war between Iran and Iraq in the Middle East. We have seen America in a combat role in Vietnam and the Soviets in Afghanistan for years.

The US and the former Soviet Union had locked horns in a fierce Cold War for decades! The Koreas have remained divided twelve years after the end of tile Cold War. The unification of China and Taiwan has not taken place year -after the Chinese economic reforms and the Taiwanese political reforms. Compared to all these realities of international affairs, Indo-Pak hostility does not look as bad as people around the world generally feel.

These are several silver linings in the dark cloud over the Indian subcontinent. But it is the need of the hour for -both Indians and Pakistanis to recognize that other people's owes do not set an admirable example for us. ! n fact, Pakistan would not have been in a precarious position today but for its flawed India policy. And India would certainly have a much more prosperous economy but for the troubles created by Pakistan due to the litter's inferiority complexes vis-a-vis India-

The significant first step in dealing with the Indo-Pak problems is perhaps not seeking resolution of

Kashmir issue, not nuclear confidence building, not enhancing trade and investment relations and not even cessation of fire along the long border. All these have been tested and have failed. The first step need not be a dialogue between the political leaders or government officials either.

The beginning should be encouraging unrestricted travel of people from India to Pakistan and vice versa. The old leadership in both the countries has failed to resolve the problem. The chance should perhaps be given to younger generations to interact openly with one another. Selective cultural exchange programmes, educational exchange programmes and second track level deliberations are important but not adequate. May be the younger generations in both the countries can establish a friendly chemistry, which in turn can slowly lead towards a path of bilateral cooperation and mutual esteem.

The sence of publci outrage at the terrorist attacks on the Indian Parliament on 13 December 2001 and on the Jammu and Kashmir legislature on 1 October has deeply scarred the collective psyche of the Indian nation. The Indian government's response reflects this sense of overwhelming anger at Pakistan's unwillingness to clamp down on terrorist groups that are creating havoc in South Asia, and beyond. More critically, however, New Delhi's moves articulate a growing frustration at its relations with Islamabad and its inability, despite persistent efforts, to inject 'a modicum of civility and stability in bilateral relations. The Pakistan conundrum presents perhaps the most intriguing example in the history of state-to-state relations since the Treaty off Westphalia.

Neither military defeat, nor constructive engagement, nor unilateral gestures, nor passive disregard and nor even international pressure seem to be able to reduce the pathological hostility that the Pakistani state bears towards India, and which goes much beyond the problems in Kashmir. .

Consider the history of India-Pakistan relations, and the manner in which the whole spectrum of policies adopted-by-New Delhi towards Islamabad -have floundered because of oppugnant Pakistani behaviour. Twice since 1998, New Delhi -has publicly engaged., Pakistan.

The Lahore summit of February 1999 raised expectations that a new detente in the subcontinent was in the offing, and indeed the summit documents included an imaginative set of cooperative measures particularly on the nuclear issue. So much so that several do-gooders prematurely nominated Prime Ministers Vajpayee and Sharif for the Nobel peace prize.

But even more prudent analysts seemed to have been convinced that the overt nuclearization of the sub-continent would help Pakistan to acquire the confidence and maturity to normalize its relations with India without being burdened by existentialist fears that had plagued it since 1947 but particularly since 1971.

In the event, Pakistan-instead of seeking to project, itself as a responsible nuclear power-sought to use the cover of nuclear weapons to escalate-the conflict in Kashmir, burying the Lahore process under the heights of Kargil. Similarly, the Agra summit failed primarily because Pakistan was unwilling to concede that no normalization of relations is possible until Islamabad continues with its policy of sponsoring violence and terror across the border. Indeed, it is believed that India had been willing to concede at Agra much more than it had done during the last decade, including setting up of high level bilateral group to discuss Kashmir and only Kashmir. But whatever was left of the spirit of Agra evaporated after the 11 September terrorist attacks and particularly after the terrorist attack in Srinagar on 1 October.

But Lahore and Agra were only the public face of a policy of engagement that New Delhi has been attempting to construct at various levels. More important, India has not been shying away from discussing what Pakistan has termed as the core issue of Kashmir. It is now well known that a special envoy of the Prime Minister Vajpayee had been discreetly meeting a Pakistani counterpart, in the weeks after the Lahore summit, to discuss a possible resolution of the Kashmir issue: ~It is even believed that the two interlocutors had been mandated by their respective Prime Ministers to find a solution for Kashmir before the dawn of the 21st century, and met several times in Islamabad and New Delhi before Kargil and the military coup by General Musharraf derailed the process.

Similarly, New Delhi has persisted in its efforts to initiate a peace process with Kashmiri separatists, even with.that section which it knows is deeply beholden to Pakistan and is in constant communication with elements within the Pakistani establishment. Even before K.C. Pant was designated as a special interlocutor earlier this year, a quiet dialogue wilt Kashmiri, separatists and militant had been continuing for at least a year.

But it became clear that any time that there was a real chance of translating discreet drawing room parleys, into a more public political, Pakistan would use all means at its.disposal, indirect physical threats, to subvert the process. In other words. Islamabad was unwilling to even let Kashmiri leaders, who it had sponsored, sustain a meaningful dialogue with New Delhi's representatives. Neither have unilateral gestures of goodwill and - cooperation made a difference.

India's continued treatment of Pakistan as a most favoured nation has not been reciprocated by Islamabad and, it is believed, that the report of the SAARC Eminent Persons Group, which recommends imaginative time-bound steps to promote regional economic integration, have been given short shrift by Pakistan, despite the presence of one of its former foreign secretaries as part of the group. New Delhi's decision.

Before the Agra summit, to unilaterally relax visa rules or its decision to open further crossing points on the border- have failed or had little effect in the absence of Pakistani reciprocity. Pakistani unwillingness to give visas to Indian artistes, its attempts at blocking Indian television channels, have meant that the hope that there could be a detente from below, a genuine breakthrough because of greater people-to people contact, too have been dashed.

Ignoring the military regime in Pakistan has always seemed to be an attractive option. For more than year, after the Kargil war-and before the Agra summit. India passively disregarded Islamabad. There were those within India who were convinced that Pakistan was in such a deep, internal crisis that it was best left alone. Economically it was on the verge of collapse, politically it had descended into yet another praetorian phase and socially it was one of the most divided societies in the world. On paper, this option may have seemed desirable, but in reality it was an option. that was- unsustainable. It is extremely difficult to ignore Pakistan if Islamabad does not want to be left alone. As long as Pakistan continues its support for militancy and terrorism in Kashmir and other places, and seeks to portray South Asia as a .region on the brink of a nuclear war, it will be almost impossible to look the other way.

If both a policy of constructive .engagement and passive disregard have failed, so has the policy of military defeat and international pressure. Although it would have been unrealistic to expect General Musharraf, the architect of Kargil to concede that the war of 1999 led to a total humiliation of Pakistan, militarily and diplomatically, it is a fact conceded even by a wide range of Pakistani commentators. But the lessons of Kargil, have not led to any change in Pakistani- attitude towards India. Indeed, .in the past, even the defeat of 1971,.and the dismemberment of the country, led to no rupture in Pakistani thinking.

Nor has Pakistan's global isolation, until I 1 September, its description as a failed state, or persistent international pressure, most memorably reflected in American President Clintons statements during. his four hour stop in Islamabad last year, seem to have forced the guardians of the Pakistan state to change their India policy.

What then arc the options open for India? Will the future be different from the past? Very unlikely. In the long term, the only hope is that the Pakistani state and society, through internal introspection, will move from its anti-Indian identity to becoming a country that has come to terms with it and is able to construct itself in more humane, if not more modern terms. But in the short term, India will have to live with persistent Pakistani hostility even while it may attempt, in vain~if past experience is good evidence, a new cycle of policies, ranging from military action to constructive engagement. What, however. about the Kashmir issue? A permanent division of Jammu and Kashmir between.-India and Pakistan along the present Line of Control (LOC), with minor adjustments if need be, may be-in the medium term-the only realistic, practical and just settlement of the problem.

While such a move would mean that India would have to forsake its commitment to the unanimous parliamentary resolution that calls for reclaiming the territory "under Pakistan's occupation", and for Pakistan to give up its traditional claim to all of Kashmir, a conversion of the present Line of Control into art international border would settle a problem which has defied a solution for more than half a century.

The LOC corresponds, more or less, to the Cease-fire Line (CFL). Recall that the CFL was created after the suspension of armed hostilities between India and Pakistan on Jan. 1, 1949. But it was delineated on maps during the Karachi Agreement of July 27, 1949, formally known as the "Agreement Between Military\ Representatives of India and Pakistan Regarding the Establishment of a Cease-fire Line in the State of Jammu and Kashmir."

By Nov. 3. 1949, with the help of United Nations military observers, the borders on the map had been demarcated on the ground by the two sides. The CFL, however. was demarcated only from the west of the Chenab River up to map coordinate NJ 9842, and not beyond. The absence of any physical demarcation has led to competing claims over the Siachen glacier, but the legality of the CFL itself has never been questioned.

The CFL, with minor changes, became the LOC after the Shimla Agreement of July 2, 1972. It was delineated on maps and demarcated by top military officers from both India and Pakistan. Until the Pakistani intrusion in Kargil. the sanctity of the LOC had been accepted and respected as such by the governments in Islamabad and New Delhi and their military commanders on the border. In short. the CFL/LOC has been the de facto border for 50 years.

There have been at least three occasions on which there seems to have been a near agreement between top Indian and Pakistani leaders that Jammu and Kashmir be partitioned along the CFL/LOC, with some adjustments. In 1955, Prime Minister Jawaharlal Nehru and Pakistani Governor General Ghulam Mohammad are believed to have agreed to a division along the- CFL with minor adjustments. Between December 1962-and May. 1963.

Pakistan's then Foreign Minister Zulfiqar Ali Bhutto and Sardar Swaran Singh, a senior Indian cabinet minister, discussed a plan for partitioning, along the CFL, with India conceding an addition 3.000 square miles west and north of the Kashmir valley, including Tithwal and Handal forests and the river Kishanganga.

These plans too did not translate into an agreement. In 1972, Prime Ministers Indira Gandhi and Zulfiqar Ali Bhutto, too, seemed to have arrived at an understanding that converting the LOC into the international border was the only way out of the Kashmir conundrum. Bhutto, it is believed however, did not want an agreement in black and white since he "wanted time" to prepare his people for the "deal." The Pakistanis. Bhutto claimed had been traumatized by the defeat in the 1971 war and the dismemberment of Pakistan, Bhutto reneged on this understanding within months. Most of Indira Gandhi' advisers, however, knew about the secret agreement. While her-secretary, P.N. Dhar, has written about it, her closest adviser during that period, P.N. Haksar, was aware of the understanding.

History apart, there are at least four reasons why converting the LOC into the international border is still the most practical solution to the Kashmir issue. First, a solution to the Kashmir problem cannot be provided on the basis of absolutes. Absolute victory is not possible for either India or Pakistan. It is unrealistic for New Delhi or Islamabad to imagine that it can, with either force or diplomacy, reunify the whole of Jammu and Kashmir.

3

Jammu and Kashmir: Burning Issues

The Kashmiri community, which was closely interwoven, was targeted. Those not supporting the militants were accused of being traitors and un-Islamic; they were forced to quit or remain quiet. It became taboo to interact with anyone within the national framework. Fear of societal rejection and suppression of dissent resulted in ambivalence of the Kashmiri mindset, depriving them of clarity of perception. Pakistan has been successful in creating a crisis of ideology and identity in Kashmir. This 'confusion' needs to be seriously addressed for winning their support and confidence. An additional factor augmenting suppression was the constant fear of the ISI (Inter Services Intelligence of Pakistan).

With informers and dissenters being cruelly dealt with, specifically denying burial to the dead, the 'ghost of ISI' has entered deep into the Kashmiri psyche. Further, Pakistan has succeeded in transferring suspicion, hostility and anger from one generation to another. Efforts to relieve the Kashmiris of the constant fear of being 'watched' is fundamental to reconstruction of the society. Notwithstanding the various economic measures that can yield specific results, a crucial sector that needs to be focused upon remains the class of entrepreneurs who find the business of militancy to be lucrative. This class lacks the skills for alternate means of employment and needs to be tackled.

The issue of Human Rights in Kashmir has failed to deliver the desired results that Pakistan was expecting. Following elaborate plans that were conceived in the Islamabad Institute of Strategic Studies in 1988, to include Jammu and Kashmir in the UN agenda on Human Rights, Pakistan systematically focused on the human rights situation in Kashmir in all international forums. Ironically, it made use of studies conducted by Indian activists and scholars, who unwittingly played into their hands.

Between the period 1990-94, Pakistan was successful in its propaganda and, in 1995, attempts were made to introduce a resolution in the UN censuring India on human rights violation in Kashmir. However, after 1995, international interest in the issue waned after realization of the ground reality. Human rights groups also adopted a more cautious approach on the subject.

Pakistan has lost control over the various Jihadi groups operating on its soil. Initially, Musharraf attempted to portray a moderate outlook and rein in these groups. However, all his attempts have failed due to intense pressure within the military to support the jihad groups. With increasing propaganda that heaven was assured for martyrs, more people are now ready to send their children for jihad; that this section of the people is increasing does not augur well for India or for Pakistan. The fact that Pakistan is in no position to control these groups need to be borne in mind when charting out a strategy to address this problem.

Grievous lapses by India have given Pakistan leverage to commit the atrocities mentioned above. Which, if they were avoided could have gained popular support for to India. Mishandling of the Centre's relationship with Sheikh Abdullah has been the most prominent of these mistakes. Post partition there were feelings of pro-independence and pro-India/accession; pro-Pakistan sentiments were significantly absent. Sheikh Abdullah headed the majority pro-accession group and worked against the strong wave of communalism. The Indian government should have cultivated his position to promote pro-India sentiments.

However, this not being done, with prevailing social and political conditions deteriorating, Sheikh Abdullah was forced to think of the third option of accession to Pakistan and issue statements tantamount to rethinking the policy of accession. The pro-India constituency in Kashmir was left uncultivated, but worse, squeezed out without having the opportunity to establish itself politically. Liberal leaders, expelled from the National Conference, were forced to reconcile with Sheikh Abdullah, and all attempts to organize an opposition were stifled.

This eroded a good check-and-balance system but also the emergence of a political alternative. Methods of rehabilitation of militants and their leaders have also been a blunder. Rehabilitating them in a manner beyond and above their status has robbed them and their commanders of social and political credibility. This has been a strategic and political lapse on the part of India in failing to cultivate the full potential of these surrendered militants.

On the issue of autonomy, the Indian Government should have been sensitive to the feelings of the people and not outrightly have rejected the resolution. It could have been delayed, discussed and debated before final rejection. The debate could have encapsulated devolution for the entire country, and not just a particular state.

The status of the entire state of Jammu and Kashmir, including territories in Pakistani and Chinese possession, needs attention. In a sense, Kashmir is a trilateral issue not a bilateral one. China holds the Shaksgam valley ceded to it by Pakistan in the sixties. China also holds Aksai Chin and the Deosai plains which India claims. This reality has to be factored into any discussion on territory. Current Indian thought bifurcates the Pakistani from the Chinese problem, and treats the Line of Actual Control with China separately. Diplomatically, this makes sense, but not geo-strategically. The other question is that India has been pushing hard to get everybody to accept the "reality" of the Line of Control between India and Pakistan.

The US has apparently accepted this formulation, for its own reasons. If this reality is to be transformed into fact, India and Pakistan will have to ponder over what happens to Siachen, i.e. the territory beyond Pt. NJ 9842, where there is no LOC but only what India calls the Actual Ground Position Line (AGPL). This, of course, detracts attention from the fact that Pakistan committed aggression in Kashmir in1947 and was emboldened to do so again in 1999 in Kargil.

The bilateral aspect of Indo-Pak relations are currently focused on India's pre-conditions for resuming a dialogue with Pakistan on the latter ending cross-border terrorism. This is vital for any trust to be established, but is inexorably linked to internal violence ending. This is where a political dialogue between all political parties is required. Several forums have begun this process, but more needs to be done to end the cult of the gun. A political dialogue is also a dialogue with the people, people of all shades of opinion and religions. It is a dialogue that has to be constantly undertaken. It also involves people from the Northern Areas and Pakistan Occupied Kashmir, this much Pakistan has to accept.

Without it the dialogue would be incomplete. In fact not enough has been done to focus world attention on conditions in the Northern Areas and POK; this is a challenge for Indian diplomacy. This is where also governance and coordination in counter-insurgency operations also become imperative. The key is realising that, in the long run, allowing the insurgency in the state to become a money spinning business like in India's North-East is detrimental to national interests.

Socio-economic issues

The revival of the state, both socially and economically can happen only when violence ends. People will return, this applies to Kahmiris who have left the State and tourists, only when the atmosphere is calm. Too much should not be expected from those who left Kashmir in the early phases of the insurgency and have settled elsewhere. It is those who are living in refugee camps that the government must focus on. Provide incentives to return. Rebuild houses and villages ravaged by decades of insurgency. Take up road building on a large scale. Improve communications. And get people to participate. All this is premised on violence receding from the Kashmiri psyche. Once India is clear about the internal-external dynamic and seeks a solution on these lines, evolving a national consensus on Jammu and Kashmir may become easier.

A charade has been played by the Indian media and Government by terming the armed conflict in Jammu & Kashmir (J&K) as the handiwork of Kashmiri militants fighting for Independence. This is not realistic or preventative of the true state of affairs. Firstly, labeling them as Kashmiris is incorrect as only the Valley Muslims are involved. The other Muslims in Jammu and Ladakh are not involved. Secondly, the Valley Muslims' militancy was contained by the security forces by 1998, and the situation was moving towards normalcy. Pakistan became rattled by the waning of the militancy due to disgust of the average Valley Muslim with atrocities on their women folk and disruption of their lives by the "Pakistani Jehadis," which spawned the Kargil War.

The diversion of our security forces from the Valley to Kargil enabled Pakistan to put into place two nefarious schemes. They pumped hundreds of Pakistani Jehadis, Afghan Mujahidden and Islamic fundamentalists into the Valley. Their main tasks were liquidation of erstwhile militants who had joined the mainstream and escalate violence and armed conflict, not only in the valley, but also in Jammu and Doda regions. An additional task was to carry out ethnic cleansing of minorities from these regions.

The situation in Kashmir today is not one of Valley Muslims' militancy but a full scale armed conflict launched by Pakistan to undo the accession of J&K to India in 1947. Pakistan is using Islamic fundamentalist mercenaries of all hues in J&K namely Pakistani Jehadis from 'madrassas', Afghan Mujahideen mercenaries and Islamic fundamentalist mercenaries from other Islamic countries. Military operations against these mercenaries needs to be guided by the following operational principles:

1. Islamic fundamentalist mercenaries are neither Indian citizens nor soldiers of an opposing army participating in a declared state of War.
2. Thus, these mercenaries do not qualify for any humane treatment under Human Rights Codes, nor do they qualify under the Geneva Conventions.
3. They must be dealt with ruthlessly. If captured, the death penalty by firing squad is the least punishment they deserve.
4. This should apply also to those Indian citizens, Kashmiri or otherwise, who aid, abet or assist Islamic Fundamentalist mercenaries in J&K. Such Indian citizens forfeit their citizenship when they aid the enemy, waging war against the Indian State.

Islamic Fundamentalist mercenaries operating in J&K have the following vulnerabilities:

- They operate in small bands, and are incapable of offering sustained armed resistance in pitched battles.
- Present targeting patterns indicate suicide bomber attacks against Headquarters of security forces,

communication set-ups, use of IEDs against convoys, and liquidation of Government informers with specific targeting of erstwhile militants.

- Ethnic cleansing in the Valley and Doda.
- They have limited logistic sustainability unless supported by ammunition and explosives catches located in inaccessible areas. Islamic Fundamentalist mercenaries have shown preference for the Pir Panjal ranges and Doda Distt.

These vulnerabilities need to be exploited by the security forces. Broad operational techniques by Security Forces to deal with threat are as follows:

1. Greater resort to helicopter-borne operations, both surveillance and assault on mercenaries hideouts in the Pir Panjal, Doda and Kupwara areas. The Pir Panjal ranges are devoid of forests and facilitate such operations.
2. Special Forces of the Indian Army are under-utilized both in peace and war. It is high time the entire weight of these forces is brought to bear against these mercenaries.
3. Mining of preferred routes of infiltration /exfiltration used by these mercenaries.
4. Mercenaries cannot stay indefinitely in J&K, they have to exfiltrate at some stage and be replaced by new Jehadis. The exfiltration process and the routes used are most vulnerable and need to be exploited to inflict casualties on the mercenaries.
5. Armed police forces like the BSF and CRPF are neither trained nor equipped to deal with Islamic mercenaries. Greater reliance will have to be placed

on Army and Rashtriya Rifles resources. Requirement exists for raising more such battalions and those of the Territorial Army.

6. The Indian Air Force needs to be co-opted and integrated into the Army's efforts to combat Islamic mercenaries by surveillance, bombing of hideouts and air assaults using helicopter gun ships.

7. The Army must devise its own intelligence set up in J&K over and above the RAW and IB so that it has actionable intelligence readily available.

8. Since the Islamic mercenaries have to depend on local support, the Government must task the IB for penetrating anti-Indian political groups supporting Pak designs. They could thus get information of infiltration/exfiltration plans also.

The situation in J&K today is neither militancy nor insurgency. It is an all out war imposed by Pakistan against India by using Islamic fundamentalist mercenaries with the rallying cry of Islam in danger. It is a pity that Indian secularists and the liberal fraternity have closed their eyes to this aspect. Obliviousness to this danger spells for the Indian nation state. The Islamic fundamentalist mercenaries in J&K need to be targeted and liquidated ruthlessly.

The Line of Control

Even after instigating the proxy war in Jammu and Kashmir for more than ten years, the Pakistani military establishment's dream of bleeding the Indian security forces white has not been realised. Their resolute fighting compelled Pakistan to beat a retreat from Kargil and foiled its attempts to sponsor armed mercenaries to destabilise Kashmir. Pakistan's obsession with Kashmir however, has taken more than 50,000 lives during the last decade. The time has finally arrived for Pakistan to realise its folly which, has bled it, converted it into a failed state on the brink of political and economic breakdown.

Since a military solution has obviously not succeeded, the answer lies in having peaceful relations with India by recognising the sanctity of the existing Line of Control (LoC) and eventually transforming the de facto line of control to a de jure international border between the two South Asian nations. The LoC was known earlier as the Cease Fire Line before the Simla Accord, and as a result of UN Security Council resolutions in 1949. Immediately after gaining freedom in August 1947, Pakistan's army in the guise of Pathan tribals had attacked the former princely state of Kashmir; its ruler had legally acceded to India after signing an Instrument of accession under the provisions of the Indian Independence Act passed by the British Parliament earlier that year. The line of control is more than 700 kilometers long, from the Akhnoor sector in the south, proceeding north and north-eastwards and, ending up at Point NJ 9842 near Thang, south of the Siachen glacier. Thereafter, it was left unmarked up to the natural border of India in the extreme north as this region was considered inaccessible.

The Indian Parliament has passed a resolution a couple of years back declaring the whole state of Jammu and Kashmir, including the part across the LoC under Pakistan's military occupation, as an integral part of India. With the passage of time, this resolution had disappeared from public memory. But the tough stance of the BJP led the government, especially after the toppling of the democratic government in Pakistan has revived it.

The Indian Prime Minister had also expressed his government's resolve to liberate the Pakistan occupied territories of Kashmir. Such rhetorical statements only add to tensions between the two hostile neighbours, now armed with nuclear weapons. This may be one of the several compulsions propelling the US to emphasise the sanctity of the LoC. to avoid a military flare up in South Asia. The US pressure may force India and Pakistan to find a final solution to the Kashmir problem by converting the LoC into a permanent international border. A territorial status quo in Jammu and Kashmir will definitely be to India's advantage. The ceasefire line, since converted into a LoC, is not the natural border separating POK from J&K. But it certainly delineates the ethnic, cultural and linguistic divide in the state.

On the Indian side the Kashmiri and Dogri ethos is apparent, and corresponds with Pan-Indian secularism; but the population on the other side is ethnically closer to Pakistan's heartland focussing around Lahore and Rawalpindi. The Americans, Europeans and other powers have repeatedly advised Islamabad to respect the LoC and desist from armed intervention in the State, but, the Pakistani leadership has been justifying 'jehad' as the means to liberate Kashmir.

The highly fundamentalist vision of Islamabad's policy makers sees the territory of J&K as crucial to Pakistan's existence on the basis of the Muslim League's two-nation theory. The bitter truth needs to be appreciated by Islamabad is that any government in New Delhi which tries to withdraw from Kashmir hoped for by Islamabad, would not survive in office.

In recent weeks there have been some positive signs that the Central government and All Party Hurriyet Conference (APHC) might enter a dialogue on resolving the crisis in Kashmir. There has been no official confirmation, but it is believed that Mir Qasim, former Chief Minister of Jammu and Kashmir has been asked by the Central government to negotiate with the various Kashmiri groups. The Defence Minister, George Fernandes, also met the Chief Minister of Jammu and Kashmir, Dr. Farooq Abdullah, during the last week of April. Sayeed Abbas Naqvi, a BJP leader, visited the state during the first week of May, meeting various sections of the people. The APHC also seems to be responding cautiously but positively. There has been enormous pressure on the Centre to negotiate with the Kashmiri people.

The end of the Kargil war witnessed a change in the nature of militancy in Kashmir, with the security forces and installations becoming the primary targets of militant attacks. The Chittisinghpura massacre, in which the Sikh community became the target of the militant groups, add a communal angle to the militancy emphasising the need for a fresh approach. Moreover, the alienation of Farooq Abdullah's government from the people has made the Centre realise that over reliance on the National Conference, though a part of the BJP's National Democratic Alliance (NDA), will worsen the situation. Besides, the sudden passing of the State Autonomy Committee and Regional Autonomy Committee Reports by the Farooq government must have unnerved the Centre. Finally, the external pressures on the Indian government, especially after the US President Clinton's visit, has made the Centre realise the need for a internal dialogue with people in Jammu and Kashmir.

The APHC was also under pressure, especially after Clinton's visit. Clinton had made it very clear that the 1948 UN Resolution on Jammu and Kashmir has been overtaken by time; ruled out American intervention in Kashmir; and stated that a solution must be found be "within the frame work of India's unity." Thus lack of support from the US would have made APHC to realise the change in the political environment. The APHC also would have realised that the various militant groups operating inside Kashmir, have started functioning independently. With the APHC being a platform of over more than 30 different political parties, religious and militant groups always struggled to reach any unanimous decisions. Having failed to achieve anything substantially in the past, other than conducting hartals, the APHC would have realised the significance of a dialogue with the Centre to gain its importance. Though everyone has emphasized the need for dialogue, both the parties have their limitations in initiating a dialogue.

The Centre wants the dialogue to be held within the constitutional provisions and shuns any third party involvement. The APHC insists on a tripartite dialogue, with Pakistan being the third party. It would be difficult for the APHC to agree on a dialogue within the "constitutional provisions", as there is a section within it, which prefers total independence whilst the other is pro-Pakistan. In fact, a section of APHC is against any dialogue with the Centre, as it believes it would affect the militant movement and all that have been gained so far. The Centre has also been sending confused signals to the APHC, with the Union Home Minister L.K. Advani saying that the Centre has no plans for a dialogue, whereas the Union Defence Minister announcing that the response of the APHC was cool.

Whatever be the hurdles, both parties should go ahead with the initiatives taken so far. The Centre has released only three APHC leaders from the jail. It can release the rest, to increase the pressure on APHC, as it has been claiming that unless all the leaders are released, it could not come to a conclusion. Secondly, though the APHC is expecting a formal offer from the Centre on the dialogue, an agreement could be reached, without making it public. In fact, there seems to be an understanding here, with Mir Qasim taking the initiative. Thirdly, the APHC should understand that, this is the right opportunity, as a section of the population seems to be interested, if not enthusiastic about the prospects of such a dialogue. The dialogue may or may not succeed in achieving any major breakthrough, but this should not hinder both the parties from conducting any meaningful negotiations. The dialogue should be institutionalized, so that even if the current round fails, there exists a forum that could be utilized in the future.

Situation in Kashmir: Report of IPCS Seminar held on 9 February 2000

The views of the panelists concerning the present situation in Kashmir were:

The last decade has seen a steady worsening of the situation in Kashmir. Though in 1996, the situation seemed to be peaceful and the popular mood was that of hope. However, these hopes were belied in the latter part of the decade. On being elected to office, the Jammu & Kashmir, Chief Minister Farooq Abdullah, had made several promises, including conducting panchayati elections, providing 20,000 jobs, activating the State

Human Rights Commission, and to publish and translate the Autonomy Committee report. However, none of this was put into practice and the alienation of the people from the government increased. Moreover, the Central government was seen as hostile to the interests of Jammu & Kashmir. The security situation in the Kashmir valley has degenerated from bad to worse, with foreign mercenaries coming into the Kashmir valley.

These mercenaries are highly motivated and attack the security installations and not the local population. The unified command of the security forces has almost broken down. Intelligence networks are in a fractured state. The local police is demoralised. The policy of rehabilitation of militants has not worked out effectively. Pakistan is determined to keep up pressure on Kashmir. Pakistan believes that sustained international pressure will bring India to the negotiating table. Pakistan is unapologetic about the Kargil conflict and this non-compromising attitude is reflective of the hardline attitude of the Pakistan military regime. India needs to strongly articulate its interests in the international arena by putting forward a coherent Kashmir policy.

Further, contrary to projecting Kashmir as a nuclear flashpoint in South Asia, India should make the international community realise that it is the role of Pakistan in South Asia that needs to be investigated. And this needs to be done in context of the mounting evidence against Pakistan about its involvement in cross-border terrorism and drug trafficking. The forthcoming visit of the American President has Kashmir on its agenda and India should use his opportunity to strongly put forward its case.

There has been a great change in the situation in the Kashmir valley between 1994 and 1998. In 1997-8, the situation in the Kashmir valley was largely under control. Tourism was picking up. Upto 1,000 militants had surrendered, and another 31,000 were dormant and seeking political participation. Further, there were many political splits among the various organisation like the JKLF, active in Kashmir. However, the government was unable to capitalise on the improving situation and squandered its gains. The Farooq Abdullah government is increasingly unpopular because of its corrupt practices. Moreover, the Centre had adopted a hostile policy to the Abdullah government, refusing to write off its debts and release the funds allocated by the Centre to the state. Owing to the lack of any economic development, the people especially the middle class in Kashmir, was becoming increasingly alienated from the government.

In fact, many possible solutions to the problems in Kashmir, such as open platform for discussions with various organisations in Kashmir, or lifting the ban on the JKLF, were ignored by the government. Since India did not capitalise on the situation, Pakistan gained from it. It renewed attacks on the Indian security forces and the number Indian casualties spiraled. In fact, at present the total number of casualties of the militancy in Kashmir may well have crossed the number of Indian army casualties in Kargil.

Pakistan's internal politics contributes to keeping the Kashmir issue alive. General Musharraf can only remain in power by continually increasing pressure on Kashmir. Otherwise, he become a liability in the predominately Punjabi-speaking Pakistan army. And he is doing so, to the extent of repeated nuclear sabre-rattling against India.

In the face of continued Pakistani support to the guerilla war in Kashmir, the Indian army needs to re-evaluate the situation in terms of the number of casualties it is willing to absorb over an indefinite period of time. If not, then it means having a decisive war with Pakistan. Third party intervention seems to be a viable option to solving the Kashmir issue. This is where the US may step in help. Clinton is of the view that South Asia is a nuclear flashpoint and hence the earlier the Kashmir issue is resolved the better.

However, one must be realistic about the fact that US will not act till such time its own interests are threatened. In fact, for India a far more productive policy would be to encourage a deal between the US and Pakistan wherein the US bail out Pakistan economically in return for a commitment to stop abetting cross-border terrorism. Kashmir is undergoing four simultaneous crises concerning its security, society, governance and that of an inadequate national response to the troubled region. The crisis of security is of recent vintage since there were some positive developments since 1996 when militancy ceased owing to the smashing of communication networks between the militants and the Pakistan army. People initially responded well to Farooq Abdullah's government and the security forces' overtures realizing that terror was becoming an end in itself. In the 1996-99 phase, militants were dormant, reorganizing through the die-hard militants. The media rediscovered its freedom while political life appeared to blossom.

Kargil changed all that, with the infiltration of Pakistani and Afghani mercenaries who have disrupted the tentative but promising relations between the armed forces and the people in the Valley. Incidents like the attack on the Badamibagh cantonment have created fear among the people all over again.

The crisis of governance apparent since 1996 has led to people following the militants on certain occasions. For instance, the attack in January on the Special Operations Group was ostensibly due to reported attempts at extracting money from the villagers and therefore the militants are perceived as saviors. The dare-devilry of the militants is both impressive and fearsome for the people. Suicide squads have existed in the Valley during the 1990 uprising as well, but the difference is that previously they were composed of local youth while foreign mercenaries exists now.

Militants are intent on creating mayhem and demoralize the Indian security forces and hence have communicated to the local populace that though they need not join them but they should not oppose them. There are uncanny similarities between the Islamist movements in Dagestan, Chechnya and Kashmir where the Wahabbi movement is very strong and proceeds on the assumption that they will liberate Muslims from foreign yoke, weed out unIslamic elements in society and use force to achieve their purposes. There is a discernible belt of Wahabbi assertion right from J&K to the Central Asian Republics.

The culture of guns has led to the crisis in society in the Valley. Violence as a social norm has ruptured familial ties. The proliferation of guns has introduced violent settling of scores and retributive justice. Deference to elders is another casualty. The constant propaganda from Pakistan Television extolling the martyrhood of 40-50,000 Kashmiris has undermined the ability of the moderates to mobilize support for a political solution.

The middle class Kashmiris who had previously supported the militants now resent the sway of violence but are unable to extricate themselves from a situation where lower-rung Kashmiris dominate the protest movement. The Abdullah government is a profile in misgovernance. Administrative anarchy is the order of the day with a complete failure of accountability. Senior officials do not even file income tax returns regularly.

The employment policies of the Abdullah government are a farce. The J&K government has appointed 100,000 people in the government sector, which logically should have amounted to the welfare of at least 600,000 people given the average family size. But this has not stemmed the alienation since local politicians dispensed the jobs through bribes.

The newly employed were mostly accommodated in security services who can actually find no work. Most do other occupations like farming and habitually arrive for work at month's end to collect paychecks which is a needless burden on the exchequer. It is generally very difficult to ensure bureaucratic integrity. Bureaucrats have arrogated to themselves the role of the politicians further marginalizing the political process. Lamentably, the rest of India tends to view Kashmir as a problem that will be solved if the Kashmiris can be made to behave. There is no denying that the situation is bad and that there is a war at hand with the terrorists but India at large must take steps to ensure that Kashmiris are on its side. No business house or associations ventured to Kashmir when things were looking up since 1996. There is no effort to integrate people at the cultural level. All that the Kashmiris are dished out are puerile television serials about militants who discover a love for India and surrender weapons. The fact that most of the valley has only 2 hours power supply a day along with two TV channels does not draw the people any closer to India.

The autonomy reports that the J&K government finalized are worth considering. There are two reports dealing with the question of state autonomy and regional autonomy. Sadly there is no inkling among the policy makers to debate the validity of these reports. A debate on autonomy is somehow perceived as a precursor to secession. The domino theory is used to eviscerate any talk of decentralization as an option in J&K.

People who hold this view forget that the mishandling of Article 356 is an issue for virtually every state in India. In any case, the current Home Minister L. K. Advani espoused the states' decentralization plan way back in 1984. Autonomy as an option has to be introduced as a discussible item if any headway is to be reached. There has always been alienation in the state bureaucracy and police in Kashmir right from 1947. Secondly, one cannot have a caste system among the various states by providing special status to Kashmir.

The Kashmir issue can only be solved through military means and for the moment governance must take as backseat. In the present international scene, a military solution to the Kashmir necessitates a favorable international opinion. We are fighting on three fronts in Kashmir. The first is a war to win the hearts and mind of the Kashmiri people. The alienation Kashmir is all pervasive because of the free hand given to the security forces in Kashmir. Politically, the Supreme Court has upheld the special status for Kashmir and to repeal Article 370 would be political denial for the Kashmiris. Secondly, the security and military analysts have to work out the best way to fight a limited war with Pakistan and explore options for making Pakistan pay for its actions in Kashmir. Thirdly, India has to garner international opinion in its favor. This requires successful diplomatic projection of India's Kashmir policy internationally.

India has to raise Pakistan's threshold for limited war. India may need to cross over the LoC, not to threaten the existence of Pakistan but to provide tactical depth for itself in fighting with the guerillas in Kashmir. India has to probe and find ways and means to do this; may be in terms of commando action in PoK or even an air attack.

The war in Kashmir is unique, hence we may needs a new force to deal with it. The militancy in Kashmir is not being funded by Pakistan alone. If Pakistan is going bankrupt, then where is the money to fund the militants in Kashmir coming from One needs to probe this issue of funding further. The US rhetoric that Kashmir is a nuclear flashpoint in South Asia does not stand in face of historical scrutiny. China and the erstwhile Soviet Union, two nuclear powers, fought a war without going nuclear. The West is with India on the issue of terrorism. However, they are asking India questions regarding governance, and human rights. Kashmiri people did not feel alienated since 1947, it set in with the economic crisis. During the last 50 years, a large middle class has emerged and they are dissatisfied with the performance of the government.

There is enough goodwill and expertise within J&K to create a domestic Track II. It will produce an informed and concerned input into policy forming. The problems of Kashmir are peculiar to the region and have to dealt with accordingly. There is no need to raise a new force to deal with the problem in Kashmir. There is tremendous support in the border districts of J&K for the security forces and an enduring fellow feeling with the Kashmiri people in PoK.

The Kashmiri people view their brethren in PoK as held under bondage and are willing to liberate them. This is proved by an incident that took place in Kashmir in April 1979. After Zulfikar Ali Bhutto was hanged in April 1979, there was a spontaneous reaction in the border areas of Kashmir. The local administration, fearing a law and order situation called in reinforcements. However, the situation unfolded to reveal that the processions were made up of the people who wanted to march into PoK to liberate it. Similar incidents have happened in the Kupwara sector in the past two years indicating great support for the army. This is representative of a difference of feelings in Srinagar and in the border areas. The autonomy reports contain nothing new that has not already been tried in Kashmir. The only contentious issues it raises are the use of Article 356 and the appointment of Sadar-e-Riyasat (a governor like position). The latter refers to a proposal to appoint the Riyazat in the state not by New Delhi's diktat by the legislative Assembly.

There is a feeling that allowing the discredited Farooq government the option to choose the Riyazat will mean that the Hurriyat Conference will have little to show for its efforts at achieving autonomy since Farooq will claim the credit. Its probably a better idea to play that "card" after Farooq exhausts himself politically. The leaders of the Hurriyat do not have adequate leverage to negotiate autonomy on behalf of the Kashmiris, since most leaders can claim barely any allegiance beyond their immediate localities. He felt that no security apparatus could win the fight against terrorism unless the people's support is enlisted. In the early 1980s the chant "Kashmir banega Afghanistan" was a laughable slogan. But going by the number of Afghani mercenaries' in Kashmir now one wonders if that might turn out to be true. Why Kashmir was given a special status by Article 370 when the instrument of accession that Hari Singh was similar in wording to instruments of accession that other princely states signed.

Though the instrument of accession was the same for all princely states, Maharaja Hari Singh appended a letter that stated that he would cede authority to the Indian Union on matters of defence, foreign policy, communications but retain a "special position" for the Kashmir province. In fact, Hari Singh wrote letters to Sardar Patel protesting the violation of Kashmir's special status.

4

Pakistan's Role in Kashmir Issues

Pakistan, therefore, had to spend more on defence as compared to other developing countries. Geographically, East Pakistan was surrounded by India from three sides. West Pakistan is wedged in-between three big neighbours, namely Soviet Union, China and India. There is no other country in the world which has geographical situation akin to Pakistan. "I know of no of other small country which has the somewhat dubious distinction of having three such mighty neighbours". This geographical position could be a source of danger for Pakistan if friendly relations were not maintained with such powerful neighbours as USSR and China.

The history of India Pak relations is witness to the fact that India has not reconciled to the existence of Pakistan? Considered objectively, defence against India has always been the major concern of Pakistan. "Pakistanis cite the long-cherished belief held among the Hindus regarding the sacred unity of India, the ancient land of Hindus. India questions the very basis of Pakistan which was established on the theory that contiguous area constituting Muslim majority would be separated from India and constitute the State of Pakistan. Pakistan was refused its due share of assets of undivided India. India practically stopped or severely restricted the flow of the river waters to the territory of Pakistan so badly needed to irrigate the cultivable areas. India played a vital role in the war of 1971.

During the September 1965 War, All-India Radio broadcast such news as the formation of a revolutionary council for the establishment of an independent republic of East Pakistan. As a result, tension or a state of cold war has always existed between the two countries. This tense situation has made the allocation of substantial portion of Pakistan Budget for defence purposes imperative. Thus, the cornerstone of Pakistan's foreign policy is the "containment of militant Hinduism, as the main concern of the West is the containment of Chinese Communism".

Pakistan being a smaller nation and having many problems was anxious to settle the disputes with India. In the first place, India refused to honour the financial settlement with Pakistan, in the wake of the partition of the subcontinent. But the most unkind cut of all was the occupation of Kashmir, Junagadh and Hyderabad. The problem of Kashmir cannot be fully comprehended without knowing its historical background.

The valley of Jammu and Kashmir was sold to Gulab Singh for seventy-five lakh of rupees by Lord Lawrence as a result of the Treaty of Amritsar. Sir Hari Singh, the successor of Gulab Singh, was the Maharaja or ruler of the State at the time of partition of the subcontinent.

According to the Census of 1947, the Muslims constituted 77 per cent of the population. The Muslims were living in miserable conditions under the Maharaja's rule. The Maharajas were alien, incompetent, dissolute and tyrannical. Agitations against the despotic rule of the Maharaja had started in early 1930s. It was in this year that the All-Jammu and Kashmir Muslim Conference was founded and a demand for basic political rights put forward. These agitations continued till 1947. The emergence of Pakistan, Lord Mountabatten, the Viceroy of India, advised the India Princes to accede to India or to Pakistan keeping in mind the geographical position of their States and the wishes of their people. This clearly meant that accession to India or Pakistan was to be dependent on two factors namely, geographical nearness and the wishes of the people.

From both these standards, Kashmir was destined to become a part of Pakistan. From geographical point of view, Kashmir had common border lines with Pakistan to the extent of 902 miles while with India it had only 317 miles of common border. The only two roads which served as a link between Jammu and Kashmir and the rest of the world passed through Pakistan.

The three main rivers which irrigate the land of Pakistan originate from Kashmir. If the accession were to be decided by the wishes of the people, Kashmir being Muslim majority area had closer affinities with Pakistan than with India.

In January 1948, India complained to the Security Council that Pakistan was giving aid to the tribesmen who had invaded a part of the valley. "Since then, the Security Council has met 136 times to consider this dispute between India and Pakistan", but without any tangible result. On the persistent demand of Pakistan, India agreed to hold a plebiscite in Kashmir to ascertain the wishes of the people in 1948.

Then she demanded the withdrawal of Pakistani troops and nationals. The plebiscite was never held because, according to India, Pakistan did not withdraw its troops which was a presupposed prerequisite for holding the plebiscite. "If an offer is made, and is not accepted or not implemented, it cannot stand for ever", was the contention of the India representative in the Security Council in response to Pakistan's demand for plebiscite. Pakistan, on the other hand, demands plebiscite in Kashmir on the basis of the right of self-determination as enunciated in the charter of the United Nations. Pakistan always agreed to the withdrawal of its troops from Azad Kashmir if India did the same in the main valley. Whenever the proposal for demilitarisation and stationing of UN Forces was put forward, Pakistan always accepted the proposal but India insisted upon the complete and unilateral withdrawal of Pakistan forces only. The same opinion was expressed by General A.G.L.McNaughton in 1950 in his report to the Security Council. He stated that Pakistan accepted the proposal for a simultaneous demilitarisation of the territories under the control of UN but "India insisted upon the complete withdrawal of Pakistan forces and the occupation of the northern area of Baltistan and Gilgit by the India Army".

In 1950, Sir Owen Dixon was appointed as Mediator to bring about an understanding between the two countries holding a plebiscite in Kashmir. He reported his failure to the United Nations. Lord Attlee put forward three alternatives during the meeting of the commonwealth Prime Ministers' Conference in January 1951. The proposals were: (1) Commonwealth Force; (2) Joint Indo-Pak force; (3) A local force to be raised by Plebiscite Administrator. Each of these proposals was accepted by Pakistan but rejected by India. On 22 February 1951 an Anglo-American resolution was brought before the Security Council suggesting that the Kashmir dispute be submitted to the International Court of Justice for arbitration. Pakistan showed her willingness, but India again refused.

In 1953, Muhammad Ali Bogra, Pakistan's Prime Minister at that time, held negotiations with Nehru, the Prime Minister of India. In the first communique, they agreed that the Kashmir dispute should be settled in accordance with the wishes of the people of that State. The most feasible way of ascertaining the wishes of the people was fair and impartial plebiscite. It was also decided that Plebiscite Administrator should be appointed who would make arrangements for holding an impartial plebiscite in the State. Meanwhile Nehru came to know that Pakistan was likely to receive military aid from USA. This gave an excuse to Nehru to delay the matter, Nehru stated, while addressing the Lok Sabha in December 1953, that India could not honour the agreement set out in the communique because "the whole context in which these arrangements were made will change if military aid comes from America". Here it should be made clear that by December 1953, Pakistan had neither received military aid from the USA nor entered into any Defence Pact.

During the Ayub regime, the Pakistan Government made all possible efforts to normalise relations with India and to settle all outstanding disputes. Ayub Khan went to the extent of proposing joint defence with India in March 1959, provided India agreed to the settlement of the Kashmir Dispute. But his gesture was not appreciated by the Indian leadership and Nehru remarked". I do not understand against whom people talk about common defence policy". India refused to settle the dispute, because-Pakistan was receiving military aid from USA, while at the same time India itself was getting massive military aid from USA and USSR. During the India-China conflict, 1962, USA, UK and some other Western governments exerted pressure on Pakistan to show morale-boosting gestures to India during this crisis. President Kennedy wrote to Ayub Khan, the them President of Pakistan, suggesting a message to the Indian Prime Minister that "he could count on Pakistan's taking no action on the frontiers to alarm India". This move was intended to show Pakistan's friendly stance so that India could concentrate all its armies against China.

The President of USA and other Western countries hoped that the "painful moments which India was then experiencing would teach them how much more important the threat from the North(...) was to the whole of subcontinent", and they also assured the President of Pakistan that action taken by him "in the larger interests of the sub-continent would do more in the long run to bring about a sensible resolution of Pakistan-India differences than anything else."As a consequence, direct talks between Ayub Khan and Nehru were arranged. On 20 November 1962, a joint statement was issued by both the Governments which expressed the desire for a "renewed effort" "to resolve the outstanding differences between the two countries on Kashmir and related matters". The statement brought a ray of hope to the people of Pakistan. But the real intentions of the Indian

Government were soon exposed when Nehru tried to modify, in a statement in the Lok Sabha, this undertaking given in the communique. His statement again put the issue into the cold storage.

Nehru had been so swiftly changing his stand on Kashmir that it became difficult to believe his words. Bhutto, then Foreign Minister of Pakistan, reacted sharply and remarked in the National Assembly while discussing the above mentioned communique that "if one were to accept them, it would follow that the joint communique is actually a deception and a fraud". Nehru had expressed his desire for renewed effort under the pressure of Chinese attack and American persuasion, otherwise he had been insisting, since 1953, that Kashmir was a settled issue. "Within weeks of the unilateral declaration of cease-fire by China, the India attitude changed completely and the talks, which had never held much promise, got bogged down in procedural wrangles and academic inanities".Negotiations with India over Kashmir continued through 1963. During these discussions, Pakistan pressed the contention that the people of Kashmir should be given a chance to decide their own future. But Indian delegation again proposed the readjustment of the existing cease-fire line. Pakistan rejected it.

The negotiations ended in failure as usual, but they caused some embarrassment to the great powers that had always supported that idea of direct talks between India and Pakistan. The attitude of the Indian Government towards the Kashmir problem was best explained by Chagla, the Indian representative, who declared in the Security Council on 5 February 1964: "I wish to make it clear on behalf of may Government that under no circumstances can we agree to the holding of a plebiscite in Kashmir". Why India has persistently refused to hold plebiscite in Kashmir was explained by the former Indian Defence Minister, Krishna Menon, who said: "Kashmir would vote to join Pakistan, and no Indian Government responsible for agreeing to plebiscite would survive". It is evident from the above-quoted statement that the people of Kashmir are in favour of joining Pakistan, and India has established its rule against the wishes of the people.

The United Nations has discussed the matter and passed resolutions many times but has failed to get them implemented. It has shaken the confidence of the people in the international organisation. As regards the big powers, they never took the problem seriously. For many years the USSR abstained from voting in the SEcurity Council and, when it came forward, it vetoed the resolutions. The obvious reason for the indifferent attitude of the USSR was Pakistan's membership of the South East Asia Treaty Organisation(SEATO) and the Central Treaty Organisation (CENTO). The Western allies on whom Pakistan depended for help did not attach much importance to the problem and never took the initiative to resolve the dispute. Instead of maintaining a balance in the subcontinent, the USA and its allies gave massive military aid to India after the Indo-China border conflict.

Pakistan protested against it and expressed the apprehensions that this military hardware would be used against Pakistan. Pakistan also pointed out the inherent danger in the military imbalance created by the Western aid. President Ayub Khan told President Kennedy during his visit to the USA, that "arms assistance to India would only encourage her to remain in occupation of areas which did not belong to her and the prospects of any just settlement of the dispute [Kashmir] would be eliminated". Despite all these protests, arms assistance to India continued.

In August 1965, the Indian Government accused Pakistan of having sent infiltrators in Kashmir and this alleged action led to the September war between the two countries. Hostilities between the two countries continued till 23 September, when a cease-fire was concluded as a result of Security Council's resolution. After the cease-fire, the Government of the USSR offered its services to mediate in the dispute. On the invitation of Kosygin, President Ayub Khan and Indian Prime Minister went to Tashkent where negotiations were commenced and the Tashkent Declaration was signed. In the Tashkent Declaration, Prime Minister of India and President of Pakistan expressed their determination to restore normal relations, create good neighbourly relations and to settle their disputes through peaceful means. As a result of this agreement the armies were withdrawn to their original positions and diplomatic relations restored. As regards the settlement of the disputes peaceful means promised by the Tashkent Declaration, the situation remained unchanged.

The Declaration brought a ray of hope to the people of Pakistan for the time being. The USSR Government did not show any interest in the problem afterwards, though it was morally bound by the Tashkent Declaration. Morals hardly hold any importance in the international politics. Though the results of direct negotiations were already known, the USSR Government insisted after the Declaration, to solve the problem through direct talks. Obviously, the Tashkent Declaration did not make any improvement upon the situation which already existed between the two countries. The people of

PAkistan at least expected some favourable change in the attitude of the USSR but in vain. Despite many protests by the Pakistan Government, the Soviet Union continued its military aid to India, which further aggravated the situation. Strengthening Indian military cannot be understood as a friendly gesture towards Pakistan. India used American and Russian weapons against Pakistan in the September War of 1965 and did not hesitate to do so in 1971. The Tashkent Declaration had been generally accepted as a diplomatic failure of Pakistan.

Pakistanis engaged in the formulation of foreign policy thus are now, and may be further, limited in choices of partners in the international relations game. The obvious options, for reasons which will be detailed later, it the United States, but this could be obviated if progress toward a nuclear weapon capability continues and leads to possession of a nuclear device. China's poor relations with India have resulted in a close Sino-Pakistan relationship, but there are occasional signs of a rapprochement between New Delhi and Beijing. Islamic and geographic ties have given Pakistan military and economic benefits from some countries of the Middle East, speciality Saudi Arabia, Pakistanis may now wish for more normal relations with the Soviet Union, as they had during Ayub Khan's regime in the sixties, but it will be difficult in present conditions for Pakistan to move ties to a level that will have practical benefits for Pakistan given the Soviets' close and long-term relations with India.

It goes without saying that the primary interest of any nation is its own survival within its current boundaries- a goal which Pakistan was unable to attain as in 1971 it became the only country since World War II to be divided though a civil war, one in which the secessionists were openly and directly aided and abetted by India. Beyond mere survival, however, Pakistan has a number of additional goals to which, at a minimum, Soviet troops are withdrawn from its western neighbor, Afghanistan; a step coupled, if possible, with a return of that country to some semblance of non-alignment.

Pakistan also has an interest in maintaining and improving its defense, capability, for which it must rely on the United States, China, and for financial assistance, Saudi Arabia. It must also secure economic assistance to sustain a quite creditable development record; this requires acceptable relations with the organization of Economic Cooperation a and development record; this requires acceptable relations with the Organization of Economic cooperation and Development (OECD) countries, the internal lending agencies and the oil-rich Middle Eastern nations. The Middle East also is important to Pakistan for the markets for both goods and labor the area represents and the religious association with these nations and throughout the Islamic world. Finally, Pakistan has a more generalized interest in enhancing its reputation in the community of nations; examples in this category could include greater attention to human rights and participatory government and a sharp decrease in its reputation as a major international source for narcotics.

Before examining these interests in more detail, note must be taken of the tools with which Pakistan can work in the field of foreign relations. Pakistan is not by any means an inconsiderable country, even though it often suffers in comparison with its huge neighbour, India. In economic terms, it is now on the threshold of breaking out of the low-income category (as measured by the

World Bank) as it gross national product per capita per annum approaches $400 (although some recent studies suggest that this figure may be overstated). A caveat is necessary in interpreting the data in that a significant proportion of this amount is the product of remittances from migrant workers, a benefit which seems to be headed downward as oil prices remain; low.

Pakistan also has been able to overcome chronic cereal deficits and now is able to export wheat and rice; the permanence of this is not ensured, but the frequent requirement for large purchases or grants of cereals from overseas seems to be a thing of the past. Overall the economy has grown at rates of the order of 6%, providing a strong underpinning for many basic needs, although the country has been notably backward in such social services as education and health delivery and faces a potentially serious energy shortage. Pakistan has been able to play its dual role of the being a part of South Asia and Southwest Asia with some skill. As will be discussed below, it has been an active and useful member of the Organization of the Islamic Conference (OIC) and, after some initial reluctance, has played an important role in the South Asian Association for Regional Cooperation (SAARC).

It has also achieved membership despite Indian objections, in the Non-Aligned Movement (NAM) and participated in such associated groups as the Group of Seventy. All of this is to say that Pakistan has developed diplomatic skills with which to enhance its positions on many issues and in many fora. This was not always the case, in this writer's opinion. He can recall, for example, many instances of Pakistani reactions to Indian presentations at conferences which did no credit to the reactor or his cause. In what is perhaps the most usual measure of power military strength, Pakistan cannot match (or, expect to match) the strength of its historic rival, India. Even with the present modernization, which is actually minimal. Probably the best Pakistan can hope for is a force which will either serve as a deterrent (with or without nuclear weapons) to any Indian adventure in the sense that India's costs would be greater than any possible gain or that with regard to both India and the Soviet Union that Pakistan could hold out for the time necessary to mobilize international activity to halt the fighting (as happened in 1965, although in that case Pakistan initiated the hostilities).

There is no prospect that Pakistan could again initiate conflict and expect to be anything other than the loser. To overcome these security shortfalls, Pakistan cannot count on either U.S. or Chinese support; diplomatic activity and the current (or somewhat improved) level of armament are the items on which Pakistan must depend. (The nuclear option will be touched on later). Another measure of power, one which is less exact in its quantification, is the unity of the country.

Here Pakistan has not done, and is not doing, well. That the country has failed in nation-building is evidenced both by the separation of Bangladesh and by the disaffection of Sindhis, Pathans and Baluch. Although the current leadership seems not to recognize it, Islam as a unifying force has been tried and found wanting. It was once said, only partly in jest that the east and west wings of united Pakistan were held together by Islam, fear of India and Pakistan International Airlines. Each may be a factor in the reasonably cordial relations today between

Pakistan and Bangladesh, but they were not a sufficiently strong cement to keep the country unified. A great danger in the present antagonism among the provinces (and, if one prefers, also the "fifth nationality", the muhajirs [refugees from India] is the ability of outside powers to exploit grievances and further to weaken the fabric of Pakistan. While this writer finds some of the dire predications regarding, say, Baluchistan exaggerated, the danger is surely there.

For example, as Soviet proposals on ending the Afghan conflict are being discussed, groups in the Frontier are reviving earlier pro-Soviet positions. India has been accused of a direct role in disturbances in Sind; this may well not be true, but the then Indian prime minister, India Gandhi, did express sympathy with the Sindhis. As mentioned earlier, the first priority in foreign relations for Pakistan must be to live peacefully, but not subserviently, with India. The two countries have been at loggerheads continuously since August 1947 and before if one considers also the conflict between the Congress and the Muslim League on their visions of what Indian would be after the withdrawal of the British. The conflict after independence has resulted in three wars, in 1948, 1965, and 1971, as well as a "skirmish" in 1965 over the Rann of Kutch.

In each case, Pakistan has failed to attain its objectives: Kashmir in 1948 and 1965 and the continued unity of Pakistan in 1971. it is interesting to note, however, that on the issue which has the greatest practical effect on present Pakistan, the division of the Indus waters, the settlement came about without armed conflict and with international mediation. Perhaps there is a lesson to be learnt from this as we look at the present areas of conflict between the two original successor states to the British Raj.

Most Pakistanis probably would identify Kashmir as the principal point of contention between India and Pakistan; many but no all, Indians might also do so. It seems, however, that Kashmir is an issue which is not only dead from the point of view of real politics, but also is an issue which has little to do with the development of either country. Pakistan's expenditure of effort and resources in 1965 gained it nothing, lost it considerably in terms of economic and military costs, and, perhaps most importantly, evoked no response from the Muslims on the Indian side of the then cease-fire line, who Pakistanis were led to believe, were waiting with bated breath to rise against their Indian oppressors. As has been confirmed as recently as the March 1987 election, the Muslims of Kashmir give very little support to alleged "pro-Pakistani elements " and a high degree of support to those parties which favor continuance of the present arrangement for the association of Kashmir with the Indian Union.

The report of the Independent Task Force of the US Council on Foreign Relations, on US policy in respect of Pakistan and India contains the following comments on democracy, armed forces and governance in Pakistan: "Both India and Pakistan are democracies... After decades of intermittent military rule, Pakistan revived democratic procedures in 1989... Democratic institutions have not developed particularly deep roots in Pakistan ... The Pakistan army continues to play a large role in shaping political life... The result of all these problems is that Pakistan's future stability, orientation, and perhaps even unity are less than certain.... Some members of the Task

Force believe, however, that unless such resolve can be mustered, Pakistan may turn into a failed state."

Pakistani media appears irritated with these comments, but has made no attempt to counter or challenge their content. The media and political parties in Pakistan reacted with pain and anger, however, to certain remarks made by their own interim Prime Minister, Malik Meraj Khalid. He had said: "We have lost Pakistan in ideological terms, despite its geographical existence... A recent UN report has painted a horrible picture of our country, fearing that Pakistan would be fragmented in the next 20 years or so. We certainly want that all the corrupt elements are prevented from being returned to our Assemblies.... A society has come into being in Pakistan where values like truth, humanity and piety have lost their meaning.... A society where there is complete deviation from Islamic teachings... Where human beings are being killed in the name of Islam... minorities are scared, and do not have courage to air their grievances."

President Leghari dismissed the Benazir government, and dissolved the National Assembly, On November 5, 1996. Prime Minister Meraj Khalid took over as interim head of government, and the next general elections were announced to be held on February 3. On January 6, came Leghari's announcement that he has constituted a new Council for Defence and National Security "to aid and advise" the government.

The President is head the Council in his capacity as the Supreme Commander of the country's armed forces. The other members will be: the PM; the Ministers of Defence, Interior, Finance and Foreign Affairs; the Chairman, Jt Chiefs of Staff Committee; the Army, Navy and Air Chiefs; the Principal Secretary to the President, the Cabinet Secretary and the Defence Secretary.

The Director-General, ISI, is to be a permanent invitee. This implies the exclusion of the Finance and Foreign Secretaries and of the Chairman of the Senate Wasim Sajjd, who in all but name, is the country's Vice-President. In General Zia's original scheme of things Wasim Sajjad's predecessor had a prominent presence in the original National Security Council. The Council's role is advisory. It will be expected to advise the Government on national security and strategy, defence policy, external and domestic policies, economic and financial policies, insofar as these affect defence and national security; questions relating to proclaiming Emergency; and any items of work referred to it by either the President or the PM—pretty much everything in the purview of the Government.

IT is not a statutory or constitutional organ. However, its significance and weight are well understood, as its creation implies that the role of the military establishment in the day-to-day governance of a Pakistan, is now formalised and has been given adequate publicity. During the post-zia years, it has become clear to Pakistan people that the country's apex management group is the informal Troika, consisting of the President PM and the Chief of Army Staff; and not the Cabinet. Pakistan are shrewd enough to understand that the final authority rests with the Army Chief. Certain things in Pakistan are unambiguously controlled by the Army Chief. These are: internal law and order; policies vis-a-vis India (especially Kashmir), USA, Afghanistan and Iran. It was in these areas that in the post-1993 period, both the Foreign Office and the Finance Ministry were argumentative and lost the trust and confidence of the military establishment.

In issues concerning nuclear and missile matters, including procurement of equipment and technology in respect of these, the decision-making is the hands of the military leadership. Most competent observers of Pakistan find that the military tends to listen far more to the ISI in these matters than to their own foreign Office. In other words the military-cum-intelligence top brass in Pakistan have acquired both influence and authority in matters that are vital in foreign policy including specially the politico-military aspects, as also the technological ones. President Leghari's notification establishing the Council for Defence and National Security, confirms and formalises this arrangement for the future. Under the terms of this order, Mr Leghari has agreed to the army also helping to manage economic and fiscal issues. This will have the effect of ensuring that Pakistani military in general, and the Army Chief in particular, will hold all the levers of state power, both in name and in deep. It will be interesting to watch how, henceforth, the military establishment influences and determines policy issues in the context of financial, fiscal and economic management.

Both the IMF and the World Bank have been demanding precisely this through the intercession of certain eminent persons who are Pakistan citizens, as also, at the same time, distinguished international civil servants, loyal to their motherland, and also to the international organisations they serve. The names of Mr Shoaib Qureishi, formerly interim PM and Mr Javed Burki the current Finance Minister, come to mind. It would appear that the military establishment, panicky about the declining credit-worthiness of the country, may be seeking to take on this aspect of national management into its own hands. Whether they will have the expertise available for this, remains to be seen. Or may be they will themselves select and name civil servants and economists to give guidance to the economic ministries.

The establishment of this Council has been cautiously welcomes by Mr. Nawab Sharif's Pakistan Muslim League. The leaders of other political parties have been critical, but none of them trenchantly or uncompromisingly so. Their pronouncements can be characterised as reservations, rather than outright rejection or condemnation of the new arrangement. Pakistan media, however, has been uncompromising in its criticism of this move. They have voiced a series of suspicions. They feel that this may well be the first step towards a quasi-constitutional grafting of a military veto on what they have always promoted as a representative and parliamentary democracy. They have been suspicious of the democratic credentials of many of the feudal, effete, and easily pliable politicians. And now they are suggesting that the present set of civilian leaders may be in the process of formally yielding real power into the hands of the military. Pakistanis, especially the intelligentsia, suffered during the Aayub, Yahya and Zia periods of military authoritarianism. Many of these intellectuals and academics are opposed to what is happening. However, they suspect that the Western industrialised powers are backing Pakistani military, because they are willing to help promote Western interests in the Central Asian Republics (being recognised increasingly as the Middle East of the future); the oil rich Persian Gulf regional and South Asia. They feel that, as a result, the Americans and others will accept these militarised decision makers as a democracy of sorts, not criticising this nation being managed by the military behind a civilian facade.

The armed force in Pakistan, must not appear working against the nation's interest in context of national security e.g. Kashmir and the nuclear and missile issues. At the same time, the Pakistani media appears convinced that any advice which the military provide in these matters to the President and the PM, will become thoroughly binding. For, after all, the military alone hold the barrel of the gun, which remains, in that country, the source of real authority. Many of them recall that in 1993 when the Pakistani Rangers (the counterpart of our BSF) had refused to do the bidding of the Pakistan's civilian government, it was only due to the Army's intervention that the Rangers later obeyed the orders of their civilian political bosses. They recall also that General Zia too had established a National Security Council in 1985; and that it had functioned for eight or ten months. That body was quietly abolished when the National Assembly's negotiators accepted the deal to pass the Eighth Amendment.

Pakistan Nuclear Weapons

Pakistan's Atomic Energy commission was founded some 15 years after the Indian program. In 1965 President Ayub Khan took some initial steps in response to the emerging of Indian nuclear threat. Zulfiqar Ali Bhutto was the founder of Pakistan's Nuclear Program, initially as Minister for Fuel, Power and Natural Resources, and later as President and Prime Minister.

Pakistan's nuclear program was launched in earnest shortly after the loss of East Pakistan in the 1971 war with India, when Bhutto initiated a program to develop nuclear weapons with a meeting of physicists and engineers at Multan in January 1972. In 1974 India successfully tested a nuclear "device." Bhutto reacted strongly to this test and said Pakistan must develop its own "Islamic bomb."

Pakistan lacks an extensive civil nuclear power infrastructure, and its weapons program is not as broad as India's. Almost all of its nuclear program is focused on weapons applications. Initially, Pakistan focused on the plutonium path for building a nuclear weapon. Plutonium can be obtained from fuel that has been reprocessed from nuclear power plants, and in October 1974 Pakistan signed a contract with France for the design of a reprocessing facility for the fuel from its power plant at Karachi and other planned facilities. However, over the next two years Pakistan's international nuclear collaborators withdrew as Pakistan's nuclear ambitions became more apparent. The French were among the last to withdraw at the end of 1976, following sustained pressure from the United States.

A major advance jump to Pakistan's nuclear program was the arrival of Dr Abdul Qadeer Khan in 1975, who brought with him the plans for uranium enrichment centrifuges, and lists of sources of the necessary technology. On this basis, Pakistan initially focused its development efforts on highly enriched uranium (HEU), and exploited an extensive clandestine procurement network to support these efforts.

A.Q. Khan evidently persuaded Pakistan to work with Uranium (as compared to Plutonium) because Plutonium involves more arduous and hazardous procedures and cumbersome and expensive processes.

Pakistan's activities were initially centered in a few facilities. A.Q. Khan founded the Engineering Research Laboratories at Kahuta in 1976, which later to became the Dr. A. Q. Khan Research Laboratories (KRL).

A number of United States laws, amendments to the Foreign Assistance Act of 1961, applied to Pakistan and its program of nuclear weapons development. The 1976 Symington Amendment stipulated that economic assistance be terminated to any country that imported uranium enrichment technology.

The Glenn Amendment of 1977 similarly called for an end to aid to countries that imported reprocessing technology—Pakistan had from France. United States economic assistance, except for food aid, was terminated under the Symington Amendment in April 1979. In 1985 the Solarz Amendment was added to prohibit aid to countries that attempt to import nuclear commodities from the United States.

In the same year, the Pressler Amendment was passed; referring specifically to Pakistan, it said that if that nation possessed a nuclear device, aid would be suspended. Many of these amendments could be waived if the president declared that it was in the national interests of the United States to continue assistance. The Soviet invasion of Afghanistan made Pakistan a country of paramount geostrategic importance. In a matter of days, the United States declared Pakistan a "frontline state" against Soviet aggression and offered to reopen aid and military assistance deliveries. When the Reagan administration took office in January 1981, the level of assistance increased substantially. Presidential waivers for several of the amendments were required. The initial package from the United States was for US$3.2 billion over six years, equally divided between economic and military assistance. A separate arrangement was made for the purchase of forty F-16 fighter aircraft.

Aside from Afghanistan, the most problematic element in Pakistan's security policy was the nuclear question. President Zia had inherited a pledge that for domestic reasons he could not discard, and he continued the nuclear development program. Zia inherited an ambitious program from Bhutto and continued to develop it, out of the realization that, despite Pakistan's newly acquired weaponry, it could never match India's conventional power and that India either had, or shortly could develop, its own nuclear weapons. Even after the invasion of Afghanistan, Pakistan almost exhausted United States tolerance, including bungled attempts to illegally acquire United States nuclear- relevant technology and a virtual public admission in 1987 by the head of Pakistan's nuclear program that the country had developed a weapon.

As long as Pakistan remained vital to United States interests in Afghanistan, however, no action was taken to cut off United States support. For the remainder of Zia's tenure, the United States generally ignored Pakistan's developing nuclear program. But the issue that after Zia's death led to another cutoff of aid was Pakistan's persistent drive toward nuclear development. Initial Pakistani attempts to handle the bilateral nuclear relationship with India led nowhere, but a significant step was a nonformalized 1985 agreement that neither India nor Pakistan would attack the other's nuclear facilities. Zia asked India to agree to several steps to end the potential nuclear arms race on the subcontinent. One of these measures was the simultaneous signing of the

Treaty on the Non-Proliferation of Nuclear Weapons. The second step was a joint agreement for inspection of all nuclear sites by the International Atomic Energy Agency. Pakistan also proposed a pact between the two countries to allow for mutual inspection of sites. And, finally, Pakistan proposed a South Asian nuclear-free zone. It appeared that Zia was looking for a way to terminate the costly Pakistani program. But in order to sell this idea in Pakistan, he required some concessions from India. Termination would also get him out of difficulties the program was causing with the United States, including the curtailment of aid in 1979.

These proposals were still on the table in the early 1990s, and were supplemented by then Prime Minister Nawaz Sharif's call for a roundtable discussion among Pakistan, India, the United States, Russia, and China on nuclear weapons in South Asia. Pakistan's dependence on China grew as Western export controls and enforcement mechanisms have grown more stringent. China's nuclear assistance predates the 1986 Sino-Pakistani atomic cooperation agreement, with some of the most critical transfers occurring from 1980 through 1985. China is reported to have provided Pakistan with the design of one of its warheads, as well as sufficient HEU for a few weapons.

The 25-kiloton design was the one used in China's fourth nuclear test, which was an atmospheric test using a ballistic missile launch. This configuration is said to be a fairly sophisticated design, with each warhead weighing considerably less than the unwieldy, first-generation US and Soviet weapons which weighed several thousand kilograms. Pakistan Foreign Minister Yakub Khan was present at the Chinese Lop Nor test site to witness the test of a small nuclear device in May 1983, giving rise to speculation that a Pakistani-assembled device was detonated in this test.

Evidently, however, the jump-start provided by A.Q. Khan's trove of documents was an insufficient basis for a dependable Uranium program. Chinese assistance in the development of gas centrifuges at Kahuta was indicated by the presence of Chinese technicians at the facility in the early 1980s. The uranium enrichment facility began operating in the early 1980s, but suffered serious start up problems. In early 1996 it was reported that the A.Q. Khan Research Laboratory had received 5,000 ring magnets, which can be used in gas centrifuges, from a subsidiary of the China National Nuclear Corporation.

Perhaps in response to the persistent problems with the Uranium program, around the time of the signing of the 1986 Sino-Pakistani atomic cooperation agreement, Pakistan evidently embarked on a parrallel Plutonium program. Built with Chinese assistance, the heavy water reactor at Khushab is the central element of Pakistan's program for production of plutonium and tritium for advanced compact warheads. The Khushab facility, like that at Kahuta, is not subject to IAEA inspections. Khushab, with a capacity variously reported at between 40 and 70 MWT, was completed in the mid-1990s, with the start of construction dating to the mid-1980s. As of the mid-1990s it was widely reported that Pakistan's stockpile consisted of as many as 10 nuclear warheads based on a Chinese design. On 28 May 1998 Pakistan announced that it had successfully conducted five nuclear tests. According to the announcment, the results were as expected, and there was no release of radioactivity. The Pakistan Atomic Energy Commission that the five nuclear tests conducted on Thursday measured up to 5.0 on the Richter scale, with a reported yield of up to 40 KT (equivalent TNT). According to local reports, these detonations took place over a two hour period.

One device was said to be a boosted uranium device, with the four other tests being low yield sub-kiloton devices. On 30 May 1998 Pakistan tested one more nuclear warhead with a yield of 12 kilotons. The tests were conducted at Balochistan, bringing the total number of claimed tests to six. It has also been claimed by Pakistani sources that at least one additional device, initially planned for detonation on 30 May 1998, remained emplaced underground ready for detonation. Pakistani claims concerning the number and yields of their underground tests cannot be independently confirmed by seismic means, and it has been suggested by Indian sources that as few as two weapons were actually detonated, each with yields considerably lower than claimed by Pakistan. However, seismic data showed at least two and possibily a third, much smaller, test in the initial round of tests at the Ras Koh range. The single test on 30 May provided a clear seismic signal.

The tests came slightly more than 2 weeks after India carried out 5 nuclear tests of its own, and after many warnings by Pakistani officials that they would respond to India (the two countries have fought 3 wars). In addition, Pakistan's President Rafiq Tarar declared a state of emergency, citing "threat by external aggression to the security of Pakistan." The United States had been attempting to persuade Pakistan not to test by offering potential economic and military benefits, but this effort did not succeed. Pakistan already had been subject to limited U.S. sanctions since 1990 under the Pressler Amendment, when $650 million in military and humanitarian aid had been cut off as a result of an inability by the President to certify that Pakistan did not possess a nuclear device. As was the case following India's nuclear tests, President Clinton, as required by law (including the Glenn Amendment, part of the Arms Export Control Act) announced that the United States would impose sanctions on Pakistan. These sanctions, among other things, could stem the flow of financial assistance into Pakistan, potentially causing severe harm to the Pakistani economy. With $37 billion in foreign debt, a monthly trade deficit of $150 million, foreign exchange reserves of only $1.3 billion, and interest payments of $200-$500 million due each month, Pakistan can ill afford any suspension or cutoff in international assistance. Overall, Pakistan is considered far more vulnerable to economic sanctions than India.

In October 1997, the International Monetary Fund (IMF) had agreed to lend Pakistan $1.52 billion—including $935 million under an enhanced, low-interest-rate, enhanced structural adjustment facility (ESAF)—over three years as part of an economic reform program. (The first $208 million tranche was released in October 1997.) The IMF money is considered important not only on its own account but also because it facilitates Pakistan's ability to borrow from commercial sources by increasing the country's financial credibility. Without the IMF, some economists believe foreign lenders could call in their loans, leading to a crisis of confidence in Pakistan's economy and a run on the country's freely-convertible currency, the rupee. Pakistan also receives money from other international lending organizations, including the World Bank. Following Pakistan's nuclear tests, IMF and World Bank assistance are now thrown into question, with the United States now saying it will oppose international lending to Pakistan. According to a preliminary analysis conducted at Los Alamos National Laboratory, material released into the atmosphere during an underground nuclear test by Pakistan in May 1998 contained low levels of weapons-grade plutonium. But Lawrence Livermore National Laboratory and other agencies contested the accuracy of this finding. The significance of the Los Alamos finding was that Pakistan had either imported or produced plutonium undetected by the US intelligence community.

Pakistan Nuclear Weapons—A Chronology

1965—Pakistani nuclear research reactor at Parr, Rawalpindi, starts functioning.

1968—Nonproliferation Treaty completed. Pakistan refuse to sign.

1974—India tests a device of up to 15 kilotons and calls the test a ``peaceful nuclear explosion." Pakistani Prime minister Zulfikar Ali Bhutto tells meeting of Pakistan's top scientists of intention to develop nuclear arms.

1974—Pakistan proposed to India the establishment of a nuclear weapons free zone in south Asia

1978—Pakistan proposed to India a joint Indo-Pakistan declaration renouncing the acquisition and manufacture of nuclear weapons

1979—The United States cut off aid to Pakistan under section 669 of the Foreign Assistance Act of 1961 FAA) after it was learned that Pakistan had secretly begun construction of a uranium enrichment facility.

1979—Pakistan proposed to India mutual inspections by India and Pakistan of nuclear facilities

1979—Pakistan proposed to India simultaneous adherence to the NPT by India and Pakistan

1979—Pakistan proposed to India simultaneous acceptance of full-scope IAEA safeguards

Early 1980's—Multiple reports that Pakistan obtained a pre-tested, atomic bomb design from China.

1980—U.S. Nuclear Export Control Violation: Reexport via Canada (components of inverters used in gas centrifuge enrichment activities).

1981—AP story cites contents of reported US State Department cable stating `We have strong reason to believe that Pakistan is seeking to develop a nuclear explosives capability Pakistan is conducting a program for the design and development of a triggering package for nuclear explosive devices.'

1981—Publication of book, Islamic Bomb, citing recent Pakistani efforts to construct a nuclear test site.

1982/3—Several European press reports indicate that Pakistan was using Middle Eastern intermediaries to acquire bomb parts (13-inch `steel spheres' and `steel petal shapes').

1983—Declassified US government assessment concludes that `There is unambiguous evidence that Pakistan is actively pursuing a nuclear weapons development program We believe the ultimate application of the enriched uranium produced at Kahuta, which is unsafeguarded, is clearly nuclear weapons.'

1984—President Zia states that Pakistan has acquired a `very modest' uranium enrichment capability for `nothing but peaceful purposes.'

1984—President Reagan reportedly warns Pakistan of `grave consequences' if it enriches uranium above 5%.

1985—ABC News reports that US believes Pakistan has `successfully tested' a `firing mechanism' of an atomic bomb by means of a non-nuclear explosion, and that US krytrons `have been acquired' by Pakistan.

1985—U.S. Nuclear Export Control Violation: Texas, krytrons (nuclear weapon triggers).

1985—U.S. Nuclear Export Control Violation: US cancelled license for export of flash x-ray camera to Pakistan (nuclear weapon diagnostic uses) because of proliferation concerns.

1985/6—Media cites production of highly enriched, bomb-grade uranium in violation of a commitment to the US.

1985—Pressler Amendment [section 620E(e) of the Foreign Assistance Act] requires a total cut-off of U.S. aid to Islamabad unless the president can certify that Pakistan does not possess a nuclear weapon, and that continued US aid will significantly decrease the probability of its developing one in the future.

1986—Bob Woodward article in Washington Post cites alleged DIA report saying Pakistan `detonated a high explosive test device between Sept. 18 and Sept. 21 as part of its continuing efforts to build an implosion-type nuclear weapon;' says Pakistan has produced uranium enriched to a 93.5% level.

1986—Press reports cite U.S. `Special National Intelligence Estimate' concluding that Pakistan had produced weapons-grade material.

1986—Commenting on Pakistan's nuclear capability, General Zia tells interviewer, `It is our right to obtain the technology. And when we acquire this technology, the Islamic world will possess it with us.'

1986—Declassified memo to then-Secretary of State Henry Kissinger states, `Despite strong U.S. concern, Pakistan continues to pursue a nuclear explosive capability If operated at its nominal capacity, the Kahuta uranium enrichment plant could produce enough weapons-grade material to build several nuclear devices per year.'

1987—Pakistan proposed to India an agreement on a bilateral or regional nuclear test ban treaty

1987—U.S. Nuclear Export Control Violation: Pennsylvania, maraging steel & beryllium (used in centrifuge manufacture and bomb components).

1987—London Financial Times reports US spy satellites have observed construction of second uranium enrichment plant in Pakistan.

1987—Pakistan's leading nuclear scientist Abdul Qadeer Khan states in published interview that `what the CIA has been saying about our possessing the bomb is correct.'

1987—West German official confirms that nuclear equipment recently seized on way to Pakistan was suitable for `at least 93% enrichment' of uranium; blueprints of uranium enrichment plant also seized in Switzerland.

1987—U.S. Nuclear Export Control Violation: California, oscilloscopes, computer equipment (useful in nuclear weapon R&D).

1987—According to photocopy of a reported German foreign ministry memo published in Paris in 1990, UK government official tells German counterpart on European nonproliferation working group that he was `convinced that Pakistan had `a few small' nuclear weapons.'

1987—China concluded a deal with Pakistan to sell M-11 missiles and launchers.

1988—President Reagan waives an aid cutoff for Pakistan due to an export control violation; in his formal certification, he confirmed that `material, equipment, or technology covered by that provision was to be used by Pakistan in the manufacture of a nuclear explosive device.'

1988—Hedrick Smith article in New York Times reports US government sources believe Pakistan has produced enough highly enriched uranium for 4-6 bombs.

1988—President Zia tells Carnegie Endowment delegation in interview that Pakistan has attained a nuclear capability `that is good enough to create an impression of deterrence.'

1989—Multiple reports of Pakistan modifying US-supplied F-16 aircraft for nuclear delivery purposes; wind tunnel tests cited in document reportedly from West German intelligence service.

1989—Test launch of Hatf-2 missile: Payload (500 kilograms) and range (300 kilometers) meets `nuclear-capable' standard under Missile Technology Control Regime.

1989—CIA Director Webster tells Senate Governmental Affairs Committee hearing that `Clearly Pakistan is engaged in developing a nuclear capability.'

1989—Media claims that Pakistan acquired tritium gas and tritium facility from West Germany in mid-1980's.

1989—ACDA unclassified report cites Chinese assistance to missile program in Pakistan.

1989—UK press cites nuclear cooperation between Pakistan and Iraq.

1989—Article in Nuclear Fuel states that the United States has issued `about 100 specific communiques to the West German Government related to planned exports to the Pakistan Atomic Energy Commission and its affiliated organizations;' exports reportedly included tritium and a tritium recovery facility.

1989—Article in Defense & Foreign Affairs Weekly states `sources close to the Pakistani nuclear program have revealed that Pakistani scientists have now perfected detonation mechanisms for a nuclear device.'

1989—Reporting on a recent customs investigation, West German magazine Stern reports, `since the beginning of the eighties over 70 [West German] enterprises have supplied sensitive goods to enterprises which for years have been buying equipment for Pakistan's ambitious nuclear weapons program.'

1989—Gerard Smith, former US diplomat and senior arms control authority, claims US has turned a `blind eye' to proliferation developments Pakistan in and Israel.

1989—Senator Glenn delivers two lengthy statements addressing Pakistan's violations of its uranium enrichment commitment to the United States and the lack of progress on nonproliferation issues from Prime Minister Bhutto's democratically elected government after a year in office; Glenn concluded, `There simply must be a cost to non-compliance—when a solemn nuclear pledge is violated, the solution surely does not lie in voiding the pledge.'

1989-1990—reports of secret construction of unsafeguard nuclear research reactor; components from Europe.

Spring 1990—Pakistan reportedly reacted to Indian Army war game maneuvers near its border by preparing to drop one of seven weapons from a specially configured C-130 cargo plane. [02 December 1992 NBC News report]

1990—US News cites `western intelligence sources' claiming Pakistan recently `cold-tested' a nuclear device and is now building a plutonium production reactor; article says Pakistan is engaged in nuclear cooperation with Iran.

1990—French magazine publishes photo of West German government document citing claim by UK official that British government believes Pakistan already possesses `a few small' nuclear weapons; cites Ambassador Richard Kennedy claim to UK diplomat that Pakistan has broken its pledge to the US not to enrich uranium over 5%.

1990—London Sunday Times cites growing U.S. and Soviet concerns about Pakistani nuclear program; paper claims F-16 aircraft are being modified for nuclear delivery purposes; claims US spy satellites have observed `heavily armed convoys' leaving Pakistan uranium enrichment complex at Kahuta and heading for military airfields.

1990—Pakistani biography of top nuclear scientist (Dr. Abdul Qadeer Khan and the Islamic Bomb), claims US showed `model' of Pakistani bomb to visiting Pakistani diplomat as part of unsuccessful nonproliferation effort.

1990—Defense & Foreign Affairs Weekly reports `US officials now believe that Pakistan has quite sufficient computing power in country to run all the modeling necessary to adequately verify the viability of the country's nuclear weapons technology.'

1990—Dr. A.Q. Khan, father of Pakistan's bomb, receives `Man of the Nation Award.'

1990—Washington Post documents 3 recent efforts by Pakistan to acquire special arc-melting furnaces with nuclear and missile applications.

October 1990—President Bush announced that he could no longer provide Congress with Pressler Amendment certification that Pakistan does not possess a nuclear weapon. Economic and military aid was duly terminated, though the Bush administration continued to permit a limited number of commercial military sales to Pakistan. Pakistan handled the cutoff with little public rancor and committed itself to freezing the nuclear program in an attempt to placate the United States.

1991—Pakistan proposed to India commencement of a multilateral conference on the nuclear proliferation in south Asia

1991—Wall Street Journal says Pakistan is buying nuclear-capable M-11 missile from China.

1991—Sen. Moynihan says in television interview, `Last July [1990] the Pakistanis machined 6 nuclear Pakistan warheads. And they've still got them.'

1991—Time quotes businessman, `BCCI is functioning as the owners' representative for Pakistan's nuclear-bomb project.'

1991—India and Pakistan enter agreement prohibiting attacks on each other's nuclear installations.

July 1991—Reliable reports from Islamabad confirm that Pakistan had frozen production of HEU and halted the manufacturing of nuclear weapons components.

1992—Pakistani foreign secretary publicly discusses Pakistan's possession of `cores' of nuclear devices.

Late 1992—The US Government determines that China had transferred items controlled under the international Missile Technology Control Regime to Pakistan.

December 1992—The US Government asked Pakistan to return eight US Navy frigates and a supply ship that had been leased to the Pakistan Navy, which accounted for more than half of Pakistan's major surface combatants.

01 December 1992—Senator Larry Pressler reportedly stated in a press interview that he had been told by the Central Intelligence Agency (CIA) that Pakistan had assembled seven weapons and could air drop one in a matter of hours [Dec. 1, 1992 NBC News broadcast].

1993—Pakistan proposed to India creation of a missile-free zone in south Asia

25 August 1993—The United States imposed "Category Two" sanctions against certain Chinese and Pakistani entities that were involved in an M-11 missile-related transfer, which is prohibited under US law.

Late 1993—The Clinton Administration, citing what it considered to be asymmetrical treatment accorded to Pakistan and India over their respective nuclear programs, proposed revising the Pressler Amendment and certain "country-specific" sections of the Foreign Assistance Act. The administration argued that by the time nuclear nonproliferation provisions had been added to the Foreign Assistance Act, India had already acquired the capability to build nuclear weapons and thus Pakistan had borne the brunt of most United States sanctions.

Early 1994_The Clinton Administration withdrew its proposal to revise the amendment because of strong criticism from a number of influential members of Congress, including Senator Pressler himself.

April 1994—Deputy Secretary of State Strobe Talbott visits Islamabad to propose a one-time sale of F-16 fighter aircraft to Pakistan. Delivery of the planes would be contingent on specific commitments from Pakistan regarding its nuclear program, including a verifiable cap on the production of fissile materials. Talbott states that there is "broad agreement" between the United States and Pakistan on the goal of "first capping, then reducing, and eventually eliminating weapons of mass destruction and ballistic missiles from South Asia."

April 1995 —Prime Minister Bhutto visits Washington.

September 1995—The Clinton Administration proposes revisions to the Pressler Amendment, citing the Amendment's roadblocks to cooperation with Pakistan's Government in areas such as combatting terrorism and furthering US commercial interests in Pakistan. Under the Brown Amendment, the US would not deliver the controversial F-16 aircraft or resume an official military supply relationship with Pakistan, but the President decided to sell the F-16 aircraft to other countries and return the proceeds to Pakistan.

01 January 1996—India and Pakistan exchange lists of atomic installations which each side has pledged not to attack under an over seven-year-old confidence-building agreement.

January 1996—The Brown amendment was signed into law to relieve some of the pressures created by the Pressler sanctions, which had crippled parts of the Pakistani military, particularly the Air Force. The Brown amendment allowed nearly $370 million of previously embargoed arms and spare parts to be delivered to Pakistan. It also permited limited military assistance for the purposes of counter-terrorism, peacekeeping, anti-narcotics efforts, and some military training.

March 1996—Pakistan commissioned an unsafeguarded nuclear reactor, expected to become fully operational in the late 1990s, that will provide it with a capability to produce weapons-grade plutonium.

Late 1996—Pakistan's main nuclear weapons laboratory, the A.Q. Khan Laboratory in Kahuta, purchased 5,000 ring magnets from China. The ring magnets would allow Pakistan to effectively double its capacity to enrich uranium for nuclear weapons production.

03 October 1996—Pakistani Prime Minister Benazir Bhutto called for the convening of a South Asia security conference that would deal with, among other things, Kashmir and the nuclear arms issue.

04 July 1997—Pakistan confirms test-firing of new indigenous Hatf missile.

06 September 1997—Pakistani Prime Minister Nawaz Sharif claims Pakistan possesses nuclear weapons, saying that: "Pakistan's nuclear capability is now an established fact. Whatever we have, we have a right to keep it...."

28 May 1998: Pakistan detonates five nuclear devices. Pakistan claimed that the five nuclear tests measured up to 5.0 on the Richter scale, with a reported yield of up to 40 KT (equivalent TNT).

30 May 1998 Pakistan tested one more nuclear warheads, with a yield of 12 kilotons, bringing the total number of claimed tests to six.

A time for tough decisions

As Pakistan is caught between the rock of American political and economic pressure and the hard place of Indian military threats, policy-makers in Islamabad need to ponder where their ill-conceived plans have led the nation.

In a private enterprise, the chief executive would have been hauled over the coals by shareholders if his policies had cost the company the huge losses we have incurred as a nation. Unfortunately, the citizens of Pakistan have very little say in the formulation of the grand strategies that impinge both directly and indirectly on the lives.

Even when they get to vote for their leaders, they find that the military is the ultimate arbiter of their fate, as elected governments and parliaments are turfed out at the whim of the general of the day.

Since Pakistan's earliest days, the army has played a preponderant role in matters pertaining to internal and external security as well as foreign affairs. Even when GHQ has not been running the country directly, it has been the key player in determining the contours of our external relations, especially with India, Afghanistan,

China and the United States. The Foreign Office has largely been reduced to the status of a messenger boy, as it has executed policies its career professionals have not always agreed with. Even elected prime ministers have often been left out of the decision-making loop. The Kargil fiasco is a case in point: it seems that in the army briefing, Nawaz Sharif was given the impression that the operation was to be a short, sharp incursion with total deniability. In the event, it was evident that the whole action had been planned and executed by the army.

So here we are now, with over five decades, two-and-a-half wars, thousands of lives and billions of dollars squandered on a policy that has clearly failed. The question is, where do we go from here? Do we lick our wounds, pick up the pieces and get on with life? Or do we sit and sulk, bemoaning the injustice of life and swearing vengeance against India and the West for having forced us to abandon a failed policy that had become the end-all and be-all of our existence?

The answer will determine whether Pakistan is to emerge from its self-imposed isolation and rejoin the community of nations as a modern, forward-looking country, or remain a pariah that breeds and exports religious extremism and terrorism. The recent arrest of an alleged American terrorist in Chicago underlines the dangers of following the second path: Padilla is known to have spent time in Pakistan where he is supposed to have received bomb-making training. Many Pakistanis will scoff at the American allegations, but the fact is that Pakistan is hardly a tourist attraction for the likes of Padilla.

Whatever his motives in spending time in our country, it was not the beauty of our mountains or the charm of Moghul monuments that drew him to Karachi, Lahore and Peshawar. It is a fact that over the years, Pakistan has attained the dubious distinction of being one of the favorite destinations of desperate and fanatical men with murder in their hearts.

After the recent nerve-jangling stand-off between the two South Asian nuclear powers and the desperate efforts of world leaders to head off yet another war over Kashmir, policy-makers in Islamabad have to realize that we can no longer sustain our present course. In diplomatic, economic and military terms, we have reached the end of the road in Kashmir. Isolated as never before, fiscally kept afloat by transfusions of aid, and unable to finance our crippling military expenditure for much longer, it is time to re-examine our single-point Kashmir agenda and take some hard decisions.

Individuals can afford to base their actions on emotions; nations do so at their grave peril. National interest must be the underlying factor in decision-making; the ability to achieve a goal must be another crucial ingredient. Thus when Zia had delusions of grandeur and declared Central Asia to be part of Pakistan's sphere of influence after the collapse of the Soviet Union, he was clearly over- reaching. But to attain his dream, it was essential for Islamabad to control Afghanistan, and hence our open-ended support for the Taliban.

Once the Soviet army had pulled out of Afghanistan, both our hawkish military planners and the foreign and local holy warriors who fought for them were convinced that their success could be replicated in Kashmir. If one of the greatest war machines in the world could be humbled, they reasoned, why could they not defeat the

Indians? Taking advantage of the purely indigenous revolt that broke out in Indian Kashmir in 1989, Pakistani, Arab and Afghan jihadis began to control the struggle. Well-financed militant organizations in Pakistan sent in arms and volunteers with covert official support. Training camps were set up in Azad Kashmir and Pakistan and funds were openly raised for the Kashmiri jihad.

The blowback from Afghanistan and Kashmir caused massive disruption and hundreds of terror attacks within Pakistan, but successive governments, both civilian and military, considered this a price worth paying for solving the dispute in our favour once and for all.

But 9/11 changed the equation decisively: New Delhi raised the stakes in the knowledge that their military action would meet with American approval. All of a sudden, armed militancy would no longer be distinguished from terrorism, and the random killing of civilians would be opposed by whatever means a state could muster. If the Americans could come across half the globe to engage the Taliban, the Indians argued that they could do the same with the Pakistanis on their borders. Despite General Musharaf's new-found popularity in Washington, the Indian argument has won the day.

There are many shrill voices in Pakistan calling for an outright rejection of Musharaf's decision to halt cross-border incursions as this is tantamount to a U-turn on Kashmir. These people talk of 'national honour' and the 'inalienable right of the Kashmiris to determine their future'. But what of the inalienable right of the people of Pakistan to peace and prosperity? By impoverishing and isolating ourselves, how have we helped the people of Kashmir? As a matter of fact, we have made life more difficult for them.

Proxy War in Kashmir and Pakistan's Economy

Pakistan has always faced economic difficulties due to several reasons – a basically agrarian economy, lack of industrial infrastructure and the sizeable diversion of financial resources to the maintenance of a military machine disproportionate to its legitimate defence requirements.

In the last 53 years of its existence, Pakistan launched four armed conflicts against India – 1947 – 48, 1965, 1971 and 1999 in Kargil. Pakistan has also sustained through its ISI separatist movements all over India, which requires sizeable resources.

The Pakistani economy in terms of exports potential and foreign exchange earnings lost out heavily when East Pakistan seceded to become Bangladesh. Pakistan is therefore, a state with limited economic means; negligible economic growth, no industrial infrastructure worth the name and yet vying to attain strategic symmetry with its powerful neighbour India. Till lately, Pakistan was the recipient of economic and military aid from USA and other advanced industrialised countries .

With the end of the Cold War, the down grading of Pakistan's front line status and its increasing shift towards Islamic fundamentalism, these financial resources are trickling off.

Pakistan's Dismal Economic Picture

Pakistan's economy is as the economic indicators below would highlight.

1. It's foreign debt amounts to $ 42 billion. The domestic debt totals $ 70 billion. The total amounts to a figure which is $ 50 billion higher than Pakistan's GDP.
2. Debt servicing amounts to 51% and military expenditure accounts for 28% of the budget.
3. Economic growth has been on a decline from 6.8% per year in Ayub's regime to 6.5% in Zia's tenure and 4.4% in Bhutto's time. It is much lower in 1999 – 2000.
4. Agriculture, which has been the mainstay of Pakistan's economy, especially cotton and other cash crops, has declined from an annual growth of 5.1% in Ayub's time and
5. 4% in Zia's time to only 2.7% in Bhutto's time. 5.Pakistan owes more than 47% of its GDP to foreign financial institutions.
6. GDP growth of about 2.7% in 1992 – 93 has dropped to 1.3% in 1996 – 97.
7. The worst indicator is that Pakistani expatriate deposits in Pakistan totalled $ 11.2 billion.

Successive governments in Pakistan have spent this money leaving no resources to pay the depositors.

Against the back drop of this dismal economic picture, Pakistan has been incurring sizeable expenditure to promote its proxy was in J & K and sustain:

- Daily shelling incidents along the entire length of the LAC.
- Financial payments to Islamic fundamentalist mercenaries from Pak Madrassas, Afghan Mujahideen and mercenaries from other Islamic countries, to keep alive the proxy War in J & K.
- Financing the ISI for its destabilisation activities in various parts of India.
- Acquisition of sizeable quantities of arms and explosives for its mercenaries in J&K and ISI in other parts of India.
- The exorbitant cost of the Kargil War.
- Nuclear weaponisation of Pakistan could run into thousands of crores.

The funds for conducting the proxy War in J & K and other destabilising activities in India cannot be found from within Pakistan's own financial resources.

It is inconceivable that any of the Western countries, Pakistan's erstwhile donors of the Cold War era, would supply funds.

Logically, the finger points at the following sources which Pakistan could be exploiting :

1. Islamic fundamentalist countries like Saudi Arabia and some of the Gulf Sheikhdoms.
2. Collections from Pakistani expatriates abroad on sentimental grounds.
3. Lastly, the most lucrative would be narcotics smuggling to Western countries which could yield sizeable resources not require public accounting.

The narcotics drug trade is being carried out clandestinely by the Pakistan Army independent of the Government, and the ISI provides the financial resources for its anti-India activities. In this, with the Talibanisation of Afghanistan the potential for additional resources becomes more pronounced.

The possibility of covert Chinese military aid for Pak Army's ventures is also a possibility. Unthinkable, but possible, in view of sizable recovery of Chinese origin weapons.

LoC not acceptable as border: Musharraf

President Gen Pervez Musharraf has said Islamabad will not accept the Line of Control dividing Kashmir between Pakistan and India as the international border. In an interview with the *Washington Post*, the president said accepting the LoC as a border or granting some sort of autonomy to Kashmir would not solve the problem. "If the Line of Control were the border, what have we fought two wars for?" he asked. President Musharraf also said that Pakistan might boost its military capabilities, citing increases by India in defence spending. "If they tilt the conventional balance, we shall have to restore it."

President Musharraf said the United States was the only country which could persuade India to start a dialogue as "bilateralism has not worked." To a question, President Musharraf said that after October elections he would retain the authority to dismiss the government if it was found that power was abused.

The following are the excerpts of the interview:

Q: Did you tell US Deputy Secretary of State Richard Armitage that you would stop cross-border terrorism and shut down the training camps that exist in Azad Kashmir and in Pakistan itself?

A: First of all, I don't call it cross-border terrorism. There is a freedom struggle going on in Kashmir. What I said is that there is no movement across the Line of Control. There was no talk of anything else. I have made clear that a response is required from the Indian side....

Q: US and Indian officials say that the number of terrorist infiltrations from Pakistan into Occupied Kashmir has decreased.

A: I have told President Bush nothing is happening across the Line of Control. This is the assurance I've given. I'm not going to give you an assurance that for years nothing will happen. We must address the root-cause, the cause of Kashmir. If you want a guarantee of peace, there are three ways: 1) denuclearize South Asia; 2) ensure a conventional deterrence so that war never takes place in the sub-continent; 3) find a solution to the Kashmir problem.

Q: So you are going to build up your conventional defences?

A: We should. Our army is deterrence enough at the moment. But the Indians are increasing their defence budget, having contracted for billions of dollars of purchases from Russia and the West. If they tilt the conventional balance, we shall have to restore it.

Q: How close did you come to a war with India recently?

A: It was very close. India and Pakistan both had moved their forces to the border. Therefore, the capability of adventurism was there. As far as Pakistan was concerned, we said we would not initiate a war, but if attacked, we will defend offensively.

Q: Do you think that some kind of autonomy is a solution for Kashmir or accepting the Line of Control as a border?

A: That is just not possible. If the Line of Control were the border, what have we fought two wars for?

Q: Is this moment a turning point for Pakistani-Indian relations or just a pause between crises?

A: This is certainly a turning point for the good. I have an assurance. I have been told by President Bush and Deputy Secretary Armitage that, yes, they (Indian officials) need to move forward on the initiation of a dialogue on Kashmir.

Q: Can Vajpayee be your partner?

A: He had become a partner in Agra (at their summit last July in India). He invited me and I gave him credit for it. The recognition of Kashmir as the core issue was very much in the communique that was drafted by me, Vajpayee, Indian Foreign Minister Jaswant Singh and my foreign minister, Abdul Sattar.

Q: Vajpayee says that Agra broke down because you wouldn't recognize the terrorists as terrorists.

A: We had four sessions. We may have discussed cross-border terrorism for 10 minutes because I said, "Prime Minister, you don't expect me to accept that what is happening in Kashmir is terrorism because the Pakistani nation will not accept that." We never spoke of it again. In the proposed communique... what was bold on the part of Prime Minister Vajpayee was that he accepted Kashmir as the main issue that needs to be resolved.

Q: It is said that you made a 180-degree turn after Sept 11, when you joined the West and dropped the Taliban. Now it is said that you may do the same in regard to the Jihadis who have operated in Kashmir with Pakistani backing.

A: Yes, on Afghanistan, we changed our policy. Before Sept 11, we had no choice but to go along with the Taliban. They occupied 90 per cent of Afghanistan. Then, the Taliban got involved in the terrorist act on Sept 11. We saw the environment and thought we should join the coalition. If you call it 180 degrees, okay. But Kashmir is our national interest. Pakistan has always given moral, political and diplomatic support to Kashmiris.

Q: You have another problem - the fundamentalist groups that have been out of control in your country.

A: There are three kinds of militancy that we are confronting. One is Afghanistan-related - Al Qaeda. We don't want a single Al Qaeda member on Pakistani territory....

Q: Vajpayee says you know where Osama bin Laden is and that the remnants of Al Qaeda are here.

A: That is how they keep maligning us. If they are hiding somewhere, we are trying to locate them. Pakistan has arrested over 300 people and handed them over. I cannot say we have freed Pakistan from Al Qaeda. But Abu Zubaida (an Al Qaeda leader now in US custody) was caught by us....

The second kind of militancy is Kashmir-related. The third is internal; domestic extremism, religious fanaticism, sectarian extremism. I moved against five political groups. Lashkar-i-Taiba and Jaish-i-Muhammad have been banned, their offices sealed and accounts frozen. It's not easy to tackle these people, and no government ever dared touch them... There is a lot of fallout. This cannot be accomplished by a few orders.

Q: Who's responsible for the attack on the US consulate in Karachi?

A: One possibility is Al-Qaeda. The other is that it's RAW-related. RAW does a lot of anti-Pakistan activity within Pakistan. So many bomb blasts have been taking place. Who is brewing this? Obviously they are RAW-inspired. They (the Indians) don't like us getting close to the US.

Q: Aren't the extreme groups a threat to you and your government?

A: Certainly, I get a lot of threats. But I'm not scared. I take principled stands whether it is an external or internal threat. Now, I'm facing both. Obviously, I am stepping on the toes of a lot of people.

Q: What is your opinion about the upcoming elections in Kashmir? It is said that Pakistani-backed groups have killed moderates like the Kashmiri leader Abdul Ghani Lone, who was assassinated recently.

A: You believe that? Mr Lone was addressing about 1,000 people. Obviously, there were (Indian) military men all around.

Q: You are saying that Indians did this?

A: Obviously. I am 100 per cent sure. He had given a statement that he was opposed to elections. Pakistan is against elections; Kashmir is a disputed territory; not a part of India.

Q: In this region, would you like to see the US try to bring about a settlement?

A: The US is the only country which can persuade India to initiate a dialogue and move toward a solution of Kashmir. Bilateralism hasn't worked.

Q: Do you believe that Pakistan's nuclear option prevented war recently?

A: No, I think it was (our) conventional deterrence.

Q: It used to be said that ISI was a rogue entity; now it's said to be under your control.

A: ISI does whatever the government wants. The problem arises whenever there is a rift between the government and the army, which happened under the previous (Nawaz Sharif's) government.... I can remove anybody from ISI so I am responsible for whatever ISI does or does not do.

Q: Do you have any thoughts about returning this country to a more democratic system?

A: We will have elections in October, though we have the most democratic system now, a functional democracy. But Pakistan has never had democracy with elected governments. I am a dictator all right, because I am not elected. But I think my functioning is most democratic.

Q: Even after October, you will still be the most powerful man in the country.

A: No, not after October. My power is as the chief executive of Pakistan, not as the president of Pakistan. Power is the power to govern, to take decisions about governing the country - on economic strategy, on education, on the distribution of the budget. Now, I make those decisions. After October, that authority will remain with the president. I am going to shed power to the prime minister. I am a believer that two people cannot share power. I will be left as the president and chief of army staff. I will retain the authority to dismiss (the government). Our experience during the past 10 years was that the government itself was looting and plundering and misgoverning. That needs to be checked.

Q: But you have the advantage of the loyalty of the army.

A: Everyone thinks being a military man means I'm an abuser of power. But I want to bring real democracy to Pakistan. We have to have elections and get a prime minister. This prime minister must perform. If he doesn't, I will guide him to a right course. I became maybe a little emotional and sentimental about many of the things you asked about but these are the realities. You can't judge actions taken here in the context of the US. You have to be in my shoes to understand the difficulties. This is a complicated place. We have four mind-sets to satisfy; First, what do Pakistanis think of various issues? Second, what does the US think? Third, what do the Kashmiris think? Fourth, what do the Indians think? I have to take the country forward in spite of the militancy to the west, to the east and in the centre. I have to do this balancing act and it is not an easy job.

Pakistan President Pervez Musharraf has denied giving an "assurance" to US of permanently ending cross-border terrorism and said it was linked to India's response to its demand for "discussion on Kashmir". "I've told President Bush nothing is happening across the Line of Control. This is the assurance I've given. I'm not going to give you an assurance that for years nothing will happen. We have to have response from India, a discussion about Kashmir," Musharraf said in an interview given to *Newsweek*.

Even during his recent discussions with American Deputy Secretary of State Richard Armitage, he said they did not talk about dismantling of terrorist training camps in the Pakistan Occupied Kashmir.

"Kashmir is witnessing a freedom struggle. What I said was that there would is no movement across the Line of Control," he said.

Musharraf also blamed Indian Intelligence Agency RAW for recent bomb blasts in Pakistan and said it was engineered as "India do not want Islamabad to get close to US".

Accusing India of buying billions of dollars worth of weapons from Russia and the West and said, "If they tilt the conventional balance, we shall have to restore it."

Asked whether he would like the United States to bring about some kind of settlement between India and Pakistan, he replied "America is the only country which can persuade India to initiate a dialogue and move towards a solution of Kashmir. Bilateralism has not worked."

Asked about reports that Indian army wanted to conduct strikes against terrorist training camps in

Pakistan occupied Kashmir, he said, "We would have taught them a lesson. This is not a small country. This is not Afghanistan."

Replying to a question, he said India and Pakistan had come very close to having a war. "As far as Pakistan is concerned, we said we will not initiate war but if attacked, will defend offensively."

Asked if this is a turning point in the relations between the two countries or just a pause between crises, he replied this is certainly a turning point for the good.

"But India needs to move forward on the initiation of dialogue on Kashmir. So we are looking for a response from India." he said.

To a question whether some kind of autonomy for Kashmir or accepting Line of Control as border would a solution to Kashmir, Musharraf replied, "That's just not possible. If Line of Control is to be border, what have we fought these two wars for?"

Asked whom he held responsible for recent bomb blasts in the country, he said Al- Qaeda is one possibility. But the other is Indian intelligence agency RAW.

"RAW does a lot of anti-Pakistan activity. So many bomb blasts are taking place. Who is brewing this? Obviously, they are RAW-inspired. They (Indians) do not like us getting close to the US. They had thought after Sept 11, Pakistan would declared a terrorist state."

5

India's Stand on Kashmir

India responded by aiding and abetting the establishment of a so-called "Provisional Government" of Junagarh on Indian territory, which attacked Junagarh with Indian connivance and support. Subsequently Indian forces also invaded Junagarh, despite protests from Pakistan, in order to "restore law and order". A farcical plebiscite was organized under Indian auspices, and India annexed Junagarh. Similarly, in Hyderabad, a Hindu majority state, the Muslim ruler of the state wanted to retain an independent status. India responded by attacking Hyderabad and annexed the state by force. India sought to justify its aggression against Hyderabad and Junagarh on the plea that the rulers of Junagarh and Hyderabad were acting against the wishes of their people. In Jammu and Kashmir state, the situation was the reverse. The ruler of the State was a Hindu, while the population was overwhelmingly Muslim and wanted to join Pakistan. In this case, India consistently pressurized the Hindu Ruler to accede to India. Apprehending that the Hindu ruler was likely to succumb to Indian pressure, the people of

Jammu and Kashmir rose against him, forcing him to flee from Srinagar, the capital of the State. They formed their own government on 24th October, 1947. On 27th of October, 1947, the Government of India alleged that the ruler had acceded to India on the basis of a fraudulent instrument of accession, sent its forces into the State and occupied a large part of Jammu and Kashmir. But Indian leaders, including Jawahar lal Nehru, the Prime Minister and Lord Mountbatten, the then Governor General of India, solemnly declared that the final status of Jammu and Kashmir would be decided by the people of the State.

This declaration was reiterated by India at the UN Security Council when the dispute was referred to that august body, under chapter 6 of the U.N Charter relating to peaceful settlement of disputes. The Security Council adopted a number of resolutions on the issue, providing for the holding of a fair and impartial plebiscite in Jammu and Kashmir under UN auspices to enable the Kashmiri people to exercise their right of self-determination and join either Pakistan or India. The UN also deployed the United Nations Military Observer Group (UNMOGIP) to monitor the cease-fire line between the Liberated or Azad Kashmir area and the Indian Held Kashmir (IHK). These resolutions were accepted by India and Pakistan and constitute an agreed legal basis for settlement of the dispute.

India, however, thwarted all attempts by the United Nations to organize a plebiscite in the State of Jammu and Kashmir. Eventually, India openly resiled from its commitments and declared that Jammu and Kashmir was an integral part of India. The Indian armed intervention in the State of Jammu and Kashmir was illegal and took place against the wishes of the Kashmiri people. Despite the decision of the UN Security Council for the holding of a plebiscite to allow the people of Jammu and Kashmir to determine their own future, India's own pledges to that effect, and reiteration of their commitment of resolving the Kashmir issue in the Simla Agreement of 1972 signed between Pakistan and India after the 1971 war, India continues to remain in illegal occupation of a large part of Jammu and Kashmir, refuses to allow the Kashmiris to decide their own future and continues its brutal suppression in the territory.

Moreover, India went on to violate other aspects of the Simla agreement, specifically the undertaking that neither side shall change the ground situation, by occupying the Chorbat La, Siachen & Qamar sectors, an area over 2500 sq. kilometres between 1972 to 1988. After more than four decades of a peaceful struggle against Indian repression, manipulation and exploitation, the Kashmiri people, convinced that India would never honour its commitments, and inspired by similar movements for freedom in other parts of the world, rose against the Indian occupation towards the later part of 1989. Their struggle was, and remains, largely peaceful. India sought to suppress their movement with massive use of force, killing hundreds of innocent men, women and children. This led some of the Kashmiri youth to take up arms in self defence.

Since 1989, more than 60,000 Kashmiri people have been killed in a reign of terror and repression unleashed by over 600,000 Indian troops. Many more languish in Indian jails where they are subjected to torture and custodial deaths. There have been numerous cases of gang rapes of Kashmiri women by the Indian forces and the deliberate burning down of entire localities and villages. These brutalities have been documented by International and even Indian Human Rights Organizations. Organizations such as Amnesty International and Human Rights Watch as well as Indian human rights NGOs have extensively documented the gross and systematic violation of human rights of the Kashmiri people by Indian military and para-military forces. Extra judicial killings, involuntary disappearances, arbitrary detentions, rapes and torture continue to be reported on a large scale. The Kashmiri leaders have been repeatedly harassed and physically intimidated. They have also been denied travel permission to prevent them from exposing Indian human rights abuses in Occupied Jammu and Kashmir. The massive suppression by India is clearly designed to silence the people of Jammu and Kashmir through sheer brutality bordering on genocide and ethnic cleansing.

India refuses to acknowledge that the people of Indian Held Kashmir (IHK) have become totally alienated and there is complete rejection of Indian occupation. Several Kashmiri political parties have formed the All Parties Hurriyat Conference (APHC) to continue the political struggle for self-determination. The APHC, therefore, constitutes the true representative of the Kashmiri people. Instead of accepting the existing reality, India has sought to blame Pakistan for allegedly promoting the Kashmiri uprising. The fact is that this movement is completely indigenous and enjoys mass support. The Indian allegations against Pakistan are a ploy to mislead the International Community and to create a smokescreen behind which they can continue repression in IHK. Pakistan has offered to enable the UNMOGIP or any other neutral force to monitor the LoC, along which India has deployed several thousands of its troops and has mined the entire area. Indian refusal to accept these proposals, exposes their false allegations. A peaceful, negotiated settlement of the Kashmir dispute in accordance with UN resolutions remains on top of Pakistan's foreign policy agenda. To demonstrate its sincerity in finding a peaceful solution to this core issue, Pakistan has always sought a meaningful and substantive dialogue with India. However, the Indians have refused to engage in meaningful talks on Kashmir, claiming the territory as an integral part of India.

Only when compelled by extraneous factors or international pressure, such as in 1962-63, 1990-94 and again after May 1998, have the Indians agreed to talks on Kashmir. But this dialogue has been sterile because the Indian objective has never been to find a settlement but to deflect international pressure by creating the facade of talks. During 1962-63, the Indians agreed to talks on Kashmir under U.S. persuasion at a time when their relations with China had deteriorated and the Sino-Indian war took place and it was necessary for India to protect its western flank with Pakistan.

Between 1990-94, India was hard pressed for a dialogue, again due to international pressure following the indigenous Kashmiri uprising which began in the end of 1989. Under pressure from the US, following the mission of the American President's Special envoy, Robert Gates to the region, India engaged in seven rounds of talks at the Foreign Secretary level. Due to continued Indian intransigence, however, this process broke down in January 1994. After a hiatus of three years, talks were resumed at the initiative of Pakistan's former Prime Minister Nawaz Sharif, after he assumed office in

March 1997. Following Foreign Secretary level talks in June 1997, an agreed agenda was adopted which includes the specific issue of Kashmir. More importantly, in the meeting between Prime Ministers of Pakistan and India in September 1998, the two leaders agreed that resolution of the Kashmir dispute is essential for peace and security in the region. During Indian Prime Minister Vajpayee's visit to Lahore in February 1999, the Lahore Declaration was adopted committing both sides to intensify efforts to resolve the Kashmir issue.

Indian willingness to hold specific talks on Kashmir has been compelled by growing international concern over the Kashmir issue following the nuclear tests by India and in response by Pakistan in May 1998. This nuclearization of South Asia has converted Kashmir into a nuclear flash point and the U.N. Security Council through resolution 1172 as well as the G-8 and P.5 countries, apart from a number of world leaders, have expressed the urgent need for a dialogue to resolve this root cause of tensions between Pakistan and India.

While the first round of talks on Kashmir was held in October 1998 between the Foreign Secretaries, as per the agreed agenda of June 1997, there was no change in the Indian position. India rejected Pakistan's frame work proposal for a structured and substantive dialogue on Kashmir, maintaining its intransigent position that the status of Kashmir was not open for discussion.

Even though India agreed in the Lahore Declaration to intensify efforts to resolve the Kashmir issue, in February 1999, it resorted to delaying tactics for holding the next round of talks. In May 1999, India dealt a severe blow to the dialogue process by launching massive military operations, involving air and ground forces, on the Kashmiri Mujahideen in the Kargil Sector and across the Line of Control on Pakistani controlled areas. The Indians also rejected our efforts to defuse the situation, including the proposal for immediate cessation of hostilities, mutual respect for the LoC and resumption of the dialogue process in accordance with the Lahore Declaration.

At the invitation of President Clinton, former Prime Minister Nawaz Sharif visited the US on 4-5 July 1999 and held indepth discussions with the US President on all aspects of the Kashmir situation. A Joint Statement issued as a result of these talks reflects identity of views on the need to resolve the current situation as well as the larger issue of Kashmir which is central to durable peace and stability in South Asia. It recognizes and underscores the need for both India and Pakistan to respect the LOC in accordance with the 1972 Simla Agreement. It also speaks about concrete steps to be taken for restoration of the LOC. As Pakistan has no presence across the LOC the only concrete step on our part can be to appeal to the Mujahideen who have already achieved their objective of bringing the Kashmir issue back to the international focus of attention.

The two leaders agreed that the Lahore process provides the best forum for resolving all outstanding issues between Pakistan and India including Kashmir. According to the Joint Statement the President of the United States stands committed to his personal involvement to expedite and intensify the process for resolving the Kashmir dispute. This is for the first time that the US has agreed to play a direct role in the search for a final settlement of the Kashmir dispute.

India continues to rely on brute force to silence the Kashmiri people. Not only has the campaign of repression been intensified in Indian Occupied Jammu and Kashmir, but additional forces were inducted in November 1998 as part of the new "pro-active" policy and later in the Kargil operation, Indian forces have now been increased to over 730,000. This clearly points to the failure of the current Indian policy to hold the Kashmiri people against their wishes by force. Pakistani public opinion remains deeply incensed with the wide-spread atrocities committed against the innocent Kashmiri people by Indian military and para-military forces.

The government's policy on the Jammu and Kashmir issue enjoys national consensus. Pakistan maintains its principled stand in accordance with the relevant UN Security Council resolutions that call for a plebiscite under UN auspices. It is in keeping with the solemn pledge made to the Kashmiri people by Pakistan, India and the international community. In order to find an early and just solution to the 50-year old Jammu and Kashmir dispute, Pakistan has welcomed offers of good offices and third-party mediation. It has encouraged the international community to play an active role and facilitate the peaceful settlement of disputes between Pakistan and India. While Pakistan is committed to a peaceful settlement of the Jammu and Kashmir dispute, adequate measures have been taken to safeguard the country's territorial integrity and national sovereignty.

Pakistan will continue to extend full political, diplomatic and moral support to the legitimate Kashmiri struggle for their right to self-determination as enshrined in the relevant United Nations resolutions. In the context of the bilateral dialogue, it calls on India to translate its commitments into reality. At the same time, it will encourage the international community to support and supplement our efforts to establish lasting peace and stability in South Asia on the basis of equitable resolution of all disputes between the two countries, in particular the core issue of Jammu and Kashmir. We hope that India will join us in our efforts to bring durable peace to the region for the common benefit of all our peoples. For half a century our region has remained mired in tensions and conflicts. It is our sincere desire to see South Asia enter the next millennium at peace with itself.

India's Struggle for Security

Pokhran II has catapulted India into a situation radically different from the past. Therefore it has become urgently necessary to abandon the mindset of yesterday in bilateral and multilateral negotiations relating to political and security concerns. Professor Martin Sherman has focused upon the theoretical rationale for a differentiation between democratic and non-democratic regimes with regard to the manner in which security dilemmas of these political systems are resolved. This analysis has far-reaching consequences for the possession of nuclear weapons by a democratic country like India, which has to face the expanding nuclear arsenal of a politically totalitarian China.

India's new self-image would need to be based on a positive and unified national perspective, of a democratic and responsible power capable of acting in a rational manner to develop the reciprocal control systems necessitated by its nuclear deterrent. There is not place here for knee-jerk reactions as we stand on the threshold of a new international reality based on our career as a non-aligned nation which led us sometimes to express a trade Union affinity with non-democratic regimes.

A prudent approach for New Delhi at this stage would be to focus on the depth and scope of the commitment of the United States to Indian military and economic security. Before any serous talk of far-reaching global arms control, we have to ensure acceptance of "minimum nuclear deterrence" for India. It is also necessary on military grounds that there should be continued missile testing pending border settlements with China and Pakistan. India should therefore emphasise that it is not interested in rushing into a deal which would solve some short-term problems but create more political turmoil in the long run. A primary and legitimate subject is India's permanent membership in the Security Council. No less important is the recognition of our legitimate interests in Indian Ocean, South-East Asia, the Gulf and Central Asia. As a nuclear weapons state India is not interested in exercising hegemonic leadership: on the contrary, it wants to be recognised publicly as a non-expansionist and constructive power in the Asia-Pacific.

The central issues with regard to the CTBT for India are: (i) that signing it should not freeze India into an intolerable position of strategic inferiority and (ii) that being the case, it should advance our generalised interest in containing the spread of nuclear weapons. With regard to the first point., the CTBT is an obstacle to designing and perfecting weapons, the latter being as much an issue of ensuring their safety and reliability as of maximising yields. Much depends on the current stare of knowledge in this field, and on the kind of agenda planned for the future.

Next on the non-proliferation agenda after CTBT is the FMCT (fissile materials cut-off treaty) which will freeze the raw material for nuclear weapons, effectively putting a limit on the number of weapons we could make in the future. It will also entail levels of inspection by international agencies which we might find offensive. If we wish to have the capacity of build a credible force de frappe vis-a-vis China's nuclear armoury, then a series of immediate decisions will need to be taken with regard to the requisite mix of sophistication in technology and raw materials that these will necessitate. It is important, therefore, not to close options, and at the same time to build a stronger scientific and technological constituency, outside the circle of defence scientists, for underlying security concerns.

Our recommendation here would be that the government appoint a high-level commission with a majority of scientific and strategic expertise from outside the current DAE/MOD set-up to evaluate these questions in a very short period of time, and reach a conclusion on whether more tests are essential. Part of the model here would be the American JASON programme that uses the expertise of non-defence scientists to make a realistic assessment of the weapons labs. An unclassified summary of their conclusions could later be made public. With regard to the second point, the answer is likely in the direction of a qualified yes, even if it is likely to have little impact on such likely sources of threat as China, Pakistan and Iran. For one thing, it will still constrain the process of proliferation in which we have no great stake beyond ourselves. Otherwise the world may be heading for a dangerous confrontation between the US and the "rogue" states, so we should not position ourselves in a manner that invites comparison ourselves in a manner that invites comparison with the latter. In this regard, the greater transparency implicit in the constitution of the above suggested commission would go a long way in projecting a more responsible profile.

Should the technical answer of the commission be that further testing is not really necessary, there should be no further objection to signing the CTBT. There remains the question of conditionalities under which the signature is given. Ideally, the decision should emerge through a consensus which would obviate the need for conditions, but if that is not possible, then it is better to ask for an engagement by the US at the level of security concerns rather than demand high technology transfers. A better understanding on strategic issues should take care of the high tech problem anyway. The real frontier over the next decade is going to be the spread of ballistic missiles and the impact of high technology on warfare. The recent Rumsfield report to the US Congress notes that several countries deeply hostile to the US may in as little as five years possess the capacity to aim an ICBM armed with weapons of mass destruction at the US directly. Needless to say, the US will respond in two ways: by strengthening its anti-missile defences and by directly preventing the deployment of such weapons on the part of the "rogues".

Israel will react similarly. Both may also evolve doctrines that call for massive retaliation against the "rogues". The theological fig leaf of the NPT will thus be dropped to expose the very real security anxieties of the remaining superpower. In the midst of all this are India and Pakistan, countries not hostile to the US as the report notes, but nevertheless contributing to this expanding and dangerous nuclear pluralism for their own reasons.

The report also notes that China, Russia and the US itself have made the problem much worse through their short-sighted policies of arming other states through both conventional and nuclear means. The CTBT area of concern is focused on the manufacture of weapons, but it is over delivery systems that the next round of battled is going to be fought. Hence, instead of rear-mirror driving and concentration on the last war, we could instead usefully think how to safeguard our security in the midst of this growing capacity of a large number of states to threaten each other. Certainly an important feature behind the present developments has been the unravelling of an inequitable international regime dominated by the US, but it is all the more imperative to think about what might come next, and whether it will be to our benefit. Therefore, the current stalemate with the United States over the CTBT should not be an excuse not to find time to rethink the need for India and the USA to work together in broad strategic concerns. For the present, the mutual interests of the US and China seem to hold centre stage, and India has every reason to feel that both countries are cooperating to impose a hegemony on the subcontinent. But there are many aspects of China's behaviour that are worrisome for Washington, and its inadequate dialogue with India is coming under increasing criticism within the United States.

Two years ago in a prophetic piece of writing Selig Harrison, the noted South Asian expert, said: "If we try to preserve the nuclear status quo, first India and then Japan will, in my view, become overt nuclear weapons powers. Not only because they face the Chinese nuclear arsenals, but also because they won't accept second class status. Both of them are capable of making ICBMs that can reach the US. Nonproliferation will simply not work unless the world is moving towards denuclearisation." India has never been in the kind of adversary relations with the United States that would warrant even thinking of aiming ICBMs at that country, but it is clear that as a nuclear weapons power it is necessary for India policy-makers to investigate casual relations between regional and international factors, and sharpen the awareness of issues involved which can produce a new strategic bargain. This bargain must take into account India's long-term goals and their compatibility with America's long-term interests. It must recognise both India's geopolitical importance and her rootedness as a democracy in the moral-political sphere.

The foregoing sections argue that India's nuclear tests were heavily influenced by the BJP's strategic assessment of China and its view that Nehruvian foreign policy poorly served New Delhi's overall strategic needs. They also argue that Pakistan's nuclear status, even without nuclear testing, was perceived by India as a deterrent to conventional escalation. Thus strategic imperatives were less critical in explaining Pakistan's nuclear tests than Prime Minister Nawaz Sharif's fears that a failure to test would be political suicide. Both sides now argue that nuclear deterrence will help to avoid war in the future. Outside actors—principally the United States—argue that other measures would contribute to South Asian security but would reinforce global security as well.

The initial U.S. reaction to India's and Pakistan's decisions to test was to impose economic sanctions. U.S. legislation mandates that economic sanctions be placed on any nation that tests nuclear weapons, other than the five declared NPT nuclear nations. The law applies across the board, regardless of the country's relationship to the

United States or the condition of its economy. As noted by Leonard Weiss, former Staff Director for the Senate Governmental Affairs Committee, where the sanctions legislation originated: "the wide array of sanctions for detonating a nuclear device ... is what I call a 'diplomatic doomsday machine' provision." It was of a piece with prior legislation that made nonproliferation more important than bilateral relations.

Where presidents in the past had been obligated to weigh the balance between opposing policies, and put one aside in favor of another, legislatively mandated foreign policy dictates that if a foreign country takes certain steps, the president is compelled to respond in a pre-planned manner regardless of the effect. The sanctions affected Pakistan more harshly than India, although both sides considered them to be a discriminatory response to their sovereign national security decisions. Many analysts feared that Pakistan would be driven into the arms of states who would seek benefit from supporting Islamabad in its hour of need, while at the same time Pakistan's domestic political structure would become more vulnerable to internal breakdown. In India, analysts feared the government might be driven into a more autarkic way of thinking, which would only play into the hands of BJP conservatives.

The White House too was uncertain about the value of the mandated sanctions; two weeks after the reciprocal tests were completed, Assistant Secretary of State Karl Inderfurth testified that the threat of sanctions was "meant primarily as a deterrent" that the administration hoped "would never have to be implemented." Even Weiss agreed that "a sanction with no exit strategy [is] a bad idea." Attention quickly shifted to how the United States might extricate itself from its somewhat counterproductive approach. The Group of 8 (G-8) and the five permanent members of the UN Security Council (P-5) collaborated to propose a set of five benchmarks for South Asia. The goal was to specify a set of objectives that, if agreed to by India and Pakistan, would mitigate, though perhaps not entirely eliminate, the negative consequences of their nuclear tests. If these objectives were met, sanctions might be lifted and a kind of status quo ante established. It was not clear what benefits India and Pakistan might accrue from the other four P-5 members, as they had not imposed sanctions, but the United States held out the prospect of enhanced cooperative relations.

In Under Secretary of State Strobe Talbott's view, these measures "would help avoid a destabilizing nuclear and missile competition, as well as more generally reduce tensions on the subcontinent and bolster global nonproliferation." The five steps were

1) to conduct no more nuclear tests and sign the CTBT;
2) to engage in good faith negotiations for a fissile material cutoff treaty (FMCT) at the Conference on Disarmament in Geneva;
3) to practice restraint in the development and deployment of delivery systems;
4) to bring national export controls into accord with international regime norms; and
5) to commence a bilateral dialogue on contentious issues.

The issue of testing was the most pressing, as a clock had been set when the CTBT was signed in 1996. Pushed most vigorously by the United States, the treaty was accepted by China only after China had completed a series of underground nuclear tests in 1995.

India and Pakistan were not party to the negotiations, but when the treaty was drafted China insisted that it should only enter into force when the three threshold states signed and ratified. This clause particularly affronted India, which argued that it was a violation of international law to include a nation that was not party to a treaty. K. Subrahmanyam interpreted the insertion of the "infamous" in the following terms:

After the conclusion of the negotiations and after India made it clear ... that while it would not sign the CTBT since it affected it's national security interests adversely it had no objection to the treaty being adopted by the others, the entry into force clause was amended at the last minute to include India in the list of 44 countries whose accession to the treaty was necessary to bring it into force. This was done at the instigation of some nuclear weapon powers ... to prevent India from becoming a nuclear weapon state and subject it to the full rigors of nuclear apartheid.

From New Delhi's point of view, the CTBT was not an invitation but a summons that it felt no duty to answer. The CTBT had originally been envisioned as a way to slow the arms race during the Cold War. The Canadian Government noted that:

In its specific function, the CTBT has a limited but important role: it helps to put a cap on technological arms races by freezing the designs of new nuclear weapons by States Party, especially designs of compact fission-boosted and two-stage thermonuclear weapons, and of miniaturizing low-yield tactical weapons. In the aftermath of the Cold War, the emphasis shifted from stopping technological arms races to stopping new proliferators from getting very sophisticated—in effect, it would deal with new proliferators rather than old ones. Given that argument, it was logical to maintain that it would not serve its purpose unless threshold proliferators were required to sign. This may have been seen as a way to force India and Pakistan's hand; few participants fully appreciated what direction that force might take or what power it placed in those hands.

Although the tests in May 1998 cannot be blamed on the CTBT—it was only signed in 1996, after the BJP had first ordered that tests be conducted—it was clear to decision-makers in New Delhi that as the date for the three-year review approached and as a long-planned visit by President Clinton to South Asia loomed, pressure would become intense. This looming shadow, however, was not sufficient to force Prime Minister Deve Gowda or I. K. Gujral to resurrect the Rao Government's aborted plan to test in 1995. If the CTBT was a precipitating event, presumably these governments would have chosen to test.

As noted earlier, the ground evidently had been prepared for a test in 1995, so little more than an order from the prime minister stood in the way of action. Indeed it has been argued that the BJP was only able to test as quickly as it did in 1998 because the Rao Government had already taken the necessary preliminary steps. Thus it is difficult to argue that the testing represented anything like a national consensus independent of party preferences. It bears repeating that the BJP had already ordered a test during its 13-day tenure in May 1996, an action that predated whatever pressure the CTBT may have created. Regardless of the effect of the CTBT on the tests themselves, its imposition on New Delhi put Indian decision-makers in no mood to sign it. Until Washington ratifies the treaty, it remains unlikely that New Delhi will affix its signature to a treaty it did not accept in the first place. But even if the United States ratifies, a decision about whether or not the CTBT serves India's interests will have to await the seating of a new government in New Delhi.

For its part, Pakistan stuck to its time-honored position that it would agree to stop testing if India paved the way. With India having evidently satisfied its technical and strategic needs, Prime Minister Vajpayee declared a moratorium on further tests. Pakistan followed suit. This half loaf was not enough to convince the United States to abandon the sanctions, but the issue tops the agenda in Indo-American bilateral talks. U.S. policymakers may have interpreted India's comments in these bilateral talks and Prime Minister Vajpayee's statements at the United Nations in October 1998 to imply that India would sign the treaty before the September 1999 deadline. With elections only scheduled for that month, however, a signature now is likely out of the question.

But once talks resume, U.S. negotiators should not misread India's thinking, as many among India's leadership have concluded by now that the United States may need India more than vice versa. The sanctions are painful for India, but the Clinton Administration faces political difficulties if the Senate does not ratify the CTBT prior to the Nonproliferation Treaty review conference in 2000. This could happen if the U.S. Congress decides to ratify the treaty only after India signs. Thus a treaty once seen by arms control advocates as a means to limit the arms race between the United States and the Soviet Union, then marketed by the Clinton Administration as a means to stop proliferation, may ultimately fail to do either: the Soviet-American arms race was never blunted by a CTBT, and Indian and Pakistani nuclear proliferation is now a matter of record. Looming behind India's refusal is another possibility, which, although remote, is nonetheless troubling. As R. Ramachandran has argued: "it stands to reason that any weaponisation programme would demand more tests not only for SCTs [sub-critical tests] but even for designing efficient weapons."

This idea is echoed by the former Indian diplomat P. R. Chari, who adds that India "... may also need to further test its nuclear devices to arm its missiles." China reacted to the first set of tests impassively; a new round might provoke a harsher response, especially in the currently troubled atmosphere between Washington and Beijing. Thus an Indian decision to sign the CTBT and to forego testing might ensure that China would not begin yet another round of testing and development of advanced weapons that would undermine Indian security. The second "practical step" is less immediate in its consequences, and therefore relatively easy for India and Pakistan alike to take. Both countries are committed to negotiating at the Conference on Disarmament in Geneva, but neither is prepared to depart from the positions they held prior to testing. India may feel some bitterness toward this particular benchmark, however, since the Conference is supposed to operate on the basis of consensus.

When, because of India's opposition, negotiations at the Conference failed to produce a consensus on the CTBT in 1995, Australia took the treaty to the General Assembly of the United Nations anyway, where it won a resounding floor vote. Calling now for India and Pakistan to negotiate in a forum that other countries are prepared to bypass if they do not get their own way may smack of hypocrisy. Procedural matters notwithstanding, negotiating positions pose problems of their own. As Lawrence Scheinman, Director of the Center for Nonproliferation Studies (CNS) Washington, D.C. notes: "India [is] averse to an FMCT that deals with pre-existing activity and nuclear material stockpiles; Pakistan's official position is that existing stocks should be part of the negotiations."

At a public lecture at Stanford University on May 19, 1999, former Pakistan Chief of Army Staff General Jehangir Karamat stated that Pakistan no longer supported accounting for nuclear stockpiles, but did oppose a moratorium on production prior to a fissile material cutoff treaty coming into effect. This may represent a change in Pakistan's policy. In any case, both India and Pakistan appear to be in the process of asking how much fissile material they require to create the minimum deterrent they argue they need. Until India and Pakistan resolve this question, participants at the Conference on Disarmament may be in for a long negotiating process over the fissile material cutoff treaty.

The chief concern motivating the argument for restraint was that by avoiding movement toward military readiness, it would be less likely that the two sides would get caught up in an arms race. It is interesting to reread Bernard Brodie's seminal work, The Absolute

Weapon, in which he argued as early as 1946 that, with the advent of nuclear weapons, the means of delivery would become extraordinarily important.

As many feared, such is the case in South Asia now, with both sides developing short and intermediate range missiles. After India conducted a number of tests of the Prithvi short-range ballistic missile (SRBM) and Agni medium-range ballistic missile (MRBM), Pakistan tested the Ghauri MRBM in April 1998.

A year later, in April 1999, India tested a longer-range Agni MRBM to a distance of 2000 km that was swiftly followed by Pakistan testing an enhanced version of the Ghauri that also went 2000 km. One day later, Pakistan tested yet another missile, the Shaheen SRBM, which Islamabad claimed had been ready to go since the nuclear tests a year prior. Although their competition may be less intense than the Soviet-American arms race during the Cold War, the tit-for-tat nuclear tests in 1998 followed by tit-for-tat missile tests in 1999 certainly look like a race to outside observers.

Thus the wished-for restraint is not evident to date. Whether India and Pakistan can put in place other elements of a nuclear restraint regime that is sufficient to influence U.S. thinking regarding sanctions and overall relations remains to be seen. In Strobe Talbott's Spring 1999 Foreign Affairs article,56 it is unclear what criteria will need to be applied in this area before the Clinton Administration feels it can modify the post-test policies. The fourth area that the United States would like to see change before it removes sanctions is the export policy of the two newly declared weapons states. In many ways this is the least contentious benchmark, but it raises some odd problems. India and Pakistan were the victims of export controls and could be expected to have mixed views at best when asked to adopt what they saw as discriminatory policies.

Notwithstanding such objections, it was already the case that India and Pakistan had recognized the need to restrict access to advanced technology. Both had export control guidelines in place, with India's extending quite broadly and Pakistan's less so. India's extensive export control guidelines are guided by a variety of legislation, notably the Atomic Energy Act of 1962 and the Foreign Trade (Development and Regulation) Act of 1992. Controls cover the acquisition, production, possession, use, disposal, export, or import of a wide variety of prescribed equipment (i.e., anything that could be used for the production or utilization of atomic energy) and prescribed substances (e.g. uranium, plutonium, thorium, beryllium, deuterium, or their derivatives). In contrast, Pakistan's guidelines are currently more limited and can be found, inter alia, in the Gazette of Pakistan for July 10, 1998 and January 6, 1984. They reflect Islamabad's unwanted position of having to import nuclear-related goods and services against the wishes of the West and in the face of extensive restrictions.

Pakistanis complain that they had to pay the price for India's nuclear detonation in 1974, which galvanized the international community and precipitated the development of extensive export controls under the Zangger Committee and the Nuclear Suppliers Group. Where India by 1974 had developed its own nuclear capability (with significant help from Western countries, Pakistanis always argue), Pakistan was lagging behind and felt that it had to take any necessary measures to catch up.

When the 1974 Indian nuclear test was followed five years later by the Soviet invasion of Afghanistan, Pakistan found itself in a difficult strategic position. It followed twin policies of seeking a nuclear deterrent to counter India and confronting Soviet forces at its doorstep. It needed U.S. help to achieve the latter, but U.S. nonproliferation policy sought to prevent the former. Given the need to work around the export controls of other states while it was pinned in the spotlight of U.S. export control policy, Pakistan found itself in no position to be a supplier of nuclear technology, much less to develop sophisticated guidelines to control technology transfers. Despite smarting at the effect of controls on their own programs, both states now appear to be willing to discuss expanding their own controls. In at least one instance India has already employed its export guidelines—in the transfer of heavy water to South Korea—while Pakistan claims that it controls even the possibility of nuclear transfer extremely tightly.

Two rounds of U.S.-Indian and U.S.-Pakistan experts meetings have already taken place, with more to follow, and it would appear unlikely that India or Pakistan would resist this benchmark very strenuously on its merits. To the extent that expanded export controls are portrayed as a form of kowtowing to the United States, however, both countries may yet resist pressure to expand controls in favor of maintaining their own standards.

The last area of concern—engaging in a bilateral dialogue—appeared to have been addressed when India's Prime Minister Vajpayee took his historic bus trip from Amritsar, India to Lahore, Pakistan crossing the border at Wagah, the scene of countless atrocities during partition in 1947. Crossing this heavily defended border by such humble means seemed to presage entirely new possibilities for peaceful engagement between the two countries.

Unfortunately, events in Kashmir have since badly tarnished the symbolism of that visit. More than the symbolism, the confidence each side might have had in the dialogue process has been corroded. India may suspect that even before the ink was dry on the Lahore Declaration, Pakistan was supplying the forces that seized the high ground near Dras and Kargil on the Indian side of the Line of Control. Islamabad's counterclaim that the forces are made up entirely of "freedom fighters" from within Indian Kashmir supports those in Pakistan who argue that Kashmir is not just one of many outstanding issues, as the Lahore Declaration implied. Dialogue thus appeared to be a major victim of the fighting. Pakistan Foreign Minister Sartaj Aziz paid a visit to New Delhi in June to discuss the fighting, as did Foreign Secretary Niaz Naik, but the result was acrimony rather than the renewed harmony Lahore promised. This acrimony was worsened when Pakistan returned the bodies of six Indian soldiers killed in the Kashmir fighting, who India immediately declared had been brutally tortured prior to execution. This dialogue clearly was not at all what was envisioned when the Lahore Declaration was signed this past February.

In New Delhi, the precariousness of coalition politics was made manifest as the BJP government was brought down more or less on the whim of one partner, the mercurial Jayalalitha Jayaraman. Similar party-based demands then torpedoed Sonia Gandhi's attempt to form a successor government, leaving India to face general elections for the third time in four years. Against such turbulence, resuming a dialogue—which has historically been sterile anyway and has now been shattered by the Kashmir conflict—is an issue that both countries will allow to slide down their priority lists. It will take a cease-fire, a new government in New Delhi, and a long time before a constructive bilateral dialogue is resumed.

This essay reviewed a number of issues and attempted to provoke further thought about the nuclear tests in India and Pakistan in 1998. A wide variety of questions remain unanswered, however, and ought to be considered in future work.

For example, the discussion above hardly settles the debate over the strategic relations between India and China. This dispute has already received extensive scholarly attention, but the nature of deterrence between India and Pakistan, the prospects for conflict that Tellis and Subrahmanyam discuss, and the strategic balance described by Subrahmanyam all deserve careful analysis. The BJP changed the strategic landscape with its tests; whether one agrees with their vision or not, their actions have forced a new relationship with China.

Most Western literature on deterrence focuses on the U.S.-Soviet Union confrontation of the Cold War, yet the conditions are much different for India and China and for India and Pakistan. Alternate conceptions of deterrence have been raised in the past, but largely in theoretical terms. Concepts such as existential deterrence, introduced by Hagerty's study, as well as recessed, nonweaponized, and minimum deterrence must all be considered under the new circumstances in South Asia.

It is not clear that either side has decided what exactly is being deterred by their overt nuclear capabilities; the May 1999 Kashmir conflict reinforces the question. The relationship between nuclear capabilities and low intensity conflict in general must be analyzed. This raises the question of deterrence stability, which can be viewed in terms of arms race, crisis, or strategic stability. The nuclear weapon capability is far more now than a demonstration of technical "progress." It demands political and strategic analysis, which heretofore has been theoretical or missing.

Some new work in this area is already underway. For example, in his Ph.D. dissertation, Jordan Seng, now a Research Fellow at Harvard's Olin Center, argues that the "'how much is enough?' argument would be moot. In a sense, minimum destruction would be maximum destruction. A little would be plenty." This echoes arguments made earlier by the late General K. S. Sundarji and a host of other scholars in India and Pakistan. But with nuclear weapons out in the open, more thought must be given to this issue. What appears to be obvious to Seng and Sundarji is not at all obvious under present circumstances in South Asia.

Certain technical obstacles may prevent rapid expansion of India's and Pakistan's nuclear and missile capabilities, but the theoretical requirements for "minimum" deterrence already range from 50 to 300 weapons, as argued by Bharat Karnad and Vijai Nair in Amitabh Mattoo's book, India's Nuclear Deterrent: Pokhran II and Beyond. General Sundarji was the chief proponent of the "less is enough" argument for India, but he also appreciated the need for some element of military involvement in strategic planning. Subrahmanyam and others in India and Pakistan have argued that command and control will not be needed, but a more thorough evaluation of the available means and structure would be well worth reviewing.

Arguments that limited overall numbers will obviate the need for extensive command and control mechanisms may be overwhelmed if the targets Karnad and Nair cite are taken seriously. Another area of greater interest now is arms control in South Asia. For example, K. Subrahmanyam has argued that "India should also offer to engage Pakistan and China in nuclear confidence-building measures, both officially and unofficially." Arms control has been an important complement to strategic policy in the Russian-American confrontation, and the utility for India and Pakistan of bilateral, regional, and international arms control measures must be considered by scholars and policymakers in New Delhi and Islamabad alike. Another interesting and important area for future research is in strategic culture and deterrence. Jaswant Singh's book reassessed strategic thinking and planning in India. He based his arguments on criticisms of the basic Indian cultural approach, which served as a useful means for criticizing the legacy of Nehru's foreign policy.

But strategic culture is again an important focus of scholarship, and brings up a host of questions with respect to how nations think about deterrence, war strategy, military readiness, civil-military relations, and so on. Scholars such as Steve Rosen at Harvard University and Iain Johnston at Stanford University are addressing the strategic cultures of India and China, and more can be done in this area under the new circumstances created by the weapon tests. The Indian and Pakistani decisions to test nuclear weapons have altered strategic analysis of the subcontinent, Asia, and the world. For India, the tests represent a transformed strategic vision that the Bharatiya Janata Party brought to power. This vision is based on a redefinition of India's strategic culture and a somber—if not paranoid—view of the long-term Chinese threat. Islamabad's response was heavily based on domestic political considerations, given the vulnerabilities of its national political leaders and given the arguments that India was already deterred by Pakistan's previously veiled nuclear capabilities.

It remains to be seen whether a new government in India will moderate the policies of the BJP, or if the BJP will return with a strengthened mandate. In either case, it is likely that China and Pakistan will treat India as the strategic power the BJP would like it to be, regardless of whatever government assumes power in New Delhi. Both India and Pakistan must now deal with the consequences of this transformed strategic landscape. They say minimum deterrence will satisfy their needs, but minimum deterrence will have to become something more than a threat or slogan. In addition to minimum deterrence, moreover, the five practical steps proposed by the United States will continue to complement deterrence—and perhaps in due course replace it. To the extent that India and Pakistan embrace the notion of arms control as a necessary supplement to nuclear strategy, the CTBT and FMCT will be important measures. Not only would they be important at the international and regional level, but they would also serve India's and Pakistan's own strategic needs.

India and Pakistan decided that nuclear capabilities better served their strategic needs than the NPT; the same conclusion about the CTBT and FMCT, however, does not necessarily follow. Both sides believe that the CTBT and FMCT will slow or stop developments on the other side as well as on their own. Progress toward stability and security will come for India and Pakistan as it did for the five NPT nuclear states—by doing less, not more.

Strategic restraint will also be important regardless of how the two states define minimum deterrence. Indeed, the very notion of minimizing nuclear developments presumes that restraint will be imposed domestically. Just as Strobe Talbott argued, both India and Pakistan wish to avoid an arms race. The first step in that direction therefore must be some sort of political check on technology developments, especially in the realm of delivery vehicles.

India and Pakistan have declared themselves to be nuclear weapon states. They now bear the burden of ensuring that the capability stays at home through comprehensive export controls. They also bear the added burden of remaining engaged diplomatically with an enemy they may not trust.

Much of nuclear deterrence involves signaling, tacit bargaining, and risk management. Indians and Pakistanis already know this. They must now act on it by institutionalizing their dialogue and insulating diplomacy from local troublemakers who would create difficulties for Indo-Pak relations for their own benefit, and not for the benefit of the mass of Indians and Pakistanis who would suffer the most if deterrence fails.

Former U.S. ambassador Karl Inderfurth, who in the Clinton administration tried to talk Pakistan out of developing nuclear weapons in exchange for military and financial aid, said the consequences of a nuclear exchange would extend beyond the borders of the two nations.

"The consequences of a nuclear war have now been studied by the Pentagon," he said. "Their conclusion was that in a full-scale exchange between these countries, 12 million people would die almost instantly."

In addition to that, he said, radiation would drift across Bangladesh and Southeast Asia and across the oceans.

"So this is not something that, even though it's far a faraway conflict, we could escape the consequences of," he said.

Inderfurth said Rumsfeld must make clear to Musharraf that it is in Pakistan's interest to avoid a nuclear war at all costs, and that "the U.S. wants to be a long-term partner with Pakistan, and that would mean dealing with Pakistan's other problems, including its economy, including the fact that it has a failed economic system, a failed educational system."

Pakistan has come under more criticism from the United States than India has, in part because it has supported groups that use terror to oppose Indian rule over Kashmir. President Bush has made clear what he thinks about that.

"[Musharraf] must stop the incursions across the Line of Control," said Bush. "He must do so. He said he would do so. We and others are making it clear to him that he must live up to his word."

The dance between the United States and Musharraf is a complex one. His decision after Sept. 11 to end support of the Taliban and back the U.S. war on terror was critical to the early American success in Afghanistan. Furthermore, the United States has counted on Pakistani forces to apprehend al Qaeda forces seeking refuge.

Musharraf, for his part, is in a tricky position himself, even with what he says in public to his own people. In a speech last week, he said in English that his government was doing its part to control extremists. But then, in switching to Urdu — the national language — he said Pakistan would struggle for Kashmir.

This reflects two things: Musharraf's own belief that Kashmir is rightfully a part of Pakistan, and that radical Muslims in his nation may move against him if he even flinches in this face-off with India.

"These infiltrators were carefully nurtured by a variety of Pakistani regimes and Gen. Musharraf did little or nothing prior to Sept. 11th to curb their activities," said University of Texas at Austin Prof. Sumit Ganguly. "He must now be willing to pay a price for his earlier decisions."

That leaves the U.S. with the task of finding a face-saving way out for Musharraf that the Indians can accept, and does not in any way appear to give in to terrorism. What might help right now is, quite literally, the climate. Monsoon season, when neither sides would like to fight a war, is about to begin. If the two sides can be kept talking for a few more weeks, until the rains start, it might give everyone an excuse to back away from the brink. No careful or unbiased observer of South Asian politics could fail to notice the asymmetry in Western reporting concerning relations between India and Pakistan. The Western public is repeatedly informed how India and Pakistan have fought four wars, but rarely is it acknowledged that in each situation, in 1948, 1965, 1971 and 1998 - Pakistan was the aggressor. While mentioning Kashmir as the bone of contention, few mention how Jammu and Kashmir's unity with India enjoyed the backing of the majority of it's people. In 1996, over 55% of the Indian state's voters participated in Indian elections braving terrorist threats and boycott calls.

Most recently, a poll conducted by an Indian polling agency affiliated with the British-based MORI revealed that 61% of those polled in Jammu and Kashmir wished to remain Indian citizens and only 6% wished to become Pakistani citizens. An overwhelming 86% want an end to the infiltration of terrorists from across the Line of Control (LoC), and an end to acts of terror. Two thirds believe that Pakistan's intervention in the last decade has been detrimental rather than helpful to the interests of the people of the region. (Significantly, the military Government of Pakistan has disallowed MORI's pollsters from conducting a similiar exercise in PoK. But rarely do Western reporters share such data with the Western public. Nor do they care to tell their readers about the oppression of the people in Gilgit and Baltistan, or that there are numerous groups opposed to Pakistan's unwanted occupation of these regions. Neither does it occur to these self-styled Western media Pundits - how utterly ridiculous it is for military despots in Pakistan to be championing the cause of "self-determination" on behalf of a people who enjoy many more democratic freedoms in Indian Kashmir than do the average citizens of Pakistan.

Does General Musharraf who seized power through a military coup have any moral or ethical right to be talking of the "rights" of the Kashmiris? What gives a general - who couldn't find a single political leader to attend his recent "all-party meeting" - the authority to negotiate for the Kashmiri people? But such questions rarely trouble the minds of most Western reporters or editorial columnists. In fact, after having expelled virtually all the Hindus and Sikhs from Pakistan in a brutal campaign of terror and intimidation, what gives the right to any Pakistani to speak of self-determination for any grouping in India? If Pakistan's Sunni elites haven't even been able to ensure the safety of Shia Muslims in Pakistan, how could they possibly speak for the non-Sunni population of Jammu and Kashmir (which comprises almost half of the population of the state). Can Jammu and Kashmir be described as a "disputed" territory, simply because Pakistan's clerical and military establishment is unwilling to pare it's expansionist tendencies?

Not only do the people of India enjoy a much wider range of democratic freedoms than their Pakistani counterparts, they are also now economically better-off. That India is perhaps, the most pluralistic nation in the world, and that Pakistan has embarked on an unceasing campaign of hate and violence against India is almost never acknowledged. Western journalists cynically and routinely equate India and Pakistan. The aggressor and the victim of aggression are lumped as one.

But perhaps, most egregious is how Pakistan's nuclear brinkmanship - how Pakistan's nuclear blackmail is tacitly tolerated and even justified amongst India-bashers in the West. Time and time again, India has asserted that it will not use nuclear weapons against non-nuclear nations. That it is willing to enter into reciprocal non-use treaties with other nuclear powers. And that in general, it rejects the first-strike nuclear option. In contrast, Pakistan has repeatedly threatened the sub-continent with a nuclear holocaust. The very same journalists who are all up in arms over unsubstantiated rumors about Iraq's "weapons of mass destruction" are amazingly sanguine when it comes to reacting to Pakistan's nuclear threats. Whereas Iraq has been embargoed to the point where it's people are not even able to feed themselves, some of the military leaders of Pakistan openly boast of causing a nuclear winter. And they test nuclear-capable missiles to reinforce their chilling threats.

Will there now be some concern for Pakistan's "weapons of mass destruction"? Will the beleaguered nation of Iraq who continues to excite the most venomous hatred in the US press now get a break? Will there be a respite for the Iraqi people from talk of a renewed all-out bombing campaign? The same Western media that engaged in a vicious campaign of vilification of Yugoslavia's popularly elected leader is remarkably tolerant of officials who threaten to cause the greatest human rights disaster the world may ever see. Why is it that a popularly elected leader in one nation can be demonized as "Hitler" whereas an isolated and unpopular military hawk wins praise as a "moderate" ally in the war against terrorism?

Is the reading public so incredibly intellectually-challenged that it cannot see through such hypocrisy and duplicity? What sort of a war on "terrorism" is this that marks non-nuclear countries such as Iran (or Libya and Syria) as amongst the "most dangerous" nations in the world - but leaves out Pakistan - a nation that can't stop threatening the use of nuclear weapons? The answer is obvious. How can American analysts chastize General Musharraf''s Government for making nuclear threats when their own Pentagon has always asserted the right to a nuclear first-strike - even against nations it is supposedly trying to befriend such as Russia. Pakistan is not a wayward ally of the US, nor is it a loose-cannon as some might pretend in the West. It is merely doing what US's client states have always done - fight proxy wars and terrorize their progressive neighbors so that in the end both nations become beholden to the wishes and commands of policy-makers in Washington. Pakistan's nuclear blackmail is not that unusual when one considers how often it has been when American leaders have themselves threatened to push the nuclear button.

Whether such threats are real or merely intended as bluffs, it is immaterial. They are utterly unconscionable. And they also set a very chilling precedent. It is only a matter of time when nuclear weapons will spread to more nations. And a time may come when a nation who is not allied with the US might become emboldened or angry enough to make such a threat against the US. American analysts who are recklessly joining in the frenzy of nuclear alarmism so as to frighten and intimidate Indian leaders into inaction or submission ought to note that they are playing a very dangerous game.

A nation of a billion people with rising hopes and expectations, with justice on it's side, cannot be crushed or humiliated for ever. While Gandhian edicts (of turning the other cheek) might dominate the minds of India's older generation, India's younger generation is much less infected by such faint-hearted idealism. A time will come when India as a nation may be compelled to call the nuclear bluff. While some (or even many) in India may fall for the nuclear subterfuge today, the recalcitrance on the part of Pakistan's rulers (and Western pandering or covert encouragement of such ominous behaviour) may eventually trigger a reaction in India that might simply discount threats by Pakistan's military and diplomatic establishment of escalating a nuclear conflict. After all, even a nuclear threat can only be made so often.

But even if Pakistan's ruling class were truly ready to embark on a suicidal course of launching a nuclear attack against India, the consequences will not be confined to the subcontinent alone. The effects will be earth-shattering, and could lead to unimaginable changes in the entire world's economic system - forcing new political equations, and decisive shifts in the balance of power. Western journalists should not think that just because the Indian subcontinent lies on the other side of the globe, that their own lives will be immune from the effects of a nuclear conflagration in the Indian subcontinent. Any nuclear attack by Pakistan will invariably attempt to target India's major metros, such as Mumbai, Delhi, Bangalore, Chennai, Hyderabad, Pune, Ahmedabad, Kolkata or Thiruvananthapuram. But these are precisely the cities that have attracted billions of dollars of investments from multinational giants in the manufacturing, energy and high-technology sectors.

Consider just a brief list of companies that have expanding investments in India: Auto majors such as Japan's Toyota, Honda and Suzuki, Italy's Fiat, the US's Ford and Chrysler, Korea's Hyundai; European industrial giants such as Siemens, Philips and ABB; consumer majors like Lever Brothers and Cadbury's of Britain; technology giants such as Intel, Texas Instruments, Cisco, IBM and Oracle; energy majors such as Cairns of Australia and British Gas. Consider the multitude of traders, small businesses and suppliers that impact those that profit from Indian imports and exports; consider the airline industry which gets a sizeable share of it's revenues from it's India business.

In the last decade, there isn't a single sector of the Indian economy that hasn't attracted foreign investment or outright purchases. Do the backers or apologists for Pakistan's nuclear renegades in the West wish to see these investments go up in smoke - nuclear smoke? In the last decade, excluding China, no other economy has performed as consistently, or as well. Even as the Japanese economy has been mired in an unending recession, and the economies of the US and the EU nations struggle to grow, India's consumer market continues to expand at a handsome clip. Is there any other growing market of corresponding size and future potential that could provide an outlet for the stagnation scenario that looms before the world's leading manufacturers?

Is any Western economists willing to predict what the world-wide economic consequences of a Pakistani nuclear attack on the headquarters of trade, commerce, manufacturing and technology-design in India might be? Surely no one believes that a nuclear attack could be narrowly targeted so as to avoid Western losses? Consider too, the huge pool of Indian and Pakistani workers who provide manual and intellectual labor in the oil economies of the Persian Gulf. Imagine if the potential supply of this huge labor pool were cut by tens of millions? Is the world ready to do without this enormous supply of cheap labour that keeps oil-profits high, and energy prices relatively well-contained for Western consumers? Undoubtedly, a Pakistani nuclear attack will have profound consequences for India - but on account of the distributed nature of it's assets - both material and intellectual - India may yet rise up to see better days. But does anyone think that the pro-Western elite that rules Pakistan could itself survive?

A nuclear war will not only have a very deleterious impact on India - but it will permanently remove from the scene, the very class of English-speaking collaborators that have served Western interests so well in both nations. It is high time that the Western intelligentsia comprehends this and stops trying to use Pakistan's nuclear blackmail as a lever against India. The more the West tries to impose a duplicitous peace on India, the more it risks permanently alienating India's best brains. India and Pakistan couldn't be more different as nations. Whereas one nation looks to the future - to an era of social and technological progress, the other clings to an unapologetically medievalist outlook - where humanitarian concerns and democratic rights can be readily sacrificed (in the name of religious expansionism) at the altar of undiluted power .

It is time for the Western world to choose: between two approaches to nationhood - one that is secular, pluralistic and democratic - the other based on sectarian hatred and religious fundamentalism. They cannot both continue to coexist under the intolerable threats of Pakistani nuclear blackmail. It is up to the Western world to make the right choice, and do the right thing. Progressive forces throughout the world also need to do their part in ensuring that such nuclear blackmail is not tolerated or ignored. It is in the interests of the entire world to rein in Pakistan's nuclear cowboys. India should not and cannot be brow-beaten into tolerating an endless proxy-war at the hands of Pakistan's reckless and remorseless clerical and military elite.

It is especially important for the people of Pakistan to realize that this obsession with recovering Kashmir against the wishes of it's people is a political and economic dead-end, and in the worst case, might even lead to the complete annihilation of the Pakistani people and nation. On the other hand, a genuine respect for pluralism, democracy and religious tolerance, could lead to a new era of friendship and cooperation in the subcontinent. Even as the majority of India's people are extremely frustrated and angry with the machinations of the Pakistani leadership, they remain open to responding positively to any honest and sincere gesture towards reconciliation. Can the democratic forces in Pakistan rise to the occasion, and effect a lasting change in policy ? Or must Pakistan disintegrate once more ?

Two years ago, when India conducted the tests in Pokhran, it signaled a dramatic shift in India's nuclear posture. It brought India's nuclear capability from the realm of a quiet and covert military program to a publicly known status. India's nuclear tests set off a sanctimonious furor in Washington, London, Tokyo and Bonn. But in conducting it's tests it had broken no laws as was acknowledged by Andrew Mack in The Australian Financial Review when he wrote: "India's tests didn't legally violate the 1996 Comprehensive Test ban Treaty (CTBT) because India is not a signatory to it." Although India was the first country to propose a ban on nuclear testing, it has been unwilling to sign global treaties that were discriminatory because they allowed a few countries to hold nuclear arms indefinitely. In spite of nearly 100 resolutions of the UN General Assembly reflecting the will of most nations against this nuclear monopoly held by a few powerful nations, decisive steps for creating a nuclear weapon free world have still not been taken. In a recent statement by Indian Ambassador Savitri Kunadi to the Plenary Meeting of the Conference on Disarmament in Geneva, August 6, 1998 she said: "India has consistently maintained that the only credible guarantee against the use or threat of use of nuclear weapons lies in their total elimination. Until this objective is reached, as an interim measure, there exists an obligation on part of the nuclear weapon states to assure non nuclear weapon states against the use or threat of use of nuclear weapons, as also that these weapons will not be used as instruments of pressure, intimidation and blackmail. This obligation should be of an internationally legally binding character, clear, credible, universal and without discrimination."

It should be noted that in 1965, India, had put forward a proposal for an international non-proliferation agreement under which the nuclear weapon states would agree to give up their arsenals, provided other countries refrained from developing or acquiring such weapons. In the 1960s India had sought security guarantees against the use of nuclear weapons but the countries India turned to were unable to extend to India the expected assurances. In 1961 India supported UNGA resolution 1653 of 24th November 1961 which called on the Secretary General to ascertain the views of member states on the possibility of Convening a Special Conference for concluding a Convention on the Prohibition of Use of Nuclear Weapons. In 1978, India proposed negotiations for an international convention that would prohibit the use or threat of use of nuclear weapons. Although many editorial writers in the West dismissed statements emanating from the Indian government that India's nuclear tests had resulted from the repeated failure of many decades of determined efforts towards unconditional and universal nuclear disarmament, Peter Coombes, President of End the Arms Race seemed to echo India's concerns.

Rather than heap abuse on India's tests he wrote: "The irresponsible ones are the nuclear weapons states and countries like Canada that are 'protected' by the nuclear umbrella. Canadian officials are proud of Canada's role in renegotiating the Non-Proliferation Treaty without having any time constraints or conditions of disarmament being imposed on the nuclear states." That it is the US and it's allies who have repeatedly resisted all time bound attempts at disarmament has been sadly forgotten, even by many peace activists, who have now joined in the chorus of disapproval.

Government officials and security analysts and "experts" in the West (and their agents in the developing world) have talked at length about the "dangers" of nuclear weapons in South Asia and the "need" for India to sign the CTBT. But the CTBT (Comprehensive Test Ban Treaty) does not require the existing nuclear powers to disarm. Nor does it require nations like Australia, Germany and Japan to give up their nuclear umbrellas or prevent the US or NATO from stationing nuclear weapons on their soil.

Greg Sheridan, seemed to acknowledge this hypocrisy when he quoted Former prime minister Inder Kumar Gujral as saying: "I said to Australia, you get out from under the American nuclear umbrella, then talk to us." Greg Sheridan also quoted BJP national president Kushabhau Thakre: "Australia allowed British nuclear tests in your own country but later deplored us. Australia's attitude is not acceptable." That the West was being highly hypocritical was picked up by more than one journalist in Australia. Zbigniew Brzezinski writing in the Times of India, also appeared to attribute India's nuclear tests to the hypocritical manner in which the US and it's allies have approached the issue of nuclear disarmament: "U.S. efforts to halt the proliferation of nuclear weapons have failed for two reasons.

The first is that the United States has never pursued a genuinely universal and nondiscriminatory policy of halting proliferation. In fact, U.S. policy all along has been that of selective and preferential proliferation." In an even more damning vein, Zbigniew Brzezinski went on to point out that: "The United States openly assisted Great Britain in its acquisition of nuclear weapons.

Also, it is now known that the United States, though much more surreptitiously, helped France in its pursuit of a nuclear capability. Last but not the least, the United States very deliberately more than winked at Israeli efforts, while studiously ignoring the atmospheric nuclear test conducted "by someone" in the late 1970s near South Africa in the Indian Ocean."

The hypocrisy theme was echoed in other commentaries and editorials. Prof. Kumao Kaneko of Tokai University (Japan) while acknowledging that the international nuclear regime centering on the NPT was extremely unequal and discriminatory, admitted that Japan had adopted a policy of depending on the nuclear umbrella provided by U.S.A under the U.S.- Japan Security Treaty, thus becoming vulnerable to charges of hypocrisy on the issue.

The Australian in a June 4, 1998 piece by Malcolm Fraser headlined it's story on India's nuclear tests as "Nuclear jolt rooted in test ban disparity". The Australian Financial Review introduced it's May 19, 1998 story with the statement: "Uncle Sam and the other nuclear weapons states can't really demonize the Indians, argues Andrew Mack, because their criticisms smack of hypocrisy." Robert Scheer expressed a similar view in the Los Angeles Times stating: "It is hypocritical for the U.S. to say it has the right to possess such weapons and others don't. If it weren't so tragic, it would be a joke. India dares to test a few crude nuclear bombs and the United States, which has 8,000 strategic warheads mounted on sophisticated launching devices aimed a targets throughout the world is outraged." Robert Scheer also pointed out that: "The largest of the Indian tests involved the equivalent of 43,000 tons of TNT, a small hydrogen bomb by U.S. standards. The "father" of the hydrogen bomb Edward Teller, was honored with a national medal by President Reagan."

Bernard Feng also berated US hypocrisy in the Hong Kong Standard (19 May 98) as he pointed out that: "Thrice Americans have edged to the brink of holocaust, once during the Korean conflict, then in 1961 during the Cuban missile crisis and again four years later when President Lyndon Johnson contemplated radiating China as the Vietnam War escalated."

Tyler Marshall's piece in the Los Angeles Times (June 5 1998) was titled: "South Asia Testing May Blast a Hole in 3-Decade-Old Double Standard". "For the better part of a generation, the world's five declared nuclear powers kept themselves on the up side of a global double standard, encouraging other nations to renounce the right to atomic weapons even as they amassed huge stockpiles of them. This was a reality that the late German Chancellor Kurt Georg Kiesinger once likened to a bunch of alcoholics persuading others to vow abstinence".

The Berlingske Tidende ran a commentary by nuclear physicist and Nobel Laureate Joseph Rotblat on 29th July 1998, with the headline: "Nuclear Bombs for All - or for None" , continuing: "The atomic policies of the leading Powers of the world are marked with hypocrisy and double standards. The only reasonable purpose of nuclear weapons is to deter others from a nuclear attack, and this aspect would disappear if nobody had those weapons."

In that commentary, Joseph Rotblat quoted the Canberra Commission, and wrote: In 1996, the experts of the Canberra Commission summed up the situation quite incisively: "A handful of countries possess nuclear weapons and they insist that these weapons provide unprecedented security advantages, but they also reserve the right to keep these advantages to themselves. This situation is highly discriminative and thus untenable and cannot be maintained. The possession of nuclear arms by any country presents a constant incentive for others to acquire them."

Concerned about the US's enormous nuclear arsenal, Dr. Rashmi Mayur, Director, International Institute for a Sustainable Future, Mumbai, in a statement, said: "The world today has enough nuclear weapons to exterminate every one of the 5.9 billion human beings five times over." It is arguments such as these that perhaps persuaded Stephen Glover to title his Daily Mail, (May 19 1998) piece: "Why India should have the Bomb". Exposing the US record, he wrote: "How odd that America should take this line. What was and is good for it and the West is apparently not good for India.

The United States has carried 1,032 nuclear tests since 1945, the last being in 1992. Until it let off five last week, India had only done one test - in 1974. America is still in possession of some 12,000 nuclear warheads, whereas India is thought to have about 65 and, in the view of some defense experts, cannot even bolt these on to the missiles it has developed. The United States is a very large nuclear power. India a very tiny one."

In an interview with Rakesh Sharma of Deccan Herald News Service, former prime minister I K Gujral elaborated at length on India's security concerns. He pointed to the fact that Indian coastal borders were very extensive, nearly 7,000 miles, and were situated in an area that was heavily nuclearized. The Indian Ocean is home to the US military base in Diego Garcia which has been nuclearized by the US government. And there is constant movement of nuclear weapon carrying warships, submarines and aircraft carriers in the Indian Ocean, the Arabian Sea and the Persian Gulf. US, NATO and Australian military maneuvers have greatly increased in this region. India's security analysts are also perturbed by how after the disintegration of the Soviet Union, the world's sole super power (i.e. the US) has along with it's military allies decimated small and vulnerable nations.

The aggressive manner in which the US and it's NATO allies targeted Iraq and Yugoslavia has undoubtedly played on the minds of India's national security analysts. Dilip Lahiri, Additional Secretary (UN) hinted as much when he explicitly brought up the US bombardment of Yugoslavia at the United Nations Disarmament Commission on April 13, 1999, in New York. He stated that: "Apart from the impact which it has already had on regional peace, the implications of NATO action in the Federal Republic of Yugoslavia are far-reaching. If a group of countries or a regional arrangement take it upon themselves to act outside the UN Charter, in violation of its provisions, using violence against another sovereign state without the authorization of the Security Council, the legal foundations on which international relations have been built up since the end of the Second World War are gravely undermined. So too is the confidence of states in agreeing to disarmament measures, because if countries can be attacked without sanction, because its opponents are militarily more powerful, none would be prepared to lower its guard. Events in the Balkans therefore will inevitably have repercussions on the international disarmament agenda." It should be noted that it was the threatening and coercive presence in the Bay of Bengal of the US Seventh Fleet, (led by the nuclear-powered aircraft carrier Enterprise) during the 1971 Bangladesh war of independence that had triggered India's first nuclear test.

It is little wonder that India's nuclear tests drew overwhelming support from Indians both within India and abroad. An opinion poll published in the Times of India showed that 91 percent of urban Indians approved of the tests and 82 percent believed the country should now build nuclear arms. On the BBC web-site, as many as 86% percent of site visitors endorsed the Indian action and wrote passionately about the hypocrisy of the US and it's allies in defending a one-sided and highly discriminatory nuclear policy. Support also came from India's neighbors like Sri Lanka and old allies like Russia. Other developing nations expressed understanding, even sympathy - for even as the world's nuclear and military powers issued vitriolic statements condemning India, the G-15 summit of developing nations in Cairo did not.

A random opinion poll conducted in the city brought forward such comments as "At last, a friend of the Arabs is a nuclear power", and "It's good, Egypt can now turn to India for support". In Egypt, editorials in Al Akhbar, Al Abram and Al Ahram were all supportive of India's position.

Abdel Rehman was perhaps most enthusiastic when he titled his 20 May 98 piece in Al-Ahram as Revolution against the World and wrote: "The world only knows how to respect the language of action. Thus India carried its nuclear sword and went out to the world because it was the only way to deal with a world in which the poor suffer amidst large luxuries of the rich. Indian explosions are, in one aspect if nothing else, a social revolution against the unjust world economic order." Nawab Khan writing in the Iran Times titled his piece: Nuclear Tests, Why Not India? "The argument that Western powers are democratic and hence, their nuclear arsenals are under strict control and can never be misused, are not quite convincing. American democracy did not prevent it from dropping the atomic bomb twice on Japan." he wrote. "The lesson to be learnt from the Pokharan nuclear blasts is that there cannot be one law for the haves and another for the have-nots." he added.

It is therefore hardly surprising that there was no criticism of India by the 113 member Non-Aligned Movement (NAM) which issued a declaration describing as "highly discriminatory" the stand of the nuclear weapon states to monopolize the right to own atomic weapons. Soon after India's nuclear tests, the Indian Prime Minister had highly cordial meetings with African leaders from Zimbabwe, Namibia, Angola and the Congo. An attempt to criticize India in an ASEAN summit also failed in spite of considerable lobbying by the US and Australia.

Yet, in spite of this understanding for the Indian position in the developing world, internal critics of India's program have not been assuaged. Like many in the Western press, some Indian journalists espouse the position that India provoked Pakistan into conducting it's nuclear tests, thereby contributing to the "tensions" and "instability" in the region. More extreme critics of India have laid virtually all the blame on the Indian side for it's myriad problems with Pakistan. No serious analysis of India's nuclear policy can ignore the actual dynamics of the India-Pakistan relationship going back to it's very creation in 1947. Contrary to the commonly held view, the creation of Pakistan was not based on any popular democratic mandate - nor was it created with the perspective of protecting the interests of the sub-continent's ordinary Muslims.

It was a demand put forward by Muslim landlords and former feudal barons who were encouraged and abetted by the British in their demands for the creation of Pakistan. On September 4, 1939, Jinnah had met Lord Linlithgow and pledged to Britain the loyalty of Indian Muslim troops—nearly 40 per cent of the British Indian army — and help with Muslim recruitment. The Muslim League resolution of March 1940 demanding "independent states for the Muslims of India" (i.e. Pakistan) was passed after Jinnah, through Khaliq-ul-Zaman, obtained the support for Muslim states from Lord Zetland, the secretary of state for India. In his Times of India commentary, Narendra Singh Sarela stated: "BRITISH top secret documents of the period preceding India's independence have now been unsealed. They prove beyond doubt that Britain after 1945 supported Jinnah's demand for Partition in order to safeguard its strategic interest in Asia in the post-war world and was not safeguarding Muslim interests, as believed in India." Elsewhere in his article, he states: "The blueprint of the Partition plan was drawn up by Lord Wavell in New Delhi towards the end of 1945 and communicated in a top secret telegram to the secretary of state for India in London on February 6, 1946."

Narendra Sarela also points to British interests in controlling the oil-wealth of the Middle East, and the need of the Western powers in having a "reliable ally" that could serve as a foil to the former Soviet Union. Once it was created, Pakistan did not disappoint Britain or it's allies. After it's creation in 1947, Pakistan quickly became an important military ally of the US and Britain in South Asia by joining the US-led Baghdad Pact and later CENTO. In 1959, it signed a bilateral military pact allowing the US to set up a military base at Peshawar for American U2 planes to spy over the Soviet Union. Of particular importance is how Pakistan played a leading role in destroying the democratic revolution in Afghanistan and destabilizing the former Soviet Union.

From 1982 to 1990 the U.S. acknowledges providing Pakistan $5.4 billion in mostly military aid. (The $5.4 Billion sum is mentioned in the Congressional Quarterly, 16 May 1992, p. 1352; The actual figure may be much higher since additional aid was sent through covert channels by the CIA) Since then, Pakistan has provided troops and trained mercenaries to fight against Iraq, Somalia, Yugoslavia and Chechnya. Pakistan has also served as a proxy of the imperial powers in destabilizing India and in keeping India weak by initiating four wars with India ostensibly over Kashmir. Since 1990, it has kept up a barrage of cross-border fire along Kashmir. K. Subrahmanyam's Kargil Report to the Indian Parliament suggests that Pakistan was able to increase it's violence against India because it had acquired a credible nuclear capability by 1990. This capability was acquired through the conscious support of other nuclear powers such as China and the US. K. Subrahmanyam also speaks of Pakistan having threatened India with a nuclear attack more than once. As an example, he cites the following: "In 1987, Pakistan conveyed a nuclear threat to India at the time of Operation BRASSTACKS. This was officially communicated by Pakistan's Minister of State for Foreign Affairs, Zain Noorani to the Indian Ambassador in Islamabad, SK Singh. It was also communicated by the Pakistani nuclear scientist, Dr A.Q. Khan to the Indian journalist Kuldip Nayar." By resorting to nuclear blackmail, Pakistan has been able to conduct it's hostile activities against India with relative impunity and without fear of retaliation. Yet, many South Asian analysts continue to blame India for escalating tensions in the region.

Pakistan's nuclear blackmail of India has undoubtedly weighed on the minds of India's defense analysts. Barring a brief flirtation with jingoistic nationalism on the part of a few immature politicians, most of India's defense policy experts and foreign policy analysts have displayed caution and restraint. Since the Pokharan tests, India's nuclear analysts have worked extra hard to define a nuclear policy that is rooted in a strongly defensive posture - that can disarm it's non-nuclear friends in the developing world - offer mutually binding no-use pledges to other nuclear nations, and ameliorate the possibility of accidental launches and avoidable escalation. A series of conciliatory statements have been issued in an attempt to disarm the US and it's allies, as also China and Pakistan.

With Pakistan, India initiated the effort to undertake 'confidence building measures' which culminated in the 1999 'Lahore Declaration'. Unfortunately, Pakistan not only refused to endorse the no-first-use principle that India has repeatedly articulated, it followed the 'Lahore Declaration' with it's insidious invasion of Kargil. Since then Pakistan has used US-supplied unarmed aerial reconnaissance aircraft to assist in it's repeated inflitrations into Kashmir and attack the civilian and military infrastructure. Pakistan-aided terrorists have launched suicide attacks in Kashmir and in many other parts of India. Spy planes have frequently entered India's air-space in violation of previous treaties. The military coup by Gen. Musharraf in Pakistan that followed Pakistan's Kargil invasion served to exacerbate tensions with India. Gen. Musharraf was widely viewed as the architect of the Kargil invasion and as a hawkish anti-India baiter by Pakistan watchers in India. In a 1998 speech to Pakistan's elite military cadets, the Pakistani General stated that the acquisition of Kashmir by Pakistan could wait. What was more important was to keep the Indian army bleeding in Kashmir just as the Afghan Mujahideen kept the Soviet troops bleeding in Afghanistan.

He added that even if the Kashmir issue were resolved, there could not be normal relations between India and Pakistan because Pakistan, by frustrating India's ambition of emerging as a major Asian power on par with China and Japan, would continue to be a thorn on India's flesh.

In the US, Gen. Musharraf has been repeatedly described as a "moderate" by the CIA and Pentagon establishment - in Senate briefings and on Public Television. Michael Krepon of the Stinson Institute and advisor to US Secretary of State Madeline Albright on South Asia described him as a "moderate" while speaking before the Commonwealth Club in San Jose. While appearing before the sub-committee of the Senate foreign relations committee for South Asia under Senator Sam Brownback, Milton Bearden, the former CIA chief in Sudan and Pakistan pleaded on the General's behalf. He emphasized how the General was trained at Fort Bragg and was an early member of the elite 19th Baloch Regiment, the Pakistani SSG, that trained jointly with US army special forces a decade ago. The General's attitude of unmitigated hostility against India has quiet backing in the highest echelons of power in the US. In spite of a series of such and other negative developments, India has not been provoked into discarding it's cautious stand. India has remained firm in keeping it's nuclear posture entirely defensive. It has also continued with diplomatic efforts to move the nuclear powers towards unbiased and effective nuclear disarmament.

Reiterating India's strong stand that nuclear weapons must never be used, India has repeatedly called for a legally binding international prohibition on the use of Nuclear Weapons. This position was publicly asserted most recently in 1998 by India's Savitri Kunadi in Geneva: "We believe that a Convention on the Prohibition of the Use of Nuclear Weapons could form the bedrock of security assurances - comprehensive, legally binding and irreversible." Unlike the US which has threatened the use of nuclear weapons on as many as 25 (or more) occasions, India has stated that it does not intend to use nuclear weapons to commit aggression or for mounting threats against any country. The Prime Minister of India stated the following in the Lower House of the Indian Parliament on August 4, 1998; "India's nuclear tests were not intended for offense but for self-defense.

In order to ensure that our independence and integrity are never jeopardized in future, we will have a policy of a minimum deterrent. We have stated that we will not be the first to use nuclear weapons. We are also willing to strengthen this by entering into bilateral agreements on no-first use or a multilateral negotiations on a global no-first use. Having stated that we shall not be the first to use nuclear weapons, there remains no basis for their use against countries which do not have nuclear weapons."As a specific example of India's attempts to allay the fears of India's non-nuclear neighbors in Asia - India issued a public reassurance to the ASEAN nations in respect to their wishes for keeping the ASEAN nation nuclear free. This was expressly stated by Dilip Lahiri, Additional Secretary (UN) at the United Nations Disarmament Commission on April 13, 1999, in New York - "India has always believed that the use or threat of use of nuclear weapons transcends regional dimensions.

Nuclear Weapons Free Zones cannot do justice to the wide scope and global nature of the threat posed by nuclear weapons. India, however, respects the sovereign choice exercised by non-nuclear weapon states to safeguard their security interests through nuclear weapon free zones established on the basis of arrangements freely arrived at among the States of the region concerned. At the ASEAN Regional Forum in Manila last year, India had stated that it fully respects the status of the NWFZ in South East Asia and was ready to convert this commitment into a legal obligation."

India has also refrained from putting it's nuclear weapons at hair-trigger alerts. Defense analysts have spoken of mandatory delays in reacting to a nuclear attack in order to avoid accidental launches and allow India's Prime Minister and senior defense officials to make a deliberate and conscious decision as to when and how to retaliate if India were to confront a nuclear attack. India's Sharad Pawar spoke extensively on this subject while addressing the General Debate of the UN First Committee in New York (October 14, 1998).

In his speech, he stated his concerns regarding doctrines of first use of nuclear weapons and the substantial numbers under hair trigger alert that risked accidental or unauthorized launch of nuclear weapons: "We are concerned that even with the end of the cold war there are today more than 5, 000 nuclear weapons on hair trigger alert. Serious attention needs to be paid to various proposals for global de-alerting, de-targeting and de-activating of nuclear weapons that could contribute to confidence-building and to the improvement in the international climate for negotiation leading to the elimination of nuclear weapons. India proposes to introduce a resolution entitled 'Reducing Nuclear Danger', and we hope that this initiative of India aimed at focussing international attention on this clear and present danger, will receive wide spread support."

This speech and similar evidence presented earlier all goes to show that India has for long been one of the stoutest advocates of peace and disarmament. Until the fall of the Soviet Union, it's foreign policy was closely allied with that of other developing nations. It rarely hesitated from condemning the wars of aggression that the US and it's allies conducted throughout the world. India developed it's nuclear policy with considerable reluctance and more in reaction to the concrete threats it faced in the South Asian region. It is the British, the US, it's NATO allies, and it's regional proxies like Pakistan, who have turned South Asia into a region of tension and instability.

Like many other developing nations, India has repeatedly stated that the developing world needs an environment of peace to develop. This is especially true for the people of India and Pakistan if they are ever to reverse the destructive and debilitating effects that colonial rule imposed. Genuine lovers of peace in South Asia can help by illuminating the truth - and bringing pressure on the world's sole super-power to desist from intervening in the region in a provocative and malicious way. By categorically rejecting the first-use of nuclear weapons, India has made it abundantly clear that it has not acquired it's nuclear capability with any aggressive or hegemonic ambitions. It is up to the other nuclear powers to reciprocate with pledges to do likewise.

A no-first-use pledge has to be the first step - the essential basis of any real movement towards genuine nuclear disarmament. If every nuclear power can ascribe to the doctrine of no-first-use, then the world can take the next step of dismantling existing nuclear arsenals. Rather than argue in a manner that sustains nuclear apartheid, or preserves a nuclear caste-system of those who can and those who can't, a legally binding no-first-use pledge will automatically move the world towards nuclear disarmament. This is what the world's peace community must collectively fight for.

Finally, it should be noted that nuclear weapons are not the sole instruments of mass-destruction. The manner in which the US conducted it's wars in Korea and Vietnam cannot be ignored - the US took the war to civilians on an unprecedented scale. The UN charter clearly prohibits the deliberate targeting and destruction of civilian infrastructure but that is precisely what NATO and it's allies did in Iraq and Yugoslavia.

Sanctions alone have been responsible for over a million deaths in Iraq. The use of Depleted Uranium (DU) - (i.e .nuclear waste), in these wars has created deadly consequences for the people of Iraq and Yugoslavia. The US even refuses to endorse a convention to ban land-mines. The struggle for nuclear disarmament is hence, inseparable from the struggle against war and inhumane sanctions. The defeat of the Soviet Union has led to a uni-polar world. With their enormous and unprecedented concentration of economic and military power, the NATO powers are able to dominate the world. They are able to conduct one-sided wars and unilaterally impose military embargoes and unfair trade treaties. Such actions are increasing fears and tensions across the globe. The struggle for a more just and multi-polar world is therefore, an important component in the struggle for world peace.

Indian Defence Minister George Fernandes and his Chief of Staff are now saying that cross-border terrorism is definitely on the decrease. They should know. But consider this: In a gruesome act, LeT militants shot dead five members of a family and two children and injured three others at a village in Udhampur district on June 16. A day earlier armed militants entered a house in Badar village and killed a man, his wife and two daughters. On the same day three pilgrims returning from the holy shrine of Sharda Mata were killed by militants near Lharua village in Doda district.

Similarly, as many as 11 persons, including eight militants were killed and three injured in separate incidents in Srinagar. Perhaps they are isolated incidents. Perhaps these incidents took place without the knowledge or support of the ISI. It is also quite possible that Gen. Musharraf has no control over certain fundamentalist outfits bent on creating trouble. But one thing seems clear: the war clouds are clearing. And within Jammu & Kashmir itself a subtle change seems to be coming over the majority community. Apart from the findings of MORI International which conducted a poll in Jammu & Kashmir in the last week of April, 2001 that showed that 61 per cent of those polled felt they would be better off politically and economically as citizens of India, there are some other encouraging signs that communal harmony is slowly being restored in Kashmir.

Reports suggest that nearly 15,000 Kashmiri Pandits, mostly migrants, thronged the Khir Bhavani Temple at Tulmula in Central Kashmir on 18 June and were "welcomed with open arms" by the majority community. A Kashmir Pandit leader said that even Muslims participated in the special Yajna held at the temple for peace and prosperity. Another has been quoted as saying: "I definitely feel a change in the situation. People are very courteous and they have not yet forgotten the basics of Kashmiriyat". That is a healthy sign.

It may be mentioned here that between 3.5 to 4.0 lakhs of Kashmiri Pandits were driven out of their homes by the majority community between 1990 and 2000 in a major effort at ethnic cleansing. It now seems as if the Kashmiriyat Muslims are learning how to get back to their roots. Apart from India withdrawing its warships from close to Pakistani waters, it does seem that Musharraf is really cracking down, for example, on the Madrassas. On 19 June Pakistan tightened controls on madrassas by passing a tough new law forcing the seminaris to join a national register and declare funding sources.

According to the law, all of Pakistan's 10,000 Madrassas must sign up with the newly created Madrassas Education Board within six months and those who refuse to register themselves will not be allowed to operate. Information Minister Nisar Memon has been quoted as saying that no Madrassa will be allowed to receive financial assistance, aid or donations from foreign sources and should any Madrassa contravene the law it will attract closure or fine or both. The voice of liberal opinion also seems to be getting heard. A former editor of *Pakistan Times*, in an exclusive article to the Chandigarh-based *The Tribune* (11 June) writes that "public opinion realises that Pakistan's political about-turn will be a long and painful process" but is becoming necessary.

As he put it: "As regards the immediate problem, the demand for the cessation of Pakistani elements' infiltration into the Indian part of Kashmir, the majority of Pakistanis are ahead of General Musharraf, notwithstanding the noises being made by the militants and their apologists among retired Generals, amateur politicians and media moguls.... The change in the average Pakistani's outlook, and it is a big leap, is the realisation that the strategy of armed militancy has to be abandoned as it has become unfeasible". Then consider what Ayaz Amir, writing in Dawn has to say. He wrote: "Pakistan has gone through enough experiments. Over the last nine months it has suffered enough in spirit. It needs a period of calm and healing, to regain its buoyancy of spirit which seems missing in the national mood". Amir noted that "caught between an Indian anvil and an American pair of forceps applied relentlessly, we have finally a farewell to arms in Kashmir. It is to the past we have taken a gain leap back to 1989, India's policy of intimidations on which it embarked in December has been thus vindicated".

And Amir added: "Let us be rid of the bluster and the false notions which have plagued our national life for so long. There is no need to sugar-coat our several U-turns." Or take what Najam Sethi, editor of The *Friday Times* has to say. If Pakistan wants to defeat its ghosts, he writes, it has to look inside than westwards. Pointing out that "scores of highly qualified and public-spirited doctors have been killed in Karachi" Sethi pointed out that the groundswell of support for Musharraf when he first came to power in 1999 "had sprung from the citizen's desire to see the military putting an end to Pakistan's internal anarchy".

In that sense according to Sethi, Musharraf has been a failure. As he put it: "Unfortunately, state and society have both become more undermined since 1999 and the country is clearly unable to withstand external challenges while the government is unable to protect it from internal dangers. As the Musharraf government faces off with India, it would do well to remember that the greater challenge is at home". Economically Pakistan in desperate trouble. It has hiked its defence budget by 3.5

per cent when already its balance of payments position is in a precarious condition. The hefty Rs 15 billion hike over last year's revised budget marks more than 14 per cent increase in Islamabad's defence spending which it just cannot afford and some fear that like the Soviet Union it may collapse overnight.

Meanwhile another development of great significance is under way. A security apparatus to restrain India and Pakistan from going to war is quietly being put together at the initiative of the United States involving the full participation of Russia, Britain, France, and even Japan and China. Bush's national security adviser Condolleezza Rice has been quoted by the New York Times as describing the emerging arrangement as a "common security framework" in which the Great Powers "share a common security agenda". More than a fear of an Indo-Pak war is the fear of Jehadi elements in Pakistan seizing the country's nuclear weapons. No matter what Musharraf says about his country's military power, the fact remains that the man is in grave trouble internally. India may wish to see him collapse under the strain in the belief that it serves him right, but will it help us in the long run? The tragedy is that Musharraf, in the past has showed that he is extremely untrustworthy.

Kargil is an immediate example. But can it be that he has learnt his lesson? Should India at last hold talks with him in order to help him save his face? Should India seek the mediation of a third power or group of powers? The United States would like to help. So would Russia, or, for that matter, Britain. Delhi is presently standing on prestige. For one thing, a mediator may play a double game and lean towards Pakistan to India's dismay. India in the past, had a terrible experience in relying on fair play from western powers. So it is chary of getting the United States involved. But times have changed. The United States no longer is inclined to pacify Pakistan. But India nevertheless is wary. That is a sound attitude but calls for fresh study.

The US, Russia, Britain and France can work behind the scenes and arrange to stand guarantee against future Pakistani aggression. These powers can even work out an understanding on settling the Jammu & Kashmir issue to India's own satisfaction. If that can be done behind doors, India, by then knowing Pakistan's position, can publicly agree to outside intervention, without losing face. This calls for high-level diplomacy. There is no harm in seeking international guarantees against future Pakistani support to terrorism. Indeed that may be the best guarantee for lasting peace in south Asia. It may even be argued that the best way to guarantee peace is to invite foreign mediation. With Kashmiris themselves sick of blood-letting after over ten years of futile cross-border terrorism and in a mood to compromise with Delhi, with Pakistanis sick of internal division and sectarian conflicts and western powers coming to their own realisation that it is in their own interest to put down Islamic fundamentalism, the time seems to have come for a dialogue between India and Pakistan. India does not have to let down its defence; it does not need pretend to be accommodative. Indira Gandhi did that in Simla and the country had to pay for showing a sense of decency towards a fallen enemy.

India necessarily has to be firm on what it wants and how far it is willing to go. But if it could get the signatories of Great Powers to whatever is agreed upon, then Pakistan dare not renege on what it has committed itself to. That is a point worth remembering. Too long has India stood on prestige even if it is conceded that it has behaved like a person once bit twice shy. But India must currently rise to the occasion. Hopefully Pakistan by now has learnt what is possible and what is not, in its pursuit of the fulfillment to the futile Two Nation theory. Pakistan has now come to the end of the road. It can only retrace its steps. The Pakistanis are realising that they can never get Kashmir.

The Kashmiris themselves are fed up with endless terrorism. Now is the time to settle the Kashmir issue, preferably with the help of third parties. That will be good for India, good for Pakistan and good for the peace and prosperity of all of south Asia. And who knows, even the LTTE in Sri Lanka may come to terms with Colombo, learning from Pakistan's experience. All things are possible - and we should help in making them happen. After years of disregard, India's apprehensions about Pakistan's state-sponsored terrorism in Kashmir have finally found a receptive international community, led by the US and the UK. They now acknowledge the threat as real - and a stumbling block to a meaningful Indo-Pak dialogue.

This attitudinal shift was recently reflected in a House of Commons' address by British Foreign Secretary Jack Straw. Mr Straw not only endorsed India's claim that Pakistan's ISI was supporting numerous terrorist outfits in the Valley, but went further to say something that should sound music to our Foreign Office.a "In the last decade or so," Mr Straw observed, "the character of the conflict (in Kashmir) has changed with the incursion of armed militants across the Line of Control into India from the Pakistani side." This represents a total rejection of the Pakistani stand that Kashmir militancy is a part of freedom struggle in the State.

This quantum gain for Indian strategy vis-à-vis Pakistan is not trivial. Pakistan's military regime, cornered domestically over the collapse of its Afghan policy, has been hiking guns against India. It thought that the US, depending upon the establishment's support to uproot the Al Qaeda network, would willingly condone Pakistan's terror tactics in the Valley. The presence of the US and British soldiers in Pakistan to hunt down Al Qaeda terrorists was a heaven-sent opportunity for President Pervez Musharraf to up the ante for his "Kashmir through terror" strategy. He presumed that as long as American soldiers were stationed in Pakistan, he could provoke India because the US would prevent India from retaliating. At the same time, he could force the US to concede him the leverage over Kashmir, which has been for the Pakistani establishment the "core issue."

The NDA Government has denied Pakistan the opportunity of blackmailing the US and getting its way in Kashmir. New Delhi's response was to make it universally evident that it would not hesitate to use the weapon of war to destroy Islamabad's ability to execute its policy of crossborder terrorism. When New Delhi convincingly demonstrated its readiness to strike, the international coalition against terrorism had to take notice and call the Pakistani spade, a spade. The international community from Japan to the US was forced to focus on avoiding a war and dismantling of the terrorist apparatus in Afghanistan and Pakistan.

The main Indian demand, that Pakistan stop terrorist infiltration into India, has been conceded. As US

Deputy Secretary of State Richard Armitage told the Government here, Pakistan has agreed to end terrorist infiltration across the LoC "on a permanent basis".

Thus India's escalation of price that Pakistan will have to pay for its strategy of getting India to surrender Kashmir for fear of "being bled through a thousand cuts" seems to have paid off quite well. The same General Musharraf, who said at Agra that what was happening in Kashmir was a "freedom struggle", now had to concede that the support was far more than merely moral. The official visitors from the US to New Delhi in the last few months have been reiterating that the US will not play a mediatory role and limit itself to promoting Indo-Pak direct dialogue. The American visitors - and Mr Donald Rumsfeld was the latest - have also rejected that Pakistan had sought the US to act as monitors along the LoC.

As for Pakistan, this failure follows General Musharraf getting nothing for his nuclear bluster from the US. The NDA Government's cool response to nuclear sabre rattling by Pakistan would have shaken the hawks in Islamabad. New Delhi's reaction was that of a government sure of its facts and the people supported it by refusing to panic. New Delhi reiterated that India would be acting as a responsible nuclear weapons' power. That compelled General Musharraf to subdue his nuclear threat and assure the international community of acting responsibly. As noted Defence Analyst Jasjit Singh has observed: "In the hype created about the dangers of war, the inhumanity of terrorism and the risks of a nuclear holocaust, what is getting ignored is that New Delhi's overall comprehensive politico-diplomatic-military strategy is succeeding." While the country at large understands this success, and analysts perceive how

India's demonstrated readiness to go to war was a necessary part of the strategy, the Leftists are unable to appreciate this merely because this has been achieved by a BJP-led Government. They continue to oppose the strategic weapon and want the Vajpayee Government to confine itself to diplomatic efforts.

Both were well timed: the arrival of US Defence Secretary Donald Rumsfeld in New Delhi and the lifting of restrictions on Pakistan flights overflying our airspace and the withdrawal of naval ships. It looks as if Washington had arranged everything behind the scenes: President Pervez Musharraf's assurance to stop infiltration in India and Foreign Minister Jaswant Singh's statement commending Pakistan's response. But President Musharraf has not said anything beyond what he had stated in his address to the nation on January 12. Both sides should realise that war is never an option.

It should never be, not in the land of Mahatma Gandhi. In the case of India and Pakistan, war is too dangerous to contemplate because it can go nuclear. "If you drive us to the wall, we will use the bomb," That was more than three decades ago. Khan's words come to my mind often these days. If there is a reverse to any side, Islamabad may use the bomb. Such a possibility is very much there because India is superior to Pakistan in conventional warfare. Islamabad's UN ambassador Munir Akram has already made it clear that since they do not have the capacity to match India in conventional force, they will depend on the bomb. President Pervez Musharraf's horror over the thought of nuclear holocaust only deepens doubts. His UN ambassador could not have mentioned the use of the bomb without clearance from Islamabad.

It is no more a secret that Pakistan establishment had considered the use of the bomb at the time of the Kargil war before Prime Minister Nawaz Sharif flew to Washington to have President Bill Clinton's intervention to rescue Pakistan. It is not beyond the realm of possibility that Musharraf may use the bomb if and when he realizes he cannot cope with India's advance in Pakistan. Whatever he says now, he will also be under pressure from within Pakistan to perform. At one time, Sharif did not want to explode the bomb because of the interference which America offered but the pressure of public opinion on him was too strong to resist. Afghanistan President Hamid Karzai told the leaders of both India and Pakistan a few days ago to visit his country to see the destruction that the war caused and then decide their course of action.

He was talking about limited conventional war. When the entire international community is saying that Pakistan must stop infiltration and assuring us that proof would be coming forth, we should not be giving the impression that we are at the stage of positioning our last man before embarking upon action against Pakistan. Home Minister L.K. Advani's statement that we should have spent more on defence than education is only rhetoric. His statement is no reply to the Nobel Prize winner Amartya Sen who said that education would have helped solve India's problems. Indeed, he is right. Had we concentrated on education - 40 per cent of the country's population is illiterate - we would have solved many of our problems. Sports Minister Uma Bharti is another hawk who has no control over the language she uses. Her poem to castigate Pakistan was as hideous as the picture of her riding the shoulders of Human Resource Development Minister Murli Manohar Joshi at the time of the Babri Masjid's demotion. The hardliners on our side are as much bent upon jeopardising peace as are the jehadis and fundamentalists on the other side.

Prime Minister Atal Behari Vajpayee's suggestion of joint patrolling by India and Pakistan may turn out to be a step towards de-escalation. Earlier, Pakistani columnist Dr Ijaz Ahsan, had made a similar proposal. He said: "Pakistan should offer joint patrolling of the LoC by Indian and Pakistani soldiers. If such a scheme is implemented, it will be clear to everyone that no border crossings are taking place." Rumsfeld's proposal to associate America and Britain with the supervision of the LoC is worth considering. No doubt, it will bring back UN observers whom we stopped recognising after the 1971 war. That was the time when the Ceasefire Line became the Line Of Control. But we can specify their role and indicate a time limit which we can extend if need be. War cannot possibly lead to a solution of any problem, because war has become much too terrible and destructive. If the solution we aim at cannot be brought about by large-scale war, will small-scale war help? Surely, it will not. Partly because that itself may lead to a big-scale war and partly because it produces an atmosphere of conflict and of disruption.

It is absurd to imagine that out of the conflict, the right type of forces, which are opposed to terrorism and fundamentalism, will emerge. In Germany, both the Communist Party and the Social Democratic Party were swept away by Hitler. This may happen in our part of the world. It is the same thing for our peacenik and anti-nuclear lobby. They sought to raise the people against the Government by painting an exaggerated version of nuclear holocaust, thereby hoping to disarm the

Government on the nuclear option. The Vajpayee Government refused to relent on the issue - but at the same time it did not rattle its nuclear sabre like General Musharraf, who had to eat crow.

The Left either failed or refused to understand the specific message the Vajpayee Government was sending to the international community by not foregoing the nuclear option but yet adhering to its no-first-use policy. India's availability of the nuclear option has acted as a deterrent to the hawkish Pakistani establishment. Recent events have demonstrated the advantages of India having gone nuclear. The Prime Minister's decision to hold a demonstration of nuclear weapons was criticised as "nuclear misadventure." What do critics say now? That India has its own nuclear umbrella with its own technology is enough to deter any potential aggressor. The critics' inability to see Kashmir's domestic problems as a part of the Government's problem reveals blind anti-BJPism rather than informed analysis of the situation. If these critics are to be believed, cross-border terrorism is not the issue; the issue is that the BJP is in power.

India's new drive against terrorism

The killing of some 30 civilians and soldiers at Kaluchak in Jammu on May 14, 2002 filled the Prime Minister with the resolve to act which he had lacked till then. In a public speech in Manali where he had a tension-filled holiday two weeks ago, he admitted that he should have acted after the December 13th terrorist attack on the Parliament complex but failed to do so because of international pressure.

So, he did after Kaluchak what he had failed to do after the December 13, 2001 event. It appears that our massive deployment of force along the border and the message it carried to Pakistan that we would risk a war with the belligerent neighbour if the latter did not stop its support for terrorist activities had a desired impact on the Musharraf regime.

The strategy has worked. Pakistan has conveyed to us through US Deputy Secretary of State Richard Armitage and Defence Secretary Donald Rumsfeld that it would stop for good terrorists activities on the LoC. We believe his assurances, for the present at least, and have, therefore, reached a limited rapprochement with General Musharraf's Pakistan. The December 13, 2001 event gave us the cause to deploy force aimed at fighting a full-fledged conventional war with Pakistan. The Kaluchak event gave us an occasion to convey to Pakistan that we would use it to prevent the recurrence of such events. Capability and intention have to go together. The scope of the war was deliberately left undefined. The Vajpayee government did what the USA and Israel have done since the 9/11 event: fight wars against terror with the means they think fit and at the time of their choosing. We have unmistakably conveyed to the adversary our intention to fight a war against terror.

This strategy differs from all other strategies we have deployed in the past: it is offensive in both capability and intention. In 1965 Pakistan started the war and we contained it, by luck and the courage of General Harbux Singh at the battle of Khem Karan. In 1971 we were engaged in a defensive action on the western border to carry out the offensive on the eastern front to break up Pakistan.

In the late eighties and the nineties we and Pakistan have had several military encounters, all over Kashmir. Operation Brasstack in 1987 was an encounter that came about because of a misunderstanding on both sides. The May, 1990, confrontation came about in the wake of the outbreak of wide unrest among the Kashmiris in 1989. Our sarkari defence analysts are silent about it. Only the Americans have talked about it, only to tell us how reckless. We and Pakistan were and how Mr Robert Gates, the CIA Director, saved us from a nuclear collision. The Kargil war of 1999 was launched by Pakistan to shift the LoC in its favour. We beat them by a purely defensive action.

More than at anytime since the 9/11 event there is now a greater recognition on the part of the USA and Britain that they and us have the same enemy: Al-Qaida and other Pakistan-Afghanistan based terrorist organisations. US Defence Secretary Rumsfeld said in Delhi that Al-Qaida was operating along the LoC though later he went back on these words in Islamabad. Till now the USA and Britain had kept their fight against terror separate from India's despite our pleadings to make war on terror a common cause. After the 9/11 event Foreign Minister Jaswant Singh even offered bases to the Americans to fight terror but they politely spurned it. No doubt they needed Pakistan much more than India because that country is the home of some of the most vicious terrorist organisations. Now Pakistan is asked to witness the destruction of the predator it had reared for so long: the terrorist.

The move is brilliant, but the person against whom it is directed is also wickedly clever to see through it. General Musharraf is cooperating with the Americans but only to the extent needed to get American money and American support for his regime. Much like his predecessor, Zia-ul-Haq, he cooperates with America but without giving up his policy objective in Kashmir.

Perhaps, General Musharraf would have been able to pursue his objectives in Kashmir had we not shown a glint of steel at the LoC and told him that the cost of supporting terror could be war. It's our offensive that has made him publicly acknowledge in his recent speech that Pakistan had spawned terrorism in Kashmir. This must greatly disturb the core Pakistani leadership which has been carrying a covert war against India for so long. We can beat the terrorists in Kashmir by clearly distinguishing them and the political opponents of the present government in Srinagar. For the past 15 years since the first manifestation of political unrest in Kashmir in 1988, Delhi has regarded all dissent in Kashmir as the work of Pakistan and its collaborators in Srinagar. Kashmir is seen as a security problem which can be solved only militarily.

6

Cross-border Terrorism

The Quran is totally inflexible when it comes to toleration of the beliefs of other religions. Surah 9: ayat 123 commands, "Believers! Make war on the infields. Let them find harshness in you." Surah 9: ayat 5 lays down "when the sacred months are over, slay the idol worshipers whereever you find them, arrest them, besiege them and lie in ambush everywhere for them." Pages after pages of the Quran are full of fire and brimstone for the unbelievers. These teachings are being imparted with the greatest zeal in thousands of madarasas in Pakistan, Afghanistan, Iran and even India, which have become the breeding ground for the vicious and the unemployed and insecure Muslim youth, bereft of useful modern education. Their adamant bigotry is exemplified by the latest outrage by the Taliban destroying their own priceless heritage of two thousand years old statues of the Buddha by tanks and rockets, contemptuously defying the universal outcry against this vandalism. Further down, the fanatical leadership has benefited from such preaching. Rabita of Saudi Arabia,

ISI of Pakistan, fanatics like Osama Bin Laden and others pour in crores and crores of rupees to fuel the Jehad. Muslim youth, volunteering to fight in Kashmir which, incidentally, is a 'Gateway to India,' get Rs 1,00,000/- for the family left behind, Rs 1,00,000/- as life Insurance cover, and Rs 5,000/- per month as pay. The leaders live in great luxury in their habitat like Muridke and wield enormous political clout. Even the powerful Pakistani Army hesitates to rein them because the rank and file, and officers upto the rank of Brigadiers, have been infiltrated by fanatical elements.

The otherwise powerful Army brass could be assassinated in the manner of Anwar Sadat if they decide to curb these elements. Arms, men and methodology are available for such a scheme. Thus the vicious cycle of violence being perpetrated in Kashmir is destined to continue, unless the Indian political leadership collectively displays the resolve to fight militancy in Kashmir and elsewhere to the finish. On the ground it should be manifested by:

a) calling off all negotiations with the Hurriyat leadership and Pakistan;

b) coming down heavily on the anti-national media in Kashmir;

c) handing over development funds to the army so as to stop their siphoning off to personal coffers;

d) raising and deploying additional troops and resources to stop infiltration of mujahideens in Kashmir;

e) fencing the LOC whatever be the cost. It will not be more than the cost of the ditch cum bund stretching from Akhnoor in J&K to Fazilka in Punjab.

In the last decade, terrorist groups in Jammu and Kashmir (J&K) have killed more than 30,000 civilians and 6000 defence personnel. The political parties have not been spared either. The National Conference has lost 205 members, Congress 49, Janta Dal 10, BJP 9, CPI (M) 5 and the Awami League 5. More than 350,000 people have been rendered homeless. The terrorists have attacked 45 security forces' establishments in the last year.

Between 1990 and 2000, the security forces have recovered 20,365 AK rifles, 8,825 pistols, 959 UMGs, 308 sniper rifles, 615 rocket launchers, 1,687 rocket boosters, 75 LMGs, 757 assorted weapons and 25,000 kg of RDX. Since 1990, over 9000 militants have been killed in J&K and approximately 24,000 apprehended. The terrorists belonged mainly to Pakistan and Afghanistan; some were from Pakistan occupied Kashmir (PoK) and few others were from Bangladesh, Sudan, Turkey, Bahrain, Chechenya, Iran, Kazakhastan, Saudi Arabia and Yemen.

There are about 8000-10,000 registered madrassas (religious schools) and between 40,000 to 50,000 unregistered madrassas in Pakistan. A recent report from Pakistan suggests that as many as 1.7 million children and young men are being trained in these madrassas for jihad in J&K. These madrassas receive about 64 percent of their funding from Islamic countries like Saudi Arabia and Libya, and Pakistan provides the rest. Militant groups draw their recruits from the madrassas; some join them from the educated classes. In the first phase, the recruit receives intensive religious education and basic firearms training. In the second phase, he is sent to a training camp where he is taught to fire live ammunition, bombs, rockets and explosives. He learns to use communication equipment. About 90 terrorist training camps are operating in Pakistan and PoK; over 30 are located in PoK. The Harkat-ul-Mujahideen provides shelter, food and clothing for the trainees at these camps, whilst the Inter-Services Intelligence (ISI) of Pakistan provides weapons, ammunition, transport and specialist instructors. In the third phase, the local commander selects the best trainees and sends them to safe houses along the Line of Control (LoC). These launch pads are situated about 3 km from the LoC.

The Pakistan Army then takes them to a forward post and gives them food, ammunition and Indian currency. Thereafter, they cross the LoC accompanied by their more seasoned colleagues. Infiltration is in small groups of 3-4 men. They congregate at pre-arranged points to form bigger groups of up to 20, depending on the objective. The group penetrates into a specified area, which is under the command of an area commander who assigns them specific tasks to be carried out from their hideouts, or bases within populated areas. Presently, 6000-10,000 terrorists could be operating in J&K, with about 70 percent being foreign mercenaries. Each militant is paid between Rs. 2000 to Rs. 3000 (US$ 44 – 66) per month depending on his experience and status in the terrorist outfit.

In case a terrorist dies in action, his or her family gets compensation ranging from Rs. 20,000 to Rs. 30,000 (US$ 444 – 666). ISI agents active in Kashmir receive between Rs. 50,000 to Rs. 1,00,000 (US$ 1111 – 2222) per month as emoluments. They are accorded five-star comforts during their visits to Rawalpindi. The ISI and its cooperating Islamic organisations spend over Rs. 100 crores (US$ 22 million) a year to run their proxy war in Kashmir. Keeping the aim of a long-term struggle in view, the militants bury large quantities of weapons, explosives and ammunition wrapped in preservative materials in caves and hideouts for convenient retrieval in times of need. The attacks on posts and headquarters of the security forces are launched to force them to defend themselves rather than launch offensive action.

Much of the criticism directed against the state government for not undertaking developmental activity to win the hearts and minds of the people, is not wholly justified; under the existing circumstances, no state government can pursue such programmes with success till peaceful conditions are first created by the military. With the fundamentalists there can be no dialogue for, having heard the voice of God, they are deaf to human reason. Dialogue and a peace process can only succeed if terrorism is first crushed. There are no soft options left for India. The threat is spreading to the rest of India. Pakistan has reportedly recruited 21,000 Indian spies.

Over 10,000 Pakistani and other foreigners have already infiltrated into India. Time is the essence. Those who seek to bleed India must be defeated in the shortest possible time. Ignoring or downplaying the emerging threat would lead to faulty and irrelevant policy responses. The world must be told in unambiguous terms that India will not allow terror and intimidation to succeed. Next, Pakistan should be told to close terrorist camps in PoK within a period of, say 60 days, or, face the consequences. Military operations should be launched to isolate the terrorists, disrupt their planning and operations. Terrorists who are apprehended should face trial for their crimes.

One of the reasons why Kargil occurred was because our conventional capability had been neglected. All deficiencies must immediately be made up. If our preparations are timely and thorough, Pakistan could well see reason.

Pakistan's Military Invasions

The intrusion of Pakistani troops and Pakistani supplied mercenaries in India's Kargil region is one more bid in a long series of failed attempts to gain possession of the territory of Kashmir. Pakistan's claim to Kashmir rests on the argument that because it is a Muslim-majority state, it must therefore, be a part of Islamic Pakistan. Were India a Hindu, Sikh or Christian India, that argument might have had a reasonable basis. But India is a secular democratic republic, home to as many or more Muslims than the entire population of Islamic Pakistan, and home to more religious communities of the world than almost any other nation. As for the Muslims of Kashmir, they rejected the very ideology that forms the founding basis of Pakistan. In 1947, like the rest of India, the majority of Kashmir's Muslims overwhelmingly supported secular political forces like the National Conference, and cast their lot with secular India. In 1947 when Pakistan made its first attempt to occupy Kashmir by force, the people of Kashmir responded by rallying behind their leader, Sheikh Mohammed Abdullah, and created a 10,000 strong militia to stall the invasion, and invited India to join them in pushing back the invading forces. By their actions in 1947, and on many occasions thereafter, Muslims of Jammu & Kashmir, whether they were Kashmiri-speaking Sunni Muslims from the Kashmir Valley, or Ladakhi-speaking Shia Muslims of Kargil region, or the Gujjar (pastoral) Muslims inhabiting the mountain tracts, they have all emphatically declared their future to be with a secular India and not with a theocratic Pakistan.

In recent years, the people of Kashmir have demonstrated their identification with India in very concrete ways. In the 1996 elections, in spite of several well-publicized boycotts and even many death threats - over 55% of Kashmir (state wide) participated in the general elections. Turnout in legislative assembly elections was even higher. In several districts, turnout crossed 65%. Most recently, in the wake of the Kargil invasion by these so-called "freedom fighters", the people of Kargil have overwhelmingly supported the efforts of the Indian army in ridding the region of armed inflitrators. Given all this, one might wonder why the Pakistani state expends so much money and blood on a cause where it has no moral or legal standing; why, with only one-sixth the population of India, it spends about half as much on military expenditure as does India; and why it constantly provokes its neighbor with bellicose posturing and hostile military acts? Lately, it has even taken to warning of a possible nuclear conflict with India, even though India has renounced the use of a nuclear first strike. Although no closer to realizing it's ambition to annex Kashmir, the Pakistani establishment persists with it's policy of cross-border raids and firing at civillians and other acts of sabotage and terror.

The reasons for this retrograde policy lie in the creation of Pakistan itself; in the nature of the Muslim League that broke with the anti-colonial unity of the people of the sub-continent, and led a narrow and sectarian separatist movement calling for the creation of an Islamic Pakistan. This demand was made during the final phase of India's freedom struggle when independance was just round the corner, but the forces for a united and secular India were languishing in British jails and could not effectively counter this divisive demand.

The Muslim League was essentially the voice of reaction amongst India's Muslims and represented the interests of the Muslim feudal aristocracy. The Congress Party, which led the freedom struggle against British rule in India included every religious denomination and almost every ethnic and linguistic group in the sub-continent in a united struggle for freedom from foreign rule. This diverse composition was reflected in the Congress Party's vision of India as a secular and democratic state. As freedom neared, the Muslim League presented the undemocratic demand of a legislature divided on the basis of religion with a disproportionate number of seats reserved for Muslims Naturally, this demand was rejected by the Indian National Congress, and this rejection was correctly seen by the Muslim League as a threat to the priviliges of the Muslim feudal aristocracy, and it's continued existence as a viable political force. Over three decades and more, the Muslim League had made little headway in rallying India's Muslim masses behind it. However, with clandestine encouragement and crucial tactical support from the British colonial authorities, it eventually succeeded in achieving it's goals. A safe haven for the Muslim feudal classes was created in the Islamic state of Pakistan.

Idealogical cover for the partition of the Indian sub-continent was sought through the two-nation theory which argued that Muslims and Hindus of India were two separate nations with irreconcilable differences. This was to be the justification for the creation of Pakistan.

They did not seem to notice that the Congress had had a Muslim President in Maulana Azad and that the Congress routinely won seats that were reserved for Muslim candidates, (hardly indicative of irreconcilable differences between Hindus and Muslims!). Furthermore, it didn't bother the crusaders of Pakistan one bit that one-third of all the Muslims of the sub-continent were to remain (as a minority) in a nation that would then be dominated by Hindus (a people with whom Muslims supposedly had "irreconcilable differences"). That India were to go on and elect Muslims as Presidents twice further discredited the theory. But it's biggest failure occured in 1971 when religion failed to be a glue to hold the eastern and western wings of Pakistan together.

When Pakistan's military rulers responded to the democratic demands of the Bengali speaking people of the eastern region with a pogram in which three million people were butchered, the eastern part rebelled and broke away to become Bangladesh. Even as secular India survived several centrifugal currents, the champions of the two-nation theory fell out in less than 25 years. The two-nation theory collapsed completely. Yet, it is still used as cover for Pakistan's land grabs in Kashmir. That British and US analysts continue to give legitimacy to Pakistani propoganda regarding Kashmir simply shows that the old colonial mentality of divide-and-conquer still prevails.

The ruling classes of Pakistan ?the combine of feudal landlords and military generals - little changed since Pakistan's creation in 1947, are more than willing collaborators in this dangerous game. Having failed to respond positively to the democratic aspirations of the Pakistani people, they have had to suppress their growing discontent by taking harsh measures, and enforcing martial law. The people have been subject to long periods of military dictatorship; democratic governments have been routinely dismissed by unelected officials in the recent past, and more recently, the courts have upheld the most inhumane interpretations of "Islamic" medieval laws. Most importantly, the feudal-military ruling combine has found it necessary to create the perpetual myth of a vile and dangerous external enemy i.e. India - so as to provide a much needed distraction from the burning issues of poverty and under-development that confront the masses.

Hostility to India has thus become Pakistan's raison d etre and an "Islamic" jehad against India in Kashmir, a "holy" mission. Hostility towards India has thus remained at the core of Pakistan's foreign policy, a policy that has been implemented with varying levels of aggressiveness; military or diplomatic ?throughout the last five decades. In 1990, emboldened by it's victory in Afghanistan, Pakistan once again directed its hostile energies eastward, at Punjab and Kashmir in India, confident that its years of experience in Afghanistan would bring India down on its knees. Arming and training mercenary terrorists, planning their infiltration into India, aiding and abetting proxy wars in India's border states, fomenting an Islamic fundamentalist insurgency in Kashmir, and coordinating and organizing terrorist attacks in India has led to the death of tens of thousands of Indian citizens in the last decade. Despite these serious provocations, India's response has been measured and patient. Its efforts to counter Pakistan's hostile activities by purely defensive measures has prevented an open confrontation with Pakistan, and yet effectively defeated Pakistan's proxy war. But Pakistan has not given up.

Pakistan's new adventure in Kargil is a continuation of this old policy. The immediate goal of this quiet invasion, (which caught India napping), was to cut off Ladakh from the rest of India, and open up one more avenue for infiltration of Islamist terrorists into the Kashmir valley. If, and when India reacted, Pakistan would try and force international attention on Kashmir, thus restraining India from even taking effective defensive measures, let alone retaliating. In either case, Pakistan expected to emerge the winner.

To the extent that India has been unable to retaliate beyond the line of control, Pakistan's gambit has paid off. Unfortunately for Pakistan, the timing of the Kargil adventure has not been entirely auspicious as far as the Western imperial powers are concerned. That the U.S. has asked Pakistan to pull the intruders back seems like an unanticipated setback for Pakistan. It does not, however, mean that the U.S. has turned pro-India or that the U.S. genuinely wants the Kashmir issue to be amicably settled between India and Pakistan. The U.S. has its own interest in keeping the hostilities between India and Pakistan simmering. It gives the U.S. leverage over both the countries, and a future option to police this part of the world with a possible occupation and a base in an 'independent' Kashmir, a la Kosovo.

Surely, U.S. spy satellites must have noticed the military activity in the Kargil area as early as January or February when the Pakistani encroachment began. But the U.S. did not alert India and it is unlikely that it warned Pakistan to desist from initiating hostilities. It satisfied world public opinion by giving Pakistan a slap on the wrist only after India discovered significant intrusion into its territory.

The recent statement by the German foreign minister, that the G-7 could not stand by forever while the fighting continued in Kargil is an ominous sign and lends credence to concerns about a future Western intervention in Kashmir. It has not helped that even as the NATO powers have ignored evidence of war-crimes on the part of the Pakistani military, they have put India under considerable pressure to keep negotiating with Pakistan when there is little scope for any constructive dialogue on the matter.

And while many foreign journalists and human rights advocates give credence to Pakistan's claims on Kashmir, few report that India's 100 million plus Muslims reject Pakistan's claims to it, and wish Kashmir's Muslims to remain with them in a secular India. Few care to note that the Indian military includes many Muslims, none of whom have ever defected to Pakistan during it's may invasions of India. Vigorous anti-Pakistan demonstrations held by India's Muslims all over India belie Pakistan's claims that it has a popular mandate to speak for the Muslims of the sub-continent, or has any moral right to call for Kashmir's secession from India. Although the people of Pakistan have been led to believe that Pakistan's crusade for Kashmir is in the popular interest, the reality is quite different. Whereas the people of Kashmir enjoy democratic rights that the people of Pakistan don't, they are also better educated and less poor. 50 years after independence, literacy in Pakistan at 44% trails India's at 64%.

For several decades, India has led Pakistan in terms of lower infant mortality - an important indicator of social welfare. Even though Pakistan inherited some of the best irrigated parts of undivided India, Pakistan must now import wheat from the U.S - something India has not had to do for decades. And although a greater portion of Pakistan's population migrates to the gulf, and brings back consumer goods like TV sets and telephones, Pakistan now trails India in terms of color TV ownership, telephone access, and cable-TV connections.

Neither has Pakistan invested in mass transit or national science and technology projects to the extent India has. If anything, Pakistan's attempts at destabilizing India have weakened the economies of both countries. Both nation's currencies have been weakened, with the Pakistani economy becoming even more dependant on bailouts from the IMF and World Bank. It is most ironic that even as the people of Pakistan endure a period of enforced austerity, the military finds the budget for it's misadventures across the border.

Unfortunately, as long as Pakistan's ruling feudal-military oligarchy can continue this bloodletting in Kashmir and elsewhere with impunity, they will do so as the best guarantee of their own existence. The people of Pakistan can change this state of affairs if they rise against their feudal-military ruling class, rein in Pakistan's army, tame the parallel state of ISI, and usher Pakistan into an era of a more democratic rule.They could insist that their governement work for peace and cooperation in the Indian subcontinent. If that happened, Kashmir could cease to be a problem dividing Pakistan and India, and the peoples of both countries could breathe easier, without the fear of war constantly hanging over them.

Then, people of both nations could benefit from expanding trade and greater cooperation in science and technology. Divided families and friends could travel with ease. Both people could jointly rediscover their shared history and culture. But that rosy scenario could be decades away. In the near term, it is more than likely that Pakistan will continue on it's present path. It is also likely that India may now respond with a substantial increase in its defense spending, just as Pakistan already did in this year's budget.

Pakistan's adventurism could thus fuel an accelerated arms race in the region. That would certainly hurt India, but being six times the size of Pakistan, it could survive. It is Pakistan which might collapse and disintegrate. Financial bail-outs from the West and its agencies, such as the IMF's recent $3 billion loan, (or by Saudi Arabia) may prolong the life of Pakistan's feudal-military oligarchy but it may not prevent the ultimate disintegration of Pakistan if it's rulers continue on this suicidal course. Furthermore, continued provocation by Pakistan's rulers could exhaust the patience of India's policy-makers to the extent that they decide to retaliate against Pakistan with a tit-for-tat - (do unto others what they have done unto you) - and begin to foment ethnic conflict and insurgency in Sindh and Baluchistan. That too could herald the end of Pakistan.

The two nation theory that has divided and weakened the entire sub-continent may then find a final resting place - dead and buried with the many victims of Pakistan's wars with India; those who survive may then discover the joys of being good neighbours and old friends.

Pakistan Army's Strategy in Kashmir

There is a grand design behind Pakistan's transgression

of the Line of Control [LoC] in the Ladakh region of Jammu and Kashmir [J & K]. This Line has never been violated in the last 27 years. The LoC Agreement is enshrined in 19 mosaics and 27 maps signed on December 11, 1972. They depict the terrain and there is no scope for errors in recognising key features. The first step in elementary map reading is to relate 'map to ground' and vice versa. Pakistan was well aware of the LoC's alignment when it downed Indian aircraft and directed artillery fire onto Indian positions and roads.

It was President Zia-ul Haq who chalked out the strategy for insurgency in J & K in 1985. His intention was to inspire a popular uprising against India by inducting trained militants belonging to fundamentalist Muslim organisations. Kashmiri youth were enticed with money and false promises to go to Pakistan for training and induction. The Pak Army had contacted the J & K Liberation Front [JKLF], which agreed to cooperate on the condition that Kashmir would be granted independence after Indian control ceased over the State. As insurgency picked up, the Pak Army engineered a split in the JKLF and went back on its commitment to an Azad Kashmir. The control of anti- Indian operations later passed on to pro –Pakistan elements who made it a pro- Islamic movement and raised the slogan of Kashmir's accession to Pakistan.

The Kashmiri youth saw through Pakistan's deceit and disassociated themselves from it. It was the population of J & K imbued as it has always been with the spirit of Kashmiriat [a secular outlook, lack of bigotry, and above all generosity in the spiritual sense] that defeated Pakistan's plans. By 1997 the situation was well under control to enable the government to hold elections. May 1998 saw the nuclear tests and pressure on both India and Pakistan not to escalate tensions. Some Indian defence analysts believed that nuclear weapons would preclude a conventional war and lead to settlement of the J & K issue along the existing LoC. In the last two or three years, it has become clear to Pakistan that, in the Indian state of J & K, a mere 10 percent of the population wish to join Pakistan; the rest would opt for autonomy within the Indian Union. What is worse the Kashmiris in Pak Occupied Kashmir [POK], having been denied political and economic freedom for 50 years, desire to break loose.

Thus, the Pak Army had to do something quickly to defuse the situation. It consequently, shifted to a military approach. The essence of this strategy was to use the Pak Army to occupy important heights in the Dras-Kargil-Batalik-Turtok area and thus cut off the Ladakh Division and Siachen Brigade. It was calculated that the critical situation would force the Indian Army to divert troops from the Valley and elsewhere in J & K to meet this challenge. This would enable Pakistan to induct some 2000 to 3000 mercenaries all over J & K and whip up a fresh wave of insurgency.

Initial success would provide the impetus to the Pak Army to breach the LoC at other points. The overly stretched Indian security forces, unable to thwart this two pronged invasion, would continue to lose control, and Pakistan would be finally able to internationalise the J & K issue.

The Pakistani General Staff did not anticipate a firm Indian response, particularly the use of air power, and certainly not in high altitude terrain where a superiority of 6:1 is required to evict the intruder. Nawaz Sharif was definitely taken into confidence, but he could not rein in his generals as national security in Pakistan is the sole preserve of the Pak Army. Interference and opposition is not countenanced.

Where do we go from here. The LoC may not be transgressed at other points to keep the conflict restricted to the present area of operations. However, having undertaken an intrusion of this magnitude, it would lead to loss of face for the Pak Army to pull back across the LoC; hence, Pakistani intransigence at the Delhi talks. Infiltration will continue and the proxy war will go on. India will find it very hard to trust Pakistan again. The Indian Army is coming out with flying colours, yet it is exercising remarkable restraint in keeping the conflict localised. Although Pakistan has found little support abroad for its misadventure, the J& K issue has been internationalised. It will not be long before the United States and other Western powers begin to declare they cannot play the role of mere onlookers.

Suicide Terrorism in Kashmir

Suicide terrorism in Kashmir is bound to increase in the coming days given the internal dynamics and objectives of the various militant groups operating there..

Besides the Lashkar-e-Toiba, Hizbul Mujahideen, Jaish-e-Mohammad and Harkat-ul-Mujahideen, there are a number of minor militant groups comprising of Kashmiris, Pakistanis and Afghans. The Hizbul is considered the most indigenous militant group and its objective is very limited: it fights for an independent Kashmir and does not support the merger of Kashmir with Pakistan.

The Lashkar-e-Toiba, comprising mainly of Pakistanis, is well organized and is independent (especially financially) of the ISI (Pakistan's Inter Services Intelligence) when compared to other militant organizations. For the Lashkar, Kashmir is a means to achieve its pan-Islamic objectives. Understanding the objectives of these two organizations and their limitations, the ISI created the Jaish with Maulana Masood Azhar as its chief. Jaish has been involved in all suicide attacks carried out in Kashmir. The first ever suicide attack took place when a student rammed his car at the gate of the Badamibagh cantonment in April 2000.

A similar second attack took place in the same spot in December 2000. The Jaish, coming into being much later than other militant groups, is attempting desperately to find some 'space' for itself through spectacular acts aimed at capturing the attention of people both inside and outside Kashmir. Second, suicide terrorism results in a lot of publicity for the militant group that perpetrates the attack. In Kashmir, this publicity is very essential as militant groups need to compete with each other to gain popular support and/or prove their invincibility to their mentors and clientele. Publicity is crucial to attract more funds, especially from abroad, and boost up recruitment drive inside Kashmir; the more Kashmiris in its fold, the more support the group can garner in terms logistics, planning and escape.

Third, Kashmiri participation in militancy has been on the decline in recent years. The suicide attack at the Srinagar Legislative Assembly complex was carried out by a Pakistani; and, the Jaish and the Lashkar have been regularly carrying out the so-called fidayeen attacks with Pakistanis. The main reason for these fidayeen attacks is to keep the hopes of the Kashmiris alive reminding them that Pakistan will liberate Kashmir.

Fourth, there exists close linkages between the militant groups, especially the above-mentioned three groups and the rightist political groups of Pakistan who patronize or/and run the madrassas. Continuous indoctrination in these madrassas has produced a number of "jihadi robots", who could be used as human bombs. How to combat suicide terrorism in Kashmir? What are the options before India?

The first option is to strike the roots of terror, be it hot pursuit or surgical strike. Both these options sound easier, but would be extremely difficult in practical terms. A hot pursuit involves chasing the militants inside PoK (Pakistan occupied Kashmir). There are a number of Pakistani military posts along the Line of Control that would have to be dealt with militarily. A surgical strike, on the other hand, involves wiping out the terrorist camps in PoK based on intelligence regarding their accurate location. Besides, such a strike needs to be undertaken with missiles based on Indian soil or from air violating Pakistani airspace.

There is every possibility that such strikes could hit other targets, resulting in loss of innocent lives. Both hot pursuit and surgical strikes are bound to escalate the conflict between India and Pakistan and the possibility of an all-out war cannot be ruled out. Whereas the Indian military establishment would be eager to exercise this option, it is doubtful whether the ruling BJP, rhetorically impressive but politically spineless, would resort to it. The second option is to send specialized ground teams to physically annihilate the leaders and the camps. This requires precise information. Israel has used this option in tracking the militants even in other countries and assassinating them. Such counter attacks would, in the short run, increase militant attacks but in the long run, yield better results.

Thirdly, India should take concrete steps at the national and international levels. Instead of merely accusing Pakistan and the militant groups for the violence in Jammu and Kashmir, it is very essential that the much talked about White Paper on ISI activities in India be tabled in the Parliament. This should be followed by diplomatic pressure, instead of media statements, both at national and international levels. Finally, unnecessary criticism of the security forces in the Valley dampening their morale should be checked. Little understanding the hostile environment in which they operate, the security forces, along with their planning, intelligence and alertness, have come under unfair criticism. Given the nature of suicide bombing, it is tough for any security force to tackle a bomb, which can think, move, dodge and be ready to destroy itself.

When Afaq Ahmad Shah, a 12th class student blew himself up along with his Maruti car to attack the 15 Corps Head Quarters in Badamibagh Cantonment during the third week of May, he became the first suicide bomber in the twelve year old militancy in Kashmir. Though previous attacks by the "fidayeens" were termed suicidal, they were hit and run attacks, in which militants, fought with the security forces or/and attacked the security installations, some of whom escaped. There always existed a chance of escape. Hence those attacks were never suicidal in the real sense although the media and every one, including the government began calling them "suicide squads."

Suicide is generally an individual act and rarely is it a group act even in the history of terrorism. A single suicide bomber has always carried out suicide attacks by the LTTE in South Asia or by the Hamas in the Middle East and there have never been suicide "squads." The implications of this first ever suicide bomber in Kashmir is worth analyzing rather than discussing whether Islam permits suicide. First, the fear of the suicide bomber will have its greatest impact on the security of the leaders in the state. Though many of them have been provided adequate security and bulletproof cars, the witnessing of a suicide bomber armed with RDX blowing up everything near him, as has occured in other parts of South Asia will have an impact. This fear will result in the leaders feeling insecure and lead to further strengthening their security, which will cause inconvenience to the general public, and also alienate the leaders from the masses. Given the conditions in Kashmir, where the government is not popular, any increase in security will increase the gap between the people and its leaders.

Secondly, the entry of suicide bomber is also bound to have an impact on the morale of the security forces. It is not that the armed forces were scarred in undertaking their day-to-day counter-insurgency activities, but they would be more suspicious in dealing with the public.

In the wake of suicide bombing, a sarcastic smile or a wink, when being checked or interrogated, would cause more damage than a 20 kg RDX blowing up a security vehicle. The hostile situation, in which the security forces are operating, coupled with the fact that the nature of militancy has changed since the Kargil war, will further lead to increase in security operations, which obviously will have a negative impact on the people. Thirdly, the nature of militancy has also undergone a change. The militants have started relying on RDX, which can be used in any simple improvised explosive device (IED). Even a small quantity of RDX can throw a jeep 30 meters into the air or cause damage to not only the target, but also to the surroundings and a bulletproof car can easily be made into pieces.

More than the blast, the sight of a vehicle disintegrating into pieces or a security post being destroyed would cause maximum psychological damage. A suicide bomber can walk or cycle up to any governmental or security installation, and blow up the entire structure. Even if the suicide bomber is caught before reaching its target, the triggering of the bomb, would serve its purpose, depending on the quantity of the RDX, he or she is carrying. Finally there is the alienation in the Kashmiri people. Unlike previous hit and run cases, in which the foreign mercenaries were involved, Afaq Ahmad Shah, the suicide bomber, was a local Kashmiri youth. This fact must be underlined. It is time to reassess often repeated judgments that the militancy is Pakistan sponsored; the locals are not involved; the militants are mercenaries; the growth of madarsas in Pakistan and Kashmir are the main reason for the militancy in Kashmir and so on.

Though there is an element of truth in these assertions, the failure to understand the complete alienation among the Kashmir people, especially its youth will further increase the intensity of the ongoing conflict. Afaq, according to his relatives and friends, never showed any signs of involving himself in militancy. The fact that his father is a retired lecturer and the family is well respected would disprove another myth that only the economically and socially deprived take up militancy. This suicide bombing may be an individual act, by a disillusioned or highly motivated youth. It may or may not be followed by similar other acts. But what needs to be understood is the existence of alienation, especially among the Kashmiri youth.

The Central and State governments should earnestly attempt to remove this. The least that could be done is to start a dialogue with all sections of Kashmir society, and the state government should begin to improve its record on administration before it becomes too late.

New Dimension of Violence

Irruption of fresh violence in Kashmir wherein in a BSF Headquarters at Bandipura a brigade HQ at Kupwara and murders of some civilian leaders have taken place, is in fact hopeful sign. For two reasons. First, it is not insurgency at all. In that it does not involve the local Kashmir's except as informants under duress. The core consists of Pakistanis, Afghans and assorted mercenaries from impoverished countries. The money for these mercenaries comes from the oil rich Gulf countries and narcotic trade and the fanatics amongst them a la Osamma Bin Laden would regard incurring such expenditures as paying insurance premiums for the next world. For the poor Pakistanis where unemployment and consequent poverty is ever worse than India, the largesse of Rs. two Lakhs for a years work in India is not bad at all. This monetary remuneration along with the potent religious exhortation and visceral vengefulness is a powerful mix which the ISI astutely exploits.

It is time that the security forces specially the Army thought through the situation and evolved an effective response. For the danger is over-reaction since the sneak attacks are mounted from the surrounding inhabited areas and while immediately retaliating and later investigating the incident, the security forces are likely to become injudiciously oppressive. Therefore, various psychological and military actions have to be implemented. Villages should be provided with high fences and entry and exit to and from them should be controlled. The environ around these should be patrolled. Likely areas of hide out in the forests and hills should be occupied and neutralized by use of air power and artillery to deny intruders safe harbour to them.

The borders inside one or two kilometers behind the forward defended localities should be fenced by high wire and patrolled. On the face of it, it will appear to be a formidable job, but if we could dig up a ditch cum bund from Aknoor to Fazika in Punjab and erect barbed wire fence across the borders of Rajasthan, there is no reason why a barbed wire fence cannot be erected in Kashmir. The cost is likely to be much less than the limited a that cost us near 3000 crores in three months in Kargil. The task is daubing in view of the virulent Pakistani propaganda being disseminated by 2000 madras's and even larger number of mosques ceaselessly. The liberal composite Kashmiri culture has been seriously undermined. It is not well known that till the reign of Shah Jahan intermarriages between Muslims and Hindus were a normal feature of societal intercourse. Shah Jahan forbade it. The mysticism of Sufis which pervaded the spiritual life of the Kashmiris has been carefully done down by the fanatical elements. These old practices need to be revived. The should be done by encouraging and aiding Kashmir Sufi men to propagate their beliefs and practices. Their books, periodials and magazines should be published, seminars, lectures and 'urs' should be organized. Necessary funds should be provided by the state for the purpose.

The key to such activities are right kind of men. They should ne acknowledged scholars and leaders whose integrity and dedication to the Kashmir culture and ethos is undisputed. Distinguished secular journalists and scholars should be provided financial wherewithal to publish and circulate their newspaper in Kashmir which should reach every village. The ultimate aim should be to enable the evolution and burnishing of a distinct Kashmir culture, of which, every Kashmir Muslim should be justifiably so proud that he cannot be converted into a clone of Pakistan exported fanatic fundamentalism. This is an era of workers who impart knowledge which opens, the door to material advancement.

The madarasas should be persuaded to impart such education, if necessary, by legislation. Modern gadgets like computers and Internet facilities should be provided to these madarsas for the purpose. Young people should be exposed to the changes being wrought in modern Islamic countries like Turkey, Egypt, Jordan, Morocco, Malaysia and Brunei. They should be enabled to become doctors, engineers, scientists, architects, artists and writers. Women should be compulsorily educated and equal rights and opportunities granted to them for their personnel achievements. A major of the ordinary Kashmiri is that while India has given over 100 lakh crores in grants in aid to Kashmiri, most of it has gone to the personnel coffers of bureaucrats and political leaders. This Gordian knot should be cut. One way out is to give the developmental funds to the Army operating in that area. The Army so far has not been corrupted.

Given sufficient will and imagination it is definitely feasible to reduce the externally exported violence from Pakistan to a controllable level and then to terminate it.

Counter-Insurgency

The insurgent gun and its carnage are the biggest problems confronting Jammu and Kashmir. Restoration of normalcy cannot be achieved without defanging Jihad. The father of Jihad, Sheikh Abdullah Azzam, has raised the slogan: "Jihad and the rifle alone. No negotiations, no conferences and no dialogues." The highroad to peace lies in strengthening counter-insurgency and striking at the roots of Jihad. Village Defence Committees (VDCs) were launched in 1994 for the people of Kashmir to defend themselves against cross-border terrorism; this coincided with the hijacking of the indigenous Kashmiri agitation by Pakistan's ISI and a realization among the Kashmiris and international community that the issue at stake is terrorism and not self-determination.

Villagers and ex-servicemen from the minority communities approached the authorities and requested them to be trained and organized into self-defence cells to deter the terrorists from cleansing J&K of non-Muslims. VDCs proliferated rapidly, starting with Doda but spreading to Kathua, Udhampur, Poonch, Rajouri and Jammu. There are more than 1500 VDCs now all over the state.

VDC operations at the outset were largely defensive and restricted to repulsing terrorist attacks with light weapons and information provided by special police officers. Due to their valorous resistance against the Jihad machine, VDCs began to be identified as primary targets, and were systematically attacked by superior armed and trained mujahideen. Manhunts for talented VDC leaders became a practice for the Jihadis and the defensive and under-armed VDC members suffered severe casualties inflicted by the Lashkar-i-Tayyaba and Hizb-ul-Mujahideen. The Jihadi objectives for pulverizing the VDCs are much broader than gun snatching and minority cleansing. It is a warning to the Kashmiris that whoever dares to organize their self-defence or question the terrorist practices of Pakistani proxies will be silenced. It is a form of psychological warfare.

Being zealots and fanatics masquerading as 'freedom fighters', the mujahideen were disconcerted by grassroots people's action that opposed their 'liberation struggle'. The ISI is especially worried about VDCs and ikhwan (former militants who have now turned informers and accomplices of the Indian Army) since they question the moral foundations of the Kashmir insurgency and neutralize the Islamist indoctrination and propaganda in Pakistani and Afghan terrorist camps. Due to the counter-insurgency and psychological functions they perform, New Delhi should heed the advice proffered by counter-terrorism experts like KPS Gill and strengthen and upgrade the VDCs by increasing their honorariums and supplying them hi-tech arms, night vision and communications equipment they were promised in January 2000, but is yet to materialize. In August 2001, the government refused to give the VDCs automatic assault weapons, partly in reaction to an isolated incident when a vigilante accidentally shot dead an innocent civilian. The result indecision is a fresh wave of slaughter by the jihadis, prompting one VDC member, Surinder Singh of Jammu, to despair, "we were like sitting ducks then and now we will be dead ducks."

Massacres, kidnappings and threats to VDC members' lives have increased exponentially in the last two years; though there was a slight thaw in terrorist actions against military targets after the December 13 attack on Indian Parliament, attacks on the VDCs and civilians are more on the increase. With VDCs having to fend for themselves in an unequal battle with the professional mujahideen, the government boasts of converting the VDCs from defensive formations into frontline allies of the army for checking infiltration. The solution lies in dispelling ISI disinformation that the VDCs are "communalizing" Kashmir and helping them materially and morally.

There cannot be a more favourable moment than the present, with the world focused on reining in extremism, and terrorism in Pakistan. As international opprobrium for Jihad builds up, India must fortify its own defences to ensure that Pakistan's proxy war in Kashmir ends. Currently, the European Parliament has, in a resolution, supported India's stance on cross-border terrorism and called upon the Pakistan President, Pervez Musharraf, to "eradicate terrorist activities carried out from Pakistan, especially infiltration of terrorists". The plenary debate on the resolution was addressed by De Miguel, Spanish Minister for European Affairs, who stressed that the "commitment of Pakistan against organised terrorism must be total and unconditional and non-selective both in terms of direction and time".

The resolution called upon Gen. Musharraf to implement his commitment — outlined in his January 12,

2002 speech — "to eradicate terrorist activities carried out from Pakistan, especially to stop infiltration of terrorists across the Line of Control into Jammu and Kashmir". It also called for "the resumption of bilateral talks on the Kashmir question" and underlined "the need to strengthen moderate forces in Kashmir and to help develop a stronger civil society". All anti-India amendments, including those by the pro-Pakistan MEP (Member of European Parliament), Liz Lynn, for mediation, were rejected. Many prominent MEPs were strongly supportive of the Indian position, and there was no statement in Pakistan's support. Charles Tannock urged Pakistan to arrest and hand over to India the terrorists involved in atrocities against civilians in Jammu and Kashmir and the attack on Parliament. Sakellariou, from Germany, welcomed the measures announced by India, including the withdrawal of the ban on over-flights by Pakistani commercial aircraft, the appointment of a High Commissioner and the withdrawal of naval ships from forward positions. Mr. Sakellariou also stressed the importance of democracy. India was a democratic country, he said, expressing the hope that elections in Pakistan would also lead to a democratic government. The Chairperson of the South Asia delegation, Maria Carrilho, from Portugal, highlighted the need for maintaining a high level of vigilance. "I had the opportunity to visit India some weeks ago and I can affirm that beyond tension there is also an effective will for peace."

7

Elections in Kashmir

The turmoil caused in Jammu & Kashmir (J&K) by terrorist violence has given Pakistan and many of the secessionist groups in the state an excuse to demand a plebiscite in Jammu & Kashmir as envisaged in the United Nations Commission for India and Pakistan (UNCIP) resolutions of August 13, 1948 and January 5, 1949. It is never mentioned by the present advocates of a plebiscite that it was Pakistan which stonewalled the implementation of a plebiscite under UNCIP resolutions and that the 1972 Simla Agreement between India and Pakistan superseded all other agreements between the two countries including the UNCIP resolutions.

Yet the issue of a plebiscite, given much currency by Pakistan and by the imperialist powers, continues to haunt many well-meaning Indians who feel that India stands on morally weak ground by insisting on the Simla Agreement and rejecting a referendum. The demand for a plebiscite in J&K is highly misunderstood. There is a myth that the demand for a plebiscite reflects the aspirations of all (or a sizable majority) of the state's population, and is the only way for the people of J&K to articulate their right to self-determination. Although seemingly well-intentioned, those who see a plebiscite as a cure-all for the problems of the people of the state are in fact, ignorant of the historic and contemporary complexities surrounding this issue. Contrary to most reports in the media, Jammu & Kashmir (J&K) is not a state where only Kashmiri Muslims live. It is a multi-ethnic, multi-religious state with 64% Muslims, 33% Hindus, and 3% Buddhists, Sikhs, Christians and others. There are three distinct geographical regions - Ladakh (with 58% of the area, and 3% of the population), Jammu (26% area, 45% population) and Kashmir (16% area, 52% population: of which over 90 % of the region's minorities, i.e. 3% of the state's total population have been driven out).

The primary languages of Ladakh are Ladakhi and Balti, of Jammu: Dogri, and of Kashmir: Kashmiri. In addition, Gujari, Pahari, Punjabi, Shina and various dialects and mixed languages are also spoken by different ethnic groups within the state. Fifteen per cent of the state's Muslims live in the provinces of Jammu and Ladakh . They are non-Kashmiris, and by and large, they stand behind J&K's association with India. (There are a few small exceptions in some towns of Doda district). Of the state's 49% who reside in the Kashmir province, about 13% are Shia Muslims. Shia Muslims do not wish to have anything to do with Sunni-dominated Pakistan, knowing full well the fate that awaits them there. (Just recently, an Oct 4, Hindustan Times report cited Pakistan's Shoora Wahdat-i-Islami who condemned what it called the genocide of Shias in Pakistan.) This is especially true of the Shias of Kargil who know of the poverty and degradation experienced by their ethnic siblings in Baltistan, a part of Pakistan occupied Kashmir referred to as the "Northern Areas". 14% of the people in Kashmir province are the pastoral nomadic Gujar and Bakarwal people.

They are strong supporters of association with India and have demonstrated this by organizing Militancy Mukhalif Morcha (Anti-Militancy Front) to assist the security forces in surveillance of terrorist activity. As far as non-Muslim groups are concerned there is no reason for them to even think about living outside multi-religious and secular India. The support for secession in Jammu & Kashmir is thus largely limited to the non-pastoral Sunni Muslim population of the Kashmir Valley who constitute 22% of the state's population, (or about 1.9 million people). This segment of the population dominates the politics of the state.

The reason that many believe separatism to be a widespread sentiment in J&K is because this dominant section has succeeded in completely drowning out all other voices in the state, and has the ability to cripple the normal functioning of the society in Kashmir province; either by inaction or insufficient action against Pakistani infiltration and terror or, worst still, by sabotage. It is this section of the state's population that receives all the attention, understandably so from Pakistan and the imperialist nations, but also from the Indian press. Since the concept of self-determination must be applied to each of Jammu & Kashmir's unique population groups, there can be no equation of self-determination with secession. If, however, the undivided state (including the Pakistan occupied regions of Kashmir which Pakistan refers to s "Azad" Kashmir & "Northern Areas") were to have a referendum under truly neutral supervision, and the people were given three options - join India, join Pakistan or be independent—the results might be shocking to votaries of secession. The majority could very well go with India, because the separatists will split the vote between pro-Pakistan and pro-independence groups. Sayyed Ali Gilani, Jammu & Kashmir's Jamaat-e-Islami leader, opposes the option of independence precisely because he is afraid that this vote may split in India's favor. On the other hand, if the people of the state are given only two choices - join India or join Pakistan - the majority vote could still go in India's favor. Of the 12.8 million people in the undivided state, J&K's population is 8.5 million, "Azad" Kashmir's is 2.8 million and "Northern Areas" is 1.5 million. If 1.9 million from J&K and all of "Azad" Kashmir and "Northern Areas" vote for Pakistan, it still gives India a vote of 6.6 million and leaves Pakistan with 6.2 million!

Even if provision were made in this analysis for erosion of support for India as a result of the current turmoil, and some sprinkling of support for Pakistan from other Muslim groups in the state, the results of the referendum would be too close to call. In reality, the vote for Pakistan could be much less for the following two reasons:-

Since 1948, the Sunni population of the Valley (22% of the state's population), has dominated the legislative, political and administrative structures in the state of J&K. Kashmir province receives more weightage in the Assembly elections than does Jammu province. Based on the size of it's population Kashmir province should send 44 members to the Legislative Assembly but sends 46. Jammu province, on the other hand, should elect 39 but is allowed only 37! The government ministries and administrative bodies have also been dominated by

Kashmiri speaking Valley Sunnis. This grouping has also expropriated a disproportionate amount of resources for their own development needs. The bogey of a plebiscite and accession (in the garb of self-determination) has been raised by this group, primarily to extract concessions from the Central Governemnt in India. These have come in the form of grants, subsidies and other forms of economic aid. This has enabled this group to maintain its political dominance and has seriously distorted the democratic process in the state.

However, if the Central Government in India were to call this bluff, the whole complexion of separatist politics in J&K may change, and if a plebiscite were actually to be conducted, support for Pakistan may drop way below this 1.9 million population base in J&K.

The effectiveness of the demand for plebiscite and its propaganda value lies precisely in its rejection by India. Were the tactical utility of such a demand to be lost, wiser elements amongst the separatists may abandon Pakistan and vote for India.

It is also likely that a significant percentage of the people of the "Northern Areas" could vote for India. The population in this region is very hostile to Pakistan because of the total neglect of this area. Literacy in the "Northern Areas" is 7% compared to J&K's 59%. Since 1947, there has been little improvement in the infrastructure - schools, hospitals, paved roads, electric power and piped drinking water - are practically non-existent!

The inhabitants have no constitutional rights and are still ruled by the frontier laws inherited from the British times. There have also been reports of serf-like treatment of the poor peasants by some of the region's former monarchs. Since the population of the eastern part of "Northern Areas" is Balti speaking Shia Muslim they could very well decide to join their siblings in Kargil area and vote for India.

Considering all this, one might ask: Why doesn't India accept a plebiscite? The fact is, it did, when, it naively it took its complaint of Pakistan's aggression in J&K state to the UN, where an Anglo-American imperialist alliance turned India's complaint into a dispute between Pakistan and India, thereby equating the aggressor with the aggrieved! India waited a long time for Pakistan to fulfill the pre-conditions of plebiscite as laid down in UNCIP resolutions. Instead of complying with the resolutions, Pakistan invaded Kashmir for a second time in 1965!

"Regardless of what Pakistan did or didn't do, the people of Kashmir did have a plebiscite of sorts in 1947. This was demonstrated when Kashmiris from varied backgrounds defiantly resisted the invasion of Pakistan and Pakistan-backed raiders in October of that year. The raiders sacked Muzaffarabad, and razed the towns of Baramulla and Rajouri, slaughtering thousands of civilians, all in a matter of days." Realizing that the Valley was going to be swallowed by these Pakistani marauders, the most popular political party, the National Conference took over the de facto administration, and organized a 10,000 men and women Kashmiri militia to stall the invasion and protect critical installations.

Sheikh Mohammed Abdullah appealed to Mahatma Gandhi to send Indian troops to defend Kashmir. In the meanwhile, all civilian vehicles were requisitioned by the National Conference to be made available to the Indian army who had to be flown in by air. When the first Indian military convoy reached Srinagar by road in November 1947, the whole convoy route in Srinagar was lined with cheering crowds waving the Indian tricolor. The tricolor flew over almost all of Srinagar's homes. That was an expression of Kashmiri self-determination.

When Sheikh Mohammed Abdullah, Bakshi Ghulam Mohammed, Ghulam Mohammed Sadiq, Maulana Sayeed Masoodi, the leaders of Kashmir's freedom struggle from the autocratic rule of Maharaja spoke of Pakistan as a feudal state and about imperialism's interest in Kashmir, when they publicly expressed their contempt for the two-nation theory, when they paid glowing tributes to Indian jawans (troops) for defending Kashmir, they echoed the sentiments of the majority of Kashmiris. That too was an expression of Kashmiri self-determination.

Equating today's terrorism with a "freedom struggle" is an insult to those leaders and their sacrifices. Today, Sheikh Abdullah's grave is protected by national security forces for fear that terrorists will remove the dead leader's body and desecrate it as threatened by them. Eight years ago, one of the first victims of terrorist bullets was the octogenarian Maulana Syed Masoodi, veteran freedom fighter of Kashmir. What is happening in Kashmir today is a low intensity war by Pakistan against India spearheaded by the ideology of two-nation theory and Islamic fundamentalism. "Azadi" is a smokescreen under whose cover the "freedom fighters" actually religious zealots, with support from a theocratic Pakistan, wage war against secular India.

The fact is, that in essence, Kashmir had a plebiscite in 1947, and it's people voted for India. If India refuses to talk about a second plebiscite today, it has many valid concerns. Can a plebiscite be conducted in an atmosphere of violence and terror?

In the last two months, newspapers in Srinagar, partial to secession, have been publishing death threats aimed at those who encourage, support or participate in Indian parliamentary elections. Unless there is an atmosphere of a free and fair debate in an environment of confidence and trust - no truly representative plebiscite is possible. Moreover, free and fair campaigning and fearless participation has to be guaranteed on both sides of the border. Pakistan with it's history of muzzling the press, of military coups and arbitrary dismissals of elected governements is in simply no position to guarantee such fairness. Neither is the UN, with it's highly partisan role in world affairs. Consider how the UN has been used as a pawn in every major imperialist undertaking, from Korea to Iraq andYugoslavia.

The 1948-9 UNCIP resolutions pertaining to a plebiscite put explicit obligations on Pakistan which Pakistan has since failed to meet. Any acceptance of a new plebiscite would once again reward the very forces that have obstructed the first plebiscite. The right to self-determination cannot be equated to the right to secession in a multi-ethnic, multi-lingual and multi-religious society. Nevertheless, there are other compelling reasons to examine the idea of secession in era where imperialism is a powerful and potent force in the world. First, Kashmir did exercise it's right to self-determination in 1947, but since it was not in a format approved by the imperialist nations, there is a tendency to dismiss its validity. That encourages people like 33 year old Yasin Malik of Jammu & Kashmir Liberation Front (JKLF) in Kashmir to ask for a second referendum because he was born 19 years after the first one took place, which he therefore conveniently trashes. If one were to accept Yasin Malik's contention that the 1947 accession of Kashmir to Indian was invalid, then the whole concept of self-determination would be trivialized. The right of self-determination would then be reduced to a voting exercise conducted in an atmosphere of terror, repeated every 25-years or so, to meet the demands of a new generation, at whose whim the boundaries of a country could be redefined! It is not difficult to imagine the chaos in the world if such a recipe were to be applied worldwide.

Second, what happens to minority sentiments under a plebiscite? If 51% of the population of J&K decide to vote for a theocratic Pakistan or independant theocratic Kashmir, is it fair to the other 49% to be forced to join that state, in spite of feeling greatly threatened by that state? J&K's Hindus, Sikhs, Buddhists, Gujar and Bakarwal, and Shia people genuinely fear that they will be decimated in a Pakistani state - or a Taliban style independant state. Women fear they will lose the freedoms they have, and be forced to march backwards under a Taliban-style barbaric patriarchy. If a "majority" cannot live in a multi-religious secular India, is it fair to ask a sizable minority to live under a theocracy?

If the majority vote went for independence or accession to Pakistan, what guarantee is there that the minority interests would be safeguarded? Although a few groups like the JKLF speak of secularism, their leadership and membership is almost exclusively made up of Sunni Muslims. No Hindus, Buddhists or Sikhs comprise their membership.

Besides, the JKLF has had close ties to Pakistan's ISI - a close collaborator of the Taliban. This exposes the

JKLF as opportunists of the first rank who mask their retrograde ideology in meaningless statements about secularism and freedom. One should not be duped by JKLF's slogan of "Azadi." One needs to be reminded that in the early 1990s, the slogan: "Azadi Ka Matlab Kya? La Illah A Illal Allah" equated "Azadi" directly to Islamic rule! It should also be noted that advocates of "Azadi" have often attempted to rally their supporters behind pan-Islamic slogans that linked a future "Azad" Kashmir to such highly intolerant Islamic states as Saudi Arabia and Afghanistan. Regardless of what individual separatist leaders may say, there is a deep and unshakeable connection between the votaries of "Azadi" and Islamic fundamentalism.

Furthermore, the principle of self-determination must apply to all communities. If the Muslim majority in Kashmir province has a right to secede from India and form a separate state, the same right of secession must be extended to the Hindu minority to secede from that new state. If the Shias feel oppressed by the Sunnis, the same right must be extended to them too. The travesty of the demand by secessionists is that they want the freedom to secede, exclusively for themselves. They want freedom to deny others their freedom! As a partial solution, some may suggest a region-wise plebiscite, but a look at the map of the undivided state will show how impractical that would be. The Kashmir valley seperates the remote regions of Kargil and Ladakh to Jammu and the rest of India. The life-line for the mountains of Kargil and Ladakh winds through the Kashmir valley.

To allow the Kashmir valley to secede would destroy the lives of the people of Ladakh and Kargil. And what is worse, it could leave the Kashmir region itself divided into a patchwork of geographically disconnected principalities. By losing their seasonal mobility which could threaten their livelihood, the nomadic Gujar and Bakarwal people would be particularly affected by any such partition of Kashmir.

Thirdly, it should be noted that the demand for self-determination leading to secession has usually been advanced by an opressed people. Are the Kashmiri people oppressed? In 1947, J&K was at the bottom of the economic ladder in India. In 1960-61 it ranked 11th among 16 states of India in per capita income; in 1971-72, 14th among 24 states. But with generous Central assistance it had improved its position by 1981-82 to number 7, surpassing industrial West Bengal, A.P., Karnataka and Tamil Nadu!.

Most of the income increase had taken place in large urban areas such as around Srinagar where the Index of Social Development (which includes literacy, health care, access to other social services, etc.) is the highest of the 14 districts in the state. Yet, separatist sentiment is the strongest in this region! What is even more striking is how Indian Kashmir is better off than Pakistan. Kashmir's literacy at 59% is much higher than Pakistan's 44%. In general, India's social indices are many notches ahead of Pakistan's. Even if Kashmir's indicators were no better than the Indian average, it would be much better off with India than with Pakistan. Per capita calorie intake in India is now higher and infant mortality is lower.

India has made greater strides in developing it's infrastructure—whether it be railways, telecommunications or mass-media. Indians are now more likely to have access to a telephone, color TV or cable TV connection. They are also less indebted to the international finance community. Per capita hard currency debt in Pakistan is more than double India's. India, being a secular state has given far more importance to scientific education and research.

For example, in Pakistan, 4500 out of 5000 Ph.D.s awarded after independence, were in Islamic studies - i.e. less than 500 were in the sciences. In India, 40,000 out of 75,000 Ph.D.s awarded were in the sciences, and only a fraction of the other 35,000 were in religious studies. This means that although India's population is about 6 times that of Pakistan's, it has produced more than 80 times as many Ph.D.s in the sciences as has Pakistan.

All things considered, the people of Jammu and Kashmir have far more opportunities in India than they would, if they seceded and joined with Pakistan.

Fourthly, and most importantly: How does one factor in the role of imperialism? In spite of the seemingly "neutral" US role in the recent Kargil conflict, the U.S. is unlikely to give up Pakistan as its choice weapon against a large and "unmanageable" India unless, of course, the latter is balkanized into "manageable" segments. In addition, the U.S. has a special interest in J&K region. It is strategically placed in Asia from where events in the many neighboring states can be monitored, and when necessary, an intervention conveniently initiated, and carried out.

For this reason the US prefers an independent state of J&K over which it can exercise easy control. If political conditions do not allow independence, the US would like to keep India and Pakistan in a continuing state of simmering hostilities over the "Kashmir-problem".

Pakistani rulers who danced to the tune of their British colonial masters prior to 1947, and since, to their imperialist masters have been more than happy to oblige. After all, India-baiting is the glue that Pakistan's elite have used to keep Pakistan together.

Recent events indicate a possible "warming up" of relations between India and the U.S. It is important that India remain on guard and that it not be lulled into believing in the benevolence of imperialism. The US may adopt different tactics from time to time, but these should not be confused with being friendly towards India. It should be kept in mind that the US did not ask Pakistan to withdraw from Kargil untill it had become clear that India had reversed Pakistan's military advantage.

Reports had begun to surface of Pakistani soldiers being desperate to retreat, and Pakistani officers ordering them to hold on to their posts, or risk being shot at if they retreated. Pakistan desperately needed a cease-fire at that point. Prior to that, India was kept under constant pressure not to cross the LOC - and to negotiate with Pakistan. Soon after Kargil, the US adopted a diplomatically hostile position towards India re. the downing of Pakistan's advanced spy plane after it had repeatedly encroached Indian territory and ignored prior warnings to desist.

It is also important to keep in mind US bullying of India on trade and economic matters. India has made several concessions in WTO but the US has not reciprocated in kind. Various economic and technological sanctions against India remain. None of this points to the US emerging as any genuine friend of the Indian nation.

In this unipolar world, fragmentation of third world

countries (that are not not allied with imperialism) only helps imperialism, more so now that the counterveiling force of the Soviet Union is absent. Fragmented nations are far more likely to be more deeply indebted to foreign banks, to accept foreign military bases, vote with the US and it's allies in the UN, and so on. They are also more likely to then suppress minorities within their borders, leading to new tensions and separatist tendencies.

Unlike Pakistan, a large secular and democratic country like India offers more opportunities for different communities to express dissent and gain influence. This is not to say that democracy in India is perfect, or free from all the problems that unequal distribution of wealth entails. However, considering that none of the separatists have a progressive (or more democratic) economic platform for J&K's people, the relative benefits of aligning with India assume significance.

Consider how India's current President hails from a historically oppressed community. Consider how Mayavati - a campaigner for the political aspirations of India's most downtrodden castes became the first woman to become the Chief Minister of India's most populous state. Consider how Mulayam Singh Yadav - a leader of India's oppressed peasant castes became Defence Minister in 1996.

Consider also, India's foreign policy. For most of its history, India has conducted a principled anti-imperialist foreign policy. Recently, it opposed the criminal bombing of Yugoslavia and it opposes the deathly sanctions on Iraq. Earlier, it had condemned the bombing of Sudan, and unlike Pakistan, it did not become a proxy for US imperialism in Afghanistan or anywhere else.

Pakistan, on the other hand, played a vicious role in destroying the democratic revolution in Afghanistan, and participated in the Gulf War and in the Balkans. So it is not surprising that in the case of Jammu & Kashmir, Pakistan should play a similiar role. As imperialism's proxy in South Asia - Pakistan - has been injecting the poison of the two-nation theory ever since it was created. Those in Kashmir who are afflicted by this poison are in a minority and have been holding the majority of the state's peoples hostage. One could argue that if they feel so suffocated and oppressed by the democracy and secularism that India offers, they could simply cross the Line of Control (LoC) into Pakistan-controlled Azad Kashmir and enjoy the sort of theocracy and intolerance they wish to impose on an unwilling population in India. But instead, they malign secular India at every opportunity, even though it is their own acts of violence and terror that have caused 20,000 civillian deaths and created 300,000 displaced people in the State.

The plebiscite and secession demand comes from a politically dominant and a vocal minority of Kashmiris and needs to be exposed for what it is. The overwhelming majority of the people of Jammu & Kashmir - 70- 80% - want to be part of a secular and democratic India and they are the ones who need our unqualified support to help defeat separatism and Pakistan's proxy war in Kashmir.

A Survey of Elections in Kashmir

The six-year term of the current Jammu and Kashmir Legislative Assembly expires in October 2002. The stage for the next elections had been set by Chief Minister, Dr.

Farooq Abdullah, who had announced that elections would be held 'very soon'. With India and Pakistan not able to find any solution to the Kashmir issue, elections to the Jammu and Kashmir Legislative Assembly has assumed significance, especially in the aftermath of the September 11 and December 13 events. The Hurriyat has refused to participate in the elections and has announced its own election commission to conduct elections.

1950 Elections

Elections to the first Constituent Assembly of the Jammu and Kashmir State were held on 15 October 1950 to frame a separate Constitution for the state. The J&K Constitution envisaged 100 seats for the Legislative Assembly, with 25 seats reserved for the people living in 'Pakistan occupied Kashmir'. Elections were conducted for only 75 seats.

1951 Elections

The first election to the J&K Legislative Assembly was held on 15 October 1951. The National Conference (NC) won all the 75 seats, out of which 73 were unopposed. It was unique in the history of elections.

1957 Elections

The second Legislative Assembly elections for Jammu and Kashmir were held on 24 February and 15 March 1957, and for Ladakh and Doda Assembly constituencies at the end of May. The NC contested with a manifesto based on 'Naya Kashmir'. It captured 68 out of 75 seats with 57.4 percent of votes polled in that election, whilst the Praja Parishad got 5 seats with 24.6 percent of votes; the Harijan Mandal got 6.0 percent of votes with 1 seat, and independent secured 9.5 percent of votes and 1 seat.

The opposition parties alleged that the 1957 elections were 'rigged' and demanded fresh elections. Parties like the Plebiscite Front and Democratic National Conference (Saraf group) had even boycotted the elections on the grounds that they were not fairly conducted.

1962 Elections

The third elections to the State Legislative Assembly were held on February 24 in Jammu and March 25 in Kashmir. The NC won 70 seats and secured 67.0 percent, Praja Parishad got 17.5 percent votes and won 3 seats, the independents won 2 seats with 7.4 percent of votes. The percentage of votes polled in the election was 72.8 percent.

In May 1965, the Jammu and Kashmir constitution was amended and the denomination of 'Prime Minister', and, 'Sadar-i-Riyast' were changed to Chief Minister and Governor respectively.

1967 Elections

In the 1967 general elections, the Indian National Congress won 61seats and secured 53.0 percent out of 58.8 percent votes polled. The National Conference got 8 seats with 17.1 percent votes, Jan Sangh 3 seats with 16.5 percent votes and independents 3 seats with 8.6 percent votes. The CPI contested 3 seats but did not win any. It got only 0.54 percent of the votes polled. The PSP (Praja Socialist Party) also fielded 3 candidates but all of them lost.

1972 Elections

The fifth State Legislative Assembly election was held in March 1972. The votes polled in the election were 66.3 percent. The Indian National Congress won 58 seats with 55.4 percent votes; the Bharatiya Janata Party 3 and got 9.8 percent votes; the Jamat-e-Islami won 5 with 7.2 percent votes, and independents got 9 seats with 26.8 percent votes.

In February 1975, Sheikh Abdullah of the National Conference formed a government after a gap of 22 years along with a breakup faction of the Congress comprising Mirza Mohd. Afzal Beg, Thakurdevi Dass and Sona Monarboo.

Later, in March 1977 Sheikh Abdullah lost a no-confidence motion against his government by the Congress. The state of Jammu and Kashmir then came under Governor's rule on 27 March 1977.

1977 Elections

The 1977 Kashmir elections were held after the rout of the Indira Congress at the hands of the Janata Party following the Emergency. The NC led by Sheikh Abdullah won 47 of the 76 seats in the Legislative Assembly securing 46.2 percent of votes. In that election 67.7 percent of votes were polled. The total seats in the assembly were increased by delimitation from 75 to 76.

The Indian National Congress won 11 seats with 16.9 percent of votes, Janata party won 13 with 23.7 percent of votes, Jamat-el-islami 1 seat with 3.6 percent of votes and Jan Sangh rebels got 4 seats with 9.5 percent of votes.

Sheikh Abdullah formed the government and extended the life of the Assembly by one-year to six years by amending the Jammu and Kashmir State Constitution. In September 1982, Dr. Farooq Abdullah became the Chief Minister after the death of his father, Sheikh Abdullah.

1983 Elections

Elections were held in March 1983, in which the NC led by Dr. Farooq Abdullah came to power after winning a majority with 46 seats. It secured 47.3 percent votes out of 73.2 percent total votes polled. The Congress won 26 seats bagging 30.3 percent votes, Panthers Party (Bhim Singh) and the People's Conference (Abdul Ghani Lone) won one seat each with 4.6 percent of votes polled, the remaining 2 seats being won by independents who got 5.1 percent of votes.

Within one year of its rule, the NC split. Ghulam Mohd. Shah of the break way section of the NC came to power in July 1984, being supported by the Congress, and continued till March 1986.

In March 1986 the J&K Legislative Assembly was placed under suspended animation and the Governor assumed all the legislative and executive powers. Subsequently the state came under President's rule in September 1986; the Assembly was finally dismissed on 7 November 1986.

1987 Elections

Elections were held in March 1987, in which the Congress and the NC formed an alliance. The coalition parties swept the polls winning 63 seats in which the National Conference got 32.99 percent and Congress (I) 20.2 percent of votes. The BJP won 2 seats, Muslim Front Party (MUFP) 4 and independents won 4 seats. Elections for Bhadrawah, Leh and Kargil were held in June that year, which were also won by the Congress-NC alliance. Dr. Farooq Abdullah became the Chief Minister.

In January 1990 the Jammu and Kashmir State came under the Governor's rule again. The Assembly was placed under suspended animation and subsequently dissolved on 19 February 1990. The State remained under President's rule from July 1990 to 1996.

1996 Elections

In mid 1995, the Government of India recommended an early election in Jammu and Kashmir to the Election Commission. However, in November 1995, the three member Election Commission unanimously rejected the government's recommendations as it felt that conditions in the State were not conducive for holding them.

Later, in 1996, elections were held for 87 Legislative Assembly seats after an upward revision of the constituencies from 76 to 87. The Jammu region has 37 Assembly seats against 46 for the Kashmir valley and 4 for Ladakh. The polling percentage was 53.92 percent.

The NC contested in 81 seats and won 57 securing 34.7 percent. The BJP won 8 and got 12.1 percent of votes;

the Congress 7 and secured 20.0 percent of votes; Congress (Tiwari) 1 with 0.7 percent of votes; Janata Dal 5 seats and 10.8 percent of votes; Bahujan Samaj Party 4 and 6.4 percent of votes; Jammu and Kashmir Panthers Party with 2.25 percent of votes and 1 seat; Jammu and Kashmir Awami League 1 seat and 2.4 percent of votes, independents 2 seats with 9.3 percent of votes.

Demands for Autonomy

The demands of the Muslims of the Kashmir valley for independence as distinct from the populace of Jammu and Kashmir (J&K) has become a feature of the scene. The external aid and prompting for this demand by Pakistan and a couple if Middle East countries known. However, the demand for autonomy and reversal to the pre-1952 status, increasingly resurrected J &K. These protagonists have enlisted the support of the members of the liberal fraternity in New Delhi, including those in academia. Their argument is that conceding autonomy to J & K would neutralize the demands for Kashmir independence and reinforce India's stand that Kashmir is an internal issue.

The arguments are rather simplistic and have no relevance to ground realities. The chief argument against the autonomy demand made out by the State Autonomy Committee is that it is not supported by the Jammu and Ladakh regions. Besides there are historical, legal, political and social factors which militate against the special status sought for J & K .

Historically, the following factors need to be recollected

1. The J & K state's accession to India in 1947 was no different from that by other princely states of India.

2. The Instrument of Accession signed by Maharaja Hari Singh was neither under duress nor did it incorporate any terms for according special status to J & K.

3. Accession to India was made by the Maharaja on the lapse of paramountcy. This was not to be determined or dictated by the population of the state with riders.

4. If Sikkim, which did enjoy special treaty rights with British India, was incorporated into the Indian Union like any other state there is no justification for any special status or autonomy for J & K.

Constitutional and legal factors also militate against demands for autonomy and special status. The following points cannot be disregarded:

1. The heading of Article 370 of the Constitution reads "Temporary Provisions with Respect to the State of Jammu and Kashmir." The provisions were not intended to be permanent. Article 371 (A to H) in respect of North Eastern Status, are classified under Gujarat, Andhra etc. The authors of the Constitution envisioned the full integration of J & K into the Indian Union like other states; hence the use of the term 'temporary' i.e. till normalcy was restored.

2. The unanimously passed Special Resolution of the Parliament on J & K (including PoK) final and non-negotiable. Implicit in this Resolution is the fact that J & K is an integral part of the Indian Union, with no claims to special status or autonomy.

The socio-political factors that cannot be over-looked are:

1. J & K state is not just the Kashmir Valley. Nor is the Valley representative of the entire state. The demands for an autonomous J & K State or even independence emerges from the Valley and that too from a small section. It is not supported by the entire state.

2. The demands for autonomy are made by the Valley Muslims. No such demands are echoed by either the Shia Muslim of Ladakh or the Muslims of the Jammu region.

The ruling political elite was not oblivious of the above factors, and in a wily and mischievous bid sought to neutralise them through the Regional Autonomy Committee report to divide the state into eight regions on communal ethno-religious lines—a formulation more divisive then even the two nation formulation of the Muslim League for the partition of India. It amounts to a Muslim communalisation of the J & K state to neutralise the voice of the larger regions of Jammu and Ladakh.

Surely the liberal fraternity in New Delhi could not be blind to the implications of such moves. The security aspects are evident and do not require pointing out up.

The situation in J & K today reveals the stark reality that it is neither insurgency nor militancy as there is limited indigenous involvement. What exists there is nothing short of a state of war being waged by Pakistan by using Islamic fundamentalist mercenaries to undo the accession of J & K State to the Indian Union. Since the accession is final and non-negotiable no space exists politically or constitutionally for discussion of autonomy or special status for J & K.

The call for autonomy demands dispassionate study to place it in correct perspective. Since April 1999, the Abdullah administration has made the issue part of its Kashmiri political agenda. Farooq had set the autonomy-ball rolling, due to popular disillusionment with militancy in the valley, hoping the National Conference could reap a rich electoral harvest. He announced the formation of a 9 member State Autonomy Panel headed by Dr. Karan Singh on 29 November 1996.

A Regional Autonomy Committee, was set up to recommend measures for decentralisation of power, to be headed by Mr. Balraj Puri. The Panel was supposed to submit its report within six months, from the start, it was afflicted controversies.

On 31 July 1997, Dr. Karan Singh resigned and was replaced by Mr.Mohinuddin Shah. Again, in December 1998, Balraj Puri tabled an RAC report without the express approval of other RAC members, which resulted in his removal. On 13 April 1999, Dr. Farooq Abdullah tabled the reports of both the SAC and RAC in the State Legislative Assembly.

The central argument of the SAC was return to the pre-1952 position and restoration of Article 370 to its original 1950 position, as a 'special' and not a 'temporary' measure. This meant that, apart from defence, external affairs and communications, other matters will to be left to the State for sovereign legislation and execution.

The RAC report recommends the division of the three regions (Ladakh, Kashmir and Jammu) into eight autonomous units on ethnic-religious lines. The Ladakh region is to be divided into Buddhist Leh and Muslim Kargil; the Kashmir region into three units: Kamraz, Nundabad and Maraz; and the Jammu region into three units: Hindu majority Jammu, Muslim majority Doda and Pir Panjal.

The recommendations of the SAC have been crticised by many commentators for its seemingly defiant tone, holding to be anti-national and a potential tinderbox that could rend asunder the monolith of Indian Union.

The Central Minister for Civil Aviation, Mr. Chamanlal Gupta, who hails from the State, has ridiculed this proposition and says the demand is not viable economically 'as the state's total revenue earnings was Rs.600 crore whereas the salary bill alone amounts to Rs 2400 crore'. He claimed that the state already enjoys unfettered powers under Article 370 and it was not wise to grant more autonomy.

The recommendations of the RAC for division of the State into eight administrative units has drawn flak from commentators. Many have criticised the principle of ethnic-religious divisions and said that it would introduce the two-nation theory by the back door. Leading the argument, Balraj Puri argues that the SAC report seeks to remove checks on the powers of the state government, lest it wriggles out of its commitment to regional autonomy.

He disclosed that he had recommended regional authority with executive, legislative and taxation powers under the heads of political autonomy, cultural autonomy and economic autonomy. He held that the state government, instead of considering the report, proposed the division of Jammu and Ladakh on communal basis and a Panchayati Raj Act under which all institutions would be dominated by nominees of the government. However, the RAC has mentioned that the Districts

Councils could replace the Regional Councils. These arguments have their own logic and rationale. The demand for autonomy has been treated, the so-called Unitarians as a divisive ploy. This passion for unity has played havoc with the universal principle of genuine federalised autonomy.

However, following the Kargil conflict when Kashmir-centric nationalism is running high, the opposition to the Kashmiri demand for autonomy is very likely to be misconstrued as anti-national. Hence the Abdullah government seems poised for troubled times ahead, but opposition from the Centre to his demand might keep him politically alive as an alternative secular political force in the valley. In any case, Farooq will have to reconcile the aspirations of the Jammuites for genuine regional autonomy.The disproportionate influence that Jammu enjoys with Central government has always acted against the Abdullahs in the valley. It is time that the Farooq administration shed its valley-mindedness. Otherwise, his National Conference may well be swept out of the valley by the Hurriyat. Of late, they are being projected by many moderate commentators as an alternative worth experimenting with in Kashmir.

Kashmir Elections: Current Scenario

Farooq Abdullah, India's chief minister of Kashmir, announced June 18 that assembly elections in Indian-controlled Jammu and Kashmir would be held in October, with the new government taking power by Oct. 14. From New Delhi's point of view, the election is a crucial test of the Pakistani government's commitment and ability to control militants in Pakistan-controlled

Kashmir. Indian officials realize that Islamabad couldn't restrain the militants even if it wanted to. But New Delhi wants and needs to clearly show the rest of the world, particularly the United States, that Pakistan is an irresponsible neighbor and therefore an untrustworthy ally in the global war against terrorism.

In late May Indian media cited unnamed military officials as saying New Delhi would hold off on attacking Pakistan if Islamabad would ensure that Kashmiri militants would not interfere with the October election in Jammu and Kashmir. The military later called the report speculation. In either case, New Delhi will not draw down its troop levels along the Line of Control in Kashmir or the rest of the border with Pakistan until after October due to the possibility of more militant attacks in the run up to the election. This will keep India in a position to strike into Pakistan or Pakistan-controlled Kashmir if the situation deteriorates rapidly. And there are already signs that Pakistani-based militants are preparing to disrupt the polls. Indian forces June 18 killed a Hizbul Mujahideen militant in south Kashmir, who in addition to weapons and communication gear was carrying "stockpiles of anti-election campaign materials," the Hindustan Times reported.

For Islamabad, the pre-election period is also of critical importance. International attention continues to focus on Pakistan as the emerging center of al Qaeda operations and activity. Pakistani President Pervez Musharraf is already under increasing domestic pressure for attempting to rein in Kashmiri militants and quell al Qaeda activities. This puts him in a tough position because if his campaign is successful, it will trigger a domestic backlash, but if it is unsuccessful, it will further weaken his foreign standing.

For New Delhi, then, the Jammu-Kashmir election is shaping up as a win-win situation, especially as the All Party Hurriyat Conference, a collection of Kashmiri nationalist and pro-Pakistani parties, appears set to boycott the poll due to the ongoing standoff between India and Pakistan. This would leave the door wide open for the pro-Indian parties participating in the election.

If India avoids the militant attacks and the polls go off without a hitch, then New Delhi proves to the world that the people of Kashmir support Indian control. If the elections are compromised by militant activity, however, New Delhi has a clear case against Pakistan and may turn the United States against its former ally, allowing India or Washington to take care of the militant problem with a military olution.

International observation

The immediate criticism against international observers would be the question of India's sovereignty and the lack of precedents. In the present global structure dominated by the IMF, World Bank and a host of transnational organizations, absolute sovereignty is a myth. The second issue – lack of precedents should be evaluated appreciating of what is happening in Kashmir at present and what is needed to restore the people's confidence in the State elections.

Empty jingoism and false national pride will not take India anywhere in getting the Kashmiris back into the national fold. An allied fear is that international observers would increase the demand for international mediation to resolve the crisis in Kashmir. Apropos during the Kargil War, India was not averse to bring people from outside to see what has been happening inside Kashmir. The same logic could be extended to elections.

Many countries today are not averse to conducting elections under international observation. The role of international observers in the recently conducted national elections in Bangladesh created a positive reaction towards elections both inside and outside the country. Besides Bangladesh, Nepal and Sri Lanka also had international observers during the last elections. Today even countries like Russia are not averse to international observation of elections to their national legislatures but also their local bodies. There is no need for India to let international observers conduct elections, but India would have nothing to lose by asking an international team to observe the elections.

An international team of observers could be either voluntary or selected. Voluntary in the sense that India could issue an open invitation to the international community to come and observe the elections. Or India could ask specific countries, organizations and the media to come and observe them. Or a team could be invited under the auspices of the United Nations. There is also the Asian Network for Free Elections (ANFREL), a Bangkok-based regional network for monitoring elections in Asia. It should be emphasized that India, had sent its own observers to a number of countries in the past.

Any such international observation should not be limited only to polling. It should be expanded to include the entire election process. The international team should observe from the date of nomination to campaigning to the announcement of results. This would have many advantages especially in Jammu and Kashmir.

First, the entire international community would come to know, how free and fair the elections have been. This would ward off any unnecessary criticism about state rigging. Secondly, it would also place India, the biggest democracy in the world, on a moral high ground. It should be remembered that our election process, despite the Bihar and UP exceptions have always been wondered. Allowing international observers would be an additional credit.

Thirdly, any such international observation adversely affect the anti-election organizations. The world community especially will understand who is for democracy and who is against within Kashmir. It would also understand how anti-election organizations like the APHC and the militants hold the Kashmiris under threat not to vote. An international observation of this phenemenon, is sure to increase pressure on the militants and their mentors across the borders. Even if they do not believe in democracy, they do not have any right to prevent others from practicing it. The presence of international observers, is sure to put the anti-elections groups on the back-foot.

Fourthly, it would increase the credibility of the election process both inside and outside the state. While those who are wavering on whether to vote or not due to the credibility factor, are sure to vote, this would create an impact on those who have made up their minds not to vote. Either way, it would increase the percentage of votes polled.

International observation of election process would increase the credibility of elections and would strengthen the democratic process in the state. The case for international observation has been argued earlier.

A number of non-governmental and human rights organizations acceptable to the Kashmiris and the Indian government could also be involved in the election process. These organizations or human rights activists could be given observer status and provided access by the Election Commission of India. If the government is averse to involving human rights organizations, individuals of high reputation at the state and national levels could be asked to observe the elections.

There is a widespread belief that the NC would involve in rigging and unfair practices in the forthcoming elections; hence, it is better to have President's rule proclaimed in the State and elections conducted thereafter. The Union government should reach an understanding with the NC on this issue and conduct the lections under the President's rule. Though it would be the same Election Commission that would be conducting the elections, whether under President's rule or otherwise, psychologically it would remove fears about rigging. During the last elections, the security forces compelled people to vote. The unofficial argument of the government was that the security forces only asked people to vote, since they were threatened by the militants not to vote. Whether there is logic in this argument or not, this led to criticism by the Kashmiris that they were forced to vote.

One can understand the government's zeal to produce a better turnout, as that would indicate the return of normalcy in the state and rejection of militancy.

The government should avoid this during the forthcoming elections. What is necessary at this juncture for the future of Kashmir is to increase the people's faith in the electoral process. It is better to have a low voter turnout, which would be credible, than forcing its increase, giving room to question the credibility of the entire process.

It is also important for the security forces to be alert and prevent militant attacks that would have serious political implications. As in the past, the militants are likely to carry out attacks on the minority communities, especially the Pandits and Sikhs. The objective would be to communally polarize society and keep the minority community away from the polls. It should be remembered that after the Wandhama massacre in 1998, before the parliamentary elections, the pandits threatened to boycott the elections. The militants could pursue the same strategy in the forthcoming elections; hence, it is essential to provide extra security to select villages where the minorities may be the targets.

The militants are also sure to target those who are contesting. They should be provided greater security along with those leaders who would be potential targets. The assassination of Abdul Ghani Lone was aimed to derail any effective role that he would play in the forthcoming elections and it was criminal negligence on the part of the state police to provide such inadequate security to him and let his assassins get away. During the recent tensions between India and Pakistan, India has increased the level of its troops along the border. It is better to keep this build up intact, till the elections are over in Jammu and Kashmir.

Omar Abdullah, Farooq Abdullah's son was unanimously elected as the President of the National Conference (NC) in Srinagar at a grand conference on 23 June 2002. It is essential to analyse the change of guard as it has implications for Kashmir politics in general and the forthcoming elections in particular.

Farooq has openly announced that Omar would be leading the National Conference in the forthcoming elections and would be its Chief Ministerial candidate. The unanimous election of Omar Abdullah clearly shows that the NC stands united, and there is no internal division in the party. It is very essential for the National Conference, Kashmir and India, for that matter, that the NC fights the forthcoming elections united. The NC is the only party that has representation in the present State Legislative Assembly from all the three major regions of the State – Jammu, Kashmir and Ladakh. In the forthcoming elections, only the NC would be in a position to win seats from the three regions. Given the attempts to mobilize society by the Hindu Right and the militants on a communal basis, it is necessary for Jammu and Kashmir to have a party acceptable to all three regions, or at least to have cadres at grassroots level. Other than the NC no other party can boast of this factor, which is why it is important for the NC to fight the elections united. It should be remembered that when Farooq succeeded the great Sheikh, there was a split within the NC, thanks to the Congress! And the NC split had its implications in the Abdullah family, as their opponent happened to be GM Shah, Sheik Abdullah's son in law.

Secondly, the change in the NC leadership and the Chief Minister augurs well for both the NC and Kashmir politics, as Farooq Abdullah stands alienated today due to his inefficiency and bad governance. Both the Kashmiris and his party cadres have been looking for a change and the selection of Omar would win the support of the people and NC cadres who had lost faith in Farooq. Omar is considered a clean and honest politician; besides, he is young. This image would certainly be a positive factor in the forthcoming elections. Omar is also probably the only leader inside and outside the NC, who will be the most acceptable leader in all three regions of the state.

Thirdly, the election of Omar has also paved the way within the NC to project many young faces, who are the offspring of the old NC leadership. If this move materializes, there would be several young faces within the NC. There is some criticism, however, against Omar Abdullah. Since he was brought up outside the state, he cannot speak Kashmiri. Critics argue that he will not be acceptable to the local population. Besides the language factor, he is also seen as an outsider. However, it is doubtful, if these factors would work against Omar.

From the limited interactions that Omar has had with his people, it appears that he would be received well. His ascendancy has also been criticized in terms of "dynastic democracy" which would destroy the "grass-roots democracy." What Kashmir needs is a fresh face that is acceptable to all the regions and it does not really matter whether he or she belongs to a dynasty. Some of the most corrupt and undemocratic leaders in India, have reached the top in a "democratic" way and do not belong to any dynasty; Laloo Prasad Yadav, Jayalalitha are examples but the list will extend endlessly! When Omar was in Sanawar, he loved acting and took part in a number of plays. One hopes he fits the Kashmir stage. The All Party Hurriyat Conference (APHC) ever since its formation in 1993, has boycotted all the elections held in the state, despite calling itself as the "sole and genuine representative" of the people in the state. With elections for the Jammu and Kashmir state Legislative Assembly expected by the end of this year, successful conducting of elections depends on the participation of the Hurriyat. While many believed that there would be a divide amongst the APHC and a section would participate in the elections, this chance seems to have been lost with the assassination of Abdul Ghani Lone.

The APHC, an amalgam of more than 20 parties and groups, has never been uniform in its reasoning for not participating in elections. Three groups could be identified within the APHC on the issue of participating in elections. Syed Ali Geelani, who was recently arrested by the Indian government, leads the first group. He is totally against any elections and wants Kashmir to accede to Pakistan. Inside the APHC a sizeable percentage supports Geelani's views. Some of the former militant leaders who are now associated with the APHC also support Geelani. Moderate leaders such as Prof Abdul Ghani Bhat and Mirwaiz Omar lead the second group. This group is willing to participate in elections, but with certain conditions.

The two major conditions are – India should agree that Kashmir is a disputed territory and the elections should be held not by the government of India, but under the auspices of the UN. Abdul Ghani Lone, who was assassinated recently, led the third group. It is believed that this group was having a dialogue with the Union government and was willing to participate in the elections, if they would be held in a free and fair manner.

The APHC boycotted the 1996 elections to the State Legislative Assembly. The reason, as explained by Prof. Abdul Ghani Bhat in April 1996, was that the Hurriyat "considers election process as a gamble, which will most probably shed the blood of the people of Jammu and Kashmir." The Hurriyat considered elections as a "game plan, which is aimed at dividing the people of Kashmir with an ulterior motive to break us."

The Hurriyat also called for a total strike during the parliamentary election in May 1996 and even launched a door-to-door campaign. The Hurriyat also boycotted the 1998 parliamentary elections due to the same reasons.

The participation of the APHC in the forthcoming elections is doubtful, especially after the assassination of the Abdul Ghani Lone. The first and foremost reason is that the APHC depends on Pakistan for its ideological and political survival and it would be difficult to take any decision against the wishes of its mentor across the border. Pakistan will endeavour to never let India conduct any elections inside Kashmir in which there is participation. The militant groups led by the Jihad Council are also against the elections. None of the present leaders of the APHC have the courage to contest elections against the wishes of the militants, especially after the assassination of Lone.

The fear of losing or not forming the next government would be another reason for the APHC to keep away from the elections. Despite the APHC's self-professed statement of being the genuine representative of the Kashmiris, this statement has never been tested.

The APHC is well aware of this fact and would think twice before participating in elections, as any adverse vote would tarnish its credibility inside Kashmir. Some of the leaders of the APHC, based on their past experiences, genuinely believe that elections held by the Indian government would not be free and fair. Hence it would be better to keep away from them. This section also believes in elections being conducted under the auspices of the United Nations.

Farooq Abdullah, the Chief Minister of Jammu and Kashmir has promised elections to the State Legislative Assembly this October. Whereas parties such as the National Conference, BJP, Congress and other minor parties are sure to participate, others have announced they would boycott. One major complaint of the parties that would boycott has been that the elections conducted by the Indian government were never free and fair in the past and would never be in the future also. They repeatedly quote the rigged 1987 elections as the main reason for their non-participation. How to make the elections free and fair in Kashmir and increase faith in electoral process is the question. Obviously elections cannot be held by a third party. One option is to invite an international team to observe the election process and Farooq Abdullah, has agreed to this idea.

The immediate criticism against international observers would be the question of India's sovereignty and the lack of precedents. In the present global structure dominated by the IMF, World Bank and a host of transnational organizations, absolute sovereignty is a myth. The second issue – lack of precedents should be evaluated appreciating of what is happening in Kashmir at present and what is needed to restore the people's confidence in the State elections. Empty jingoism and false national pride will not take India anywhere in getting the Kashmiris back into the national fold. An allied fear is that international observers would increase the demand for international mediation to resolve the crisis in Kashmir. Apropos during the Kargil War, India was not averse to bring people from outside to see what has been happening inside Kashmir. The same logic could be extended to elections.

Many countries today are not averse to conducting elections under international observation. The role of international observers in the recently conducted national elections in Bangladesh created a positive reaction towards elections both inside and outside the country. Besides Bangladesh, Nepal and Sri Lanka also had international observers during the last elections. Today even countries like Russia are not averse to international observation of elections to their national legislatures but also their local bodies. There is no need for India to let international observers conduct elections, but India would have nothing to lose by asking an international team to observe the elections.

An international team of observers could be either voluntary or selected. Voluntary in the sense that India could issue an open invitation to the international community to come and observe the elections. Or India could ask specific countries, organizations and the media to come and observe them. Or a team could be invited under the auspices of the United Nations. There is also the Asian Network for Free Elections (ANFREL), a Bangkok-based regional network for monitoring elections in Asia. It should be emphasized that India, had sent its own observers to a number of countries in the past.

Any such international observation should not be limited only to polling. It should be expanded to include the entire election process. The international team should observe from the date of nomination to campaigning to the announcement of results. This would have many advantages especially in Jammu and Kashmir.

First, the entire international community would come to know, how free and fair the elections have been. This would ward off any unnecessary criticism about state rigging. Secondly, it would also place India, the biggest democracy in the world, on a moral high ground. It should be remembered that our election process, despite the Bihar and UP exceptions have always been wondered. Allowing international observers would be an additional credit. Thirdly, any such international observation adversely affect the anti-election organizations. The world community especially will understand who is for democracy and who is against within Kashmir. It would also understand how anti-election organizations like the APHC and the militants hold the Kashmiris under threat not to vote. An international observation of this phenemenon, is sure to increase pressure on the militants and their mentors across the borders. Even if they do not believe in democracy, they do not have any right to prevent others from practicing it.

8

Indo-Pak Nuclear Rivalry

India and Pakistan, nuclear doctrines, perforce have to borrow from Western concepts, which could evolve in the 40 years of the Cold War. While India has unveiled a draft Indian Nuclear Doctrine in August 1999, Pakistan has yet to announce one, stating that they are in the process. However, enough printed material on the thinking of the Pakistan elite on the subject is available, especially of the Pakistani armed forces officers. A comparative analysis of the two nuclear doctrines is therefore possible. India's Draft Nuclear Doctrine has to be viewed as a "declaratory policy" giving out broad guidelines for the proposed development and use of its nuclear arsenal-existance and under development. Hence Indian domestic critism of its not spelling out "employment strategy" or "configuration of nuclear capability" or costing" are misplaced. These aspects will never be spelt out as intentions and capabilities are always "TOP SECRET." The major policy declarations made in the Draft Nuclear Doctrine are:

1. Fundamental purpose of Indian Nuclear Weapons is to deter the use of and threat of use of nuclear weapons by any a state or entity against and its forces.
2. India will not resort to use or threat of use of nuclear weapons against non-nuclear weapons state or those not aligned with nuclear weapon powers.
3. India will not be the first to initiate a nuclear strike.
4. India shall pursue for a credible minimum, deterrent. Any nuclear attack on India and its forces shall result in punitive retaliation with nuclear weapons.
5. Nuclear weapons shall be tightly controlled and released for use at the highest political level.
6. India's nuclear arsenal will be based on the triad concept i.e. land based ballistic missiles, sea based assets and air borne platforms.

Nuclear Doctrine of India lies in its 'declaratory policy' i.e. that India will employ nuclear weapons should operational considerations so dictate, but within the guidelines and framework spelt out. India's domestic debate cannot change this nor the prevalent Indian public mood would allow a debate on this, even, if the government changes. Proponents of Pakistan's nuclear doctrine point the following backdrop which should form the basis of enunciating the official Pakistani Nuclear Doctrine:

1. Pakistan's nuclear arsenal is India specific and designed to off-set India's conventional and nuclear weapons superiority.
2. Pakistan's nuclear deterrence against India will endure as long as it has enough nuclear war heads

and delivery systems to inflict a deterrent punishment. Should deterrence fail, Pakistan's conventional forces should be strong to prevent a nuclear weapons strike.

3. Pakistan should not be lured into an arms race, but she must develop a secure, second strike capability.

Pakistan's nuclear doctrine would therefore emerge as a hybrid mix incorporating various elements of NATO's nuclear strategies of "Mutually Assured destruction," Pakistani analysts oppose acceptance of any "Not First Use" pact with India as they feel that its acceptance would negate their deterrent capabilities against India. It is also being advocated that Pakistan should not sign it until such time enough fissile materials for Pakistan's requisite number of warheads in the India-specific context is stockpiled. In terms of command and of nuclear weapons, no clear recommendations are emerging in the Pak analyses on the subject.

The talk is of apex body centered on the Defense Committee of the Cabinet. In 1994, the former Pakistani Army Chief had talked of a "National Nuclear Command Authority" (NNCA) comprising the President PM and the Army and Air Force Chief's. In effect the de-facto control will lie with the Pak Army Chief and the collegium of Pak Army's nine Corps Commanders. Pakistan's nuclear weapon weapons are unlikely to be based on the "TRIAD" concept. Delivery system will essentially comprise of land-based ballistic missiles and aircraft. The absence of the Naval Chief from the NNCA is a pointer in the direction. India's strategic perspective for its nuclear doctrine encompass a wider perspective than South Asia in keeping with its strategic potential. Pakistan's perspective as presently evident seems to be

India-specific. India swears by the "no-first-use" principle. Pakistan is averse to this.. It would not give any such guarantees, feeling that it negates its deterrence against India. India nuclear weapons system will be "TRIAD" based. Pakistan currently gets limited to land based and aircraft delivery systems. India and Pakistani doctrines, both emphasis a 'credible minimum deterrent. However, Pakistani capabilities in this direction may be questionable. India nuclear arsenal will be under civil political control. Pakistani's nuclear arsenal will under defacto control of the Army Chief. Nuclear Weaponisation of South Asia is a reality. It can neither be wished away nor rolled back even by external pressures. India has done well by being the first one to come out with its "declaratory policy."

Pakistan's inability to do so far indicates differences on opinions in its hierarchy and an existent mis-match between economic resources and development of a nuclear arsenal, comparatively. Irrespective of the rhetoric that may emerge in any forth coming official Pakistani nuclear doctrine-two dangers need to be noted by concerned international observes. Firstly, in South Asia, Pakistan may be more prone to press the nuclear button due a low nuclear threshold. Secondly, in the pursuit of nuclear arsenal symmetry with India, Pakistan could end up as a "failed state."

Stability between India and Pakistan relies on a complex interplay of many factors. There are many drivers working in tandem, and at times parallel, to each other: grand strategies, leadership capabilities, military strategy, awareness of each others' capabilities and powerful domestic public opinion. The two Southeast Asian neighbors have a history of bilateral conflict, hostile propaganda, and persisting tensions. The countries have different political systems, varying approaches to arms control regimes, and variable foreign policy preferences, and are now laboring with hitherto unsolved issues of nuclear weaponization and deployment, command and control, and military strategy.

But as the most recent crisis between India and Pakistan continues to de-escalate, questions arise whether the crisis was coercive diplomacy at its best or nuclear brinkmanship at its worst. India threatened to take military action but never initiated, it as it was testing the limits of coercive diplomacy - threatening to go to war but not actually going to war. The U.S. shuttle diplomacy managed to obtain an assurance from Pakistani President Gen. Perverz Musharraf that the infiltration into India by Muslim radicals had been ended permanently. That seemed sufficient for India in order to de-escalate. What were India's other options? Broadly speaking, there were three options for handling the Dec. 13, 2001, bombing of the Indian Parliament and the subsequent attacks in Jammu: diplomatic, economic and military.

India had initiated the diplomatic option in December when it reduced the staff at the High Commission, snapped the rail, road and air links. Stepping up its diplomatic offensive against Pakistan in the wake of the Jammu massacre, India asked Islamabad to withdraw its High Commissioner in New Delhi, Ashraf Jehangir Qazi. In addition, India repeatedly appealed to the Western world in general and the United States in particular to step up pressure on Pakistan. India also considered visa restrictions, consulate facilities and further reducing the High Commission staff. Growing impatient with the international coalition against terrorism and faced with an eager ruling alliance, the ruling National Democratic Alliance headed by the Bhartiya Janata Party considered a "go at it alone" approach. One of the few bilateral successes between the two countries has been the 1960 Indus Water Treaty. India has been scrupulous in keeping with the terms of this treaty. If India had chosen to abrogate it, the impact of the denial of water would have been quickly felt in Pakistan economically and socially. But abrogating the treaty could have caused a ripple effect, leaving the door open for Pakistan to walk out of the 1972 Simla Agreement, which emphasized bilateral settlement of disputes.

Economically, if India had taken certain measures to halt the illegal parallel trade that runs across border into Pakistan, the impact would be immediate and widespread. This would have required a major effort from the Indian states bordering Pakistan. India also had the choice of withdrawing the Most Favored Nation (MFN) status under the World Trade Organization regime. Incidentally, Pakistan has so far not given India reciprocal MFN status. Since there is very little official trade between India and Pakistan, this option was at best a blunt sword. Perhaps last in the line of options was the military option, which required India to clearly understand its politico-military objectives. High on the escalation ladder of the military options was the use of air power on terrorist training camps, which at best would have been few tents, with the trainee terrorists probably dispersed deep inside Pakistan.

The second option was the use of Indian Special Forces and dropping para-commandoes close to where these camps are. Most of these camps, like Oghi village, Ojheri camp, Para Chinar, Saidgali and Sargodha, have already shut down operations, however. A third option could have been a "hot pursuit": envisaging "salami slicing" of Pakistan administered Kashmir. India had to consider whether it was willing to occupy and retain territory, or whether closing down training camps would have been its only objective. Obviously, these camps can be quickly established elsewhere. A fourth option could have been an all out war involving regular armies.

All military options, of course, involved the risk of escalation to a nuclear level. The two countries should not lull themselves into thinking they can call each other's bluff. If India does cross the Line of Control or the international border and Pakistan decides that it is threatened and issues a warning, explicit or implicit, that it is contemplating its nuclear options (better used early enough to deter), what would be the Indian response? Would India stop the air strikes and/recall its troops, calling off the operation? Or would it go ahead and continue in the hope that Pakistan would not make good on its nuclear threats. An element of strategic uncertainty obtains here. It is precisely this kind of uncertainty that could breed misperceptions that lead to miscalculations.

As the most recent crisis was being defused, there were a spate of statements from both sides about nuclear weapons and their role in managing the crisis itself. India and Pakistan both choose to engage in the use of force short of overall armed conflict. There have been constant artillery exchanges. There were voices within India opining that "force can be stepped up in a calibrated manner to a limited war still short of full-scale general hostilities." Such statements, and the constant nuclear saber rattling particularly by Pakistan, that drew global attention, and the direct intervention of the United States.

The first direct outcome of this was the Jan. 12 speech by Musharraf pledging the cessation of support to terrorism. Later he promised to "permanently" end cross-border terrorism. The future of Pakistan is now balanced delicately on the execution of these promises. This verbal commitment should translate into closure of training camps and the communication infrastructure associated with infiltration, which could be monitored credibly by the United States, India, or both. The use of monitoring technology would go a long way toward restoring trust.

The results could mean some gains for both countries. First, war was never a positive sum game or to the advantage of either. Second, any outbreak of large-scale armed hostilities always carried the seeds of escalation. Third, Pakistan's Kashmir policy, just like its Afghan policy, has failed the country. Fourth, a war would have been detrimental to U.S. interests in the region as it would have destabilized the entire region. Once the issue of infiltration is settled, both countries will probably pull back the million troops that are on the border.

It appears that neither country wants an armed conflict for fear of uncontrolled escalation. In the meantime, each side seems determined to convince the other that it is not blustering, maintaining the threat of actual war. However "victorious" either side may feel from the standoff, one thing is clear: An unresolved Kashmir issue always carries the risk of another such crisis. Indians continue to point out that the United States has the authority to coerce Pakistan into making substantial internal policy changes. But the credibility of Washington's role as a peacemaker and the leader of the international coalition against terrorism seems, from an Indian viewpoint, to have been compromised by its inability to stop the terrorist infiltrations into India after the attack on the parliament. And some charge that now Pakistan realizes that it can get away with testing India's patience at a threshold higher than ever before.

Where does this leave India? After the present standoff, India should realize that a military buildup coupled with far-reaching political demands does not work. The next time around, India must exercise better judgment about the probability of various consequences, including its own ability to execute a threatened course of action. In crisis transparency measures aimed at instilling confidence, increasing credibility, avoiding miscommunication-that may lead to misperception and misinterpretation-and making clear policy statements are needed rather than nuclear saber rattling.

The blow-hot blow-cold approach of Indian leaders on the possibility of a nuclear war with Pakistan has baffled many in the world. The only clue to the shape of things to come lies in the careful effort to sensitize and prepare the elite as well as the general population for not only nuclear but also chemical and biological warfare, though it is commonly believed that India would be able to obliterate Pakistan without leaving it with the capacity for even a second strike. Some reports say that the Indian army has fixed the date for the Armageddon at mid-June.

But first the seeming confusion in the Indian leadership, the latest example being the offer of joint India-Pakistan patrolling of the Line of Control (LoC) that separates the Indian and Pakistan-administered sections of Kashmir. The offer for joint patrolling, which would require a high degree of mutual trust and cordiality, was made by Indian Prime Minister Atal Bihari Vajpayee during an Asian summit conference in

Almaty, the capital of Kazakhstan, where he did not even look at the president of Pakistan, General Pervez Musharraf, even while posing for pictures with him.

Soon after the prime minister's offer, Defense Minister George Fernandes rubbished the proposal, calling it impractical, even before Pakistan could declare it unlikely to work. The PMO (Prime Minister's Office) repeated the proposal the next day. Pakistan felt that it was perhaps a serious proposal worth considering, but Fernandes again dismissed it.

This story is repeated day after day. If Vajpayee expresses hopes of a breakthrough, Home Minister Lal Krishan Advani issues a belligerent statement expressing disenchantment with Pakistan and the inevitability of war. And so on. No wonder, despite India's declared policy of no first use of nuclear weapons and maintaining a minimum credible deterrent, the world can't be blamed for not taking seriously New Delhi's professions of its peaceful intentions. In an editorial (June 4) titled "South Asia's hair trigger", for instance, the New York Times accused the Indian leadership of talking recklessly about potential nuclear exchanges and commented, "Unfortunately, India's political leaders have shown little responsibility or restraint."

But what explains this seeming confusion and contradiction in Indian policy formulations and professions of its leaders? Two factors are important. One, the very nature of the hydra-headed monster that is India's ruling Hindu fundamentalism bloc. Europe had one monster that could be identified - Adolf Hitler. In India there is the Sangh Parivar (literally the family of Hindu fundamentalists), that Booker Prize-winning novelist Arundhati Roy described recently as "a traveling extravaganza, a mobile symphonic orchestra". She continued, "The hydra-headed, many-armed Sangh Parivar - with the BJP [ruling Bharatiya Janata Party], the RSS [Rashtriya Swayamsevak Sangh], the VHP [Vishwa Hindu Parishad] and the Bajrang Dal [Hindu organizations], each playing a different instrument. Its utter genius lies in its apparent ability to be all things to all people at all times.

"The Parivar has an appropriate head for every occasion. An old versifier [Vajpayee] with rhetoric for every season. A rabble-rousing hardliner [Advani] for home affairs, a suave one [Jaswant Singh] for foreign affairs, a smooth, English-speaking lawyer [Law Minister Arun Jaitley] to handle TV debates, a cold-blooded creature [Narendra Modi] for a chief minister [Gujarat] and the Bajrang Dal and the VHP, grassroots workers in charge of the physical labor that goes into the business of genocide. Finally, this many-headed extravaganza has a lizard's tail which drops off when it's in trouble, and grows back again: a specious socialist dressed up as defense minister [Fernandes], who it sends on its damage-limitation missions - wars, cyclones, genocides. They trust him to press the right buttons, hit the right note. The Sangh Parivar speaks in as many tongues as a whole corsage of trishuls [tridents]."

The second factor in the apparent confusion among leaders is to keep the world bemused about the Parivar's real intentions for Pakistan or Kashmir or Indian Muslims and Christians. While a couple of leaders will incessantly talk about democracy, human rights, good-neighborliness and so on, some others do keep reminding the world about the Parivar's real objectives. It is another matter that the world listens only to what it likes to listen to. The world, for instance, has refused to listen to what Youth and Sports Minister Uma Bharti had to say in Leh, a town in the Ladakh region of Kashmir. To an audience comprising several media personalities and cabinet ministers, including Advani (a co-accused in the Babri mosque demolition case), she reiterated (June 1) the Sangh ambition of unfurling the Indian tricolor in every Pakistani town and thus fulfilling the dream of "Akhand Bharat" (Indivisible India). If tomorrow Pakistan is vaporized and captured, the Sangh Parivar will be justified in saying, "We told you so" and the world would be just being hypocritical in expressing shock and disbelief. This would be merely a repetition of the world expressing hypocritical concern over the recent anti-Muslim genocide in Gujarat. The Sangh Parivar has never concealed its objective of cleansing India's pavitra bhoomi (sacred land) of rakshasas and malechhas (devils and demons - Muslims and Christians) who have their holy shrines and religious attachments outside India. The flurry of diplomatic activity and repeated travel advisories and orders issued by US, British, German, Australian and other governments to their citizens to leave South Asia is perhaps an indication that the world knows the Armageddon is not too far off. India's armed forces have asked New Delhi permission to carry out strikes against terrorist camps in Pakistan-occupied Kashmir (PoK) in mid-June, according to a report in the Daily Telegraph, London.

The report said Indian forces would adopt the pattern of the US attack on Afghanistan in which air strikes would be followed by helicopter-borne commando raids. The report points out that India has been building up stocks of smart bombs and "other advanced ordnance" for its Mirage 2000H and MiG-27 warplanes.

Observers have noted that Israel's National Security Adviser Uzi Dayan was in New Delhi last week. Israel reportedly equipped India's Mirages with precision-guided missiles during the Kargil war in 1999.

The Telegraph report says that India's plan of attack would be to seize and hold bits of PoK. The Indian air force would execute standing plans to strike at 50 or 75 militant bases and targets such as the Karakoram highway connecting China and Pakistan. Most Indian defense officials expect the conflict to last about a week before the world forces a ceasefire. One officer is quoted as saying, "We will call Pakistan's nuclear bluff. [The nuclear factor] cannot deter us anymore."

It seems foolish, however, to think that India would attack terrorist bases in PoK and leave it for Pakistan to retaliate, most probably with tactical nuclear weapons (TNWs) first. (India believes Pakistan has acquired a number of TNWs - smaller versions of nuclear weapons with relatively low destructive capabilities and an impact radius confined to a limited area, as against conventional nuclear warheads, which can wipe out an entire city.) If India has to attack, it has to attack Pakistan's nuclear facilities and missile bases. If Israel is helping India, it would help it mainly to take out Pakistan's nuclear facility that it feels can some day become a threat for its own survival. It is not for nothing that in addition to the military exercise on the borders, the government is apparently gearing up for a long war. It is exercising a full-scale drill involving various ministries such as Petroleum, Civil Aviation, Railways, Civil Supplies, Health and others, besides directing the border states to be more vigilant. Government officials also supported the premier's aggressive posturing in recent days. "These statements are essential to prepare the countrymen at large, political parties and as a part of diplomatic offensive," they told the pro-establishment Pioneer newspaper.

Meanwhile, the Delhi government (New Delhi is feared to be one of Pakistan's favorite targets for a nuclear attack) is bracing itself for not only nuclear but also biological or chemical attack, reports the Hindustan Times. Delhi's Health Minister Dr A K Walia met experts on Tuesday to talk out a disaster-management plan to the in place in two weeks. A three-point action plan was mooted. It has been decided to appoint the Delhi Fire Service (DFS) as the coordinating agency with the Civil Defense and Delhi Police acting as backup. The DFS has placed orders with Germany for three Hazmat (hazardous material treatment) vans. Twelve Delhi government doctors were sent to the defense research center at Gwalior for special training to fight a chemical attack in the form of hydrogen cyanide and mustard gas, among others, that can kill a person within minutes.

News magazine India Today quoted Walia as saying, "We have 2,500 extra beds ready to be stationed at various hospitals and in makeshift outdoor hospitals if the need arises. Mobile X-ray units, ultrasound units and operation-theater equipment are being brought in. Also Delhi hospitals have been told to stock extra medicines for emergency purposes for up to six months." Another newspaper, the Asian Age, quotes Walia as saying that Delhi hospitals were not prepared for a nuclear war. Between 9 million and 12 million people would be expected to die in the short term after an attack, but the real problem would be with the many more millions waiting to die. The government has no plans to help victims. There are no bunkers, even for VIPs. Experts have been quoted as saying that radiation-free bunkers had been built hundreds of feet below the ground. However, to help victims of biological warfare in the form of cholera, plague, brochillosis, tularemia, dengue, smallpox, influenza, etc a committee has been asked to identify hospitals where victims of different agents can be rushed for specialized treatment. Rapid-response teams, with a microbiologist in command, will lift samples from the spot and civil- defense personnel will take the victims to the designated hospitals. The Delhi police will secure the area.

Last week, the Maharashtra state government, too, summoned an emergency meeting of top bureaucrats, police officers, armed personnel and nuclear scientists to discuss security measures in the event of a war. The government decided to start registering volunteers in case of emergency public rescue operations and also to appoint 600 wardens to lead them. Subways, underground shopping malls, parking lots and warehouses will be converted into anti-radiation zones. A war guide is under preparation and is to be distributed to concerned agencies and public offices. Deputy Chief Minister Chhagan Bhujbal told India Today, "It's a delicate situation where we have to make the public aware without creating panic." Doctors are also being trained to handle nuclear and chemical biological warfare ailments. But Princeton University's physicist Dr M V Ramana points out that hospitals and doctors would also be wiped out in a nuclear strike. Medical help would probably have to be rushed in from other states.

Can India come back from the brink without losing face? In theory it should not be difficult to do so, now that Pakistan has called for international patrolling of the LoC. Obviously Pakistan cannot have international forces patrolling the border and at the same time seek to encourage terrorist infiltration into Indian territory. But this is not necessarily the case, and the reason is not too difficult to see. India has a strategy to counter Pakistan-backed infiltration of terrorists; but it has no strategy to tackle the success of its strategies.

Success creates its own problems. If the world acknowledges that Pakistan has stopped its meddling in the Indian part of Kashmir; it will also demand that now India start a dialogue with Pakistan. India is a past master in holding dialogues, and it has no problem in that; but the world today demands meaningful dialogue, and that is of course a problem. India has nothing to offer to Pakistan; indeed, it doesn't even want to take the PoK that it has claims to, in the event that Pakistan were to offer it to India on a silver platter.

As Vajpayee said recently, Kashmir is an integral part of India and that is the end of the issue. Will the world that considers Kashmir disputed territory and which is pressuring Pakistan to stop its proxy war accept the proposition and leave it at that? Perhaps not. That is why the moment a statement came from the US that Pakistan appeared to have reduced infiltration, Advani felt constrained to demand the handing over of 20 suspects that it has been demanding from Pakistan. Now suppose Pakistan were to fulfill even this demand substantially, then what? New goalposts would have to be invented. But for how long? Deleting Pakistan from the map would be the easier option. What is to be done, then? Is there no way out for South Asia? Should the "unrestrained and utterly irresponsible nuke-rattling", in the words of academic Achin Vanayak, be allowed to go on? Has the civilized world done its duty by ordering its own citizens to pull out? Does it need to do no more?

Where strategic thinkers have failed, a novelist seems to have the answer. If the world listens to Salman Rushdie, South Asia can perhaps still be saved. He writes in the New York Times, "Pakistan is calling on the international community to intervene, but this call must be heard with caution. For half a century, Pakistan has sought to internationalize the Kashmiri dispute, while India has consistently described that effort as interference in its internal affairs. Both sides are locked into old language, old strategies and an old game of chicken that's currently playing itself out across the LoC. Like two aged wrestlers fighting on a cliff, India and Pakistan are locked together, rolling ever closer to the edge. "But their ancient hatred is no longer a matter only for them. The risk of a nuclear battle, however improbable, makes Kashmir everybody's problem. Right now it's the most dangerous place in the world. These pathetic old fighters must be pulled apart, and soon. Yes, that probably does mean intervention by the West, though Russia seems eager to help as well, which is useful.

"This should not, however, be the intervention that Pakistan wants. The point is not to restrain Indian 'aggression', but to make the world safer for us all. The situation can only be stabilized if India and Pakistan are both forced to back away, preferably to outside of Kashmir's historic, unpartitioned borders. This 'hands off Kashmir' solution will have to be externally imposed on the reluctant principals and will require that a large peacekeeping force be sent to the region to support Kashmir as an autonomous area. But who in the West wants that - it's just the old colonialist-imperialist power trip, isn't it? And who's supposed to pay for all this peacekeeping, anyway?

"The answers to those questions are also questions: What's the alternative? Do you have a better idea? Or shall we just stand back and keep our post-colonial, non-imperialist fingers crossed? Will it take mushroom clouds over Delhi and Islamabad to make us give up our ingrained prejudices and try something that might actually work? In the immortal words of the Spice Girls, 'Will this deja vu never end?'" Tough months lie ahead in troubled South Asia, especially for Pakistani President General Pervez Musharraf. He is caught between those within his team who are pushing for Pakistan to lend outright support to the Kashmiri military struggle, and the United States and world leaders who want him to stop cross-border incursions into Kashmir at all costs, especially as he has already given his word that he will do so. The sudden removal of Pakistan's ambassador to Washington, Maleha Lodhi, and foreign minister Abdul Sattar reflect the turmoil within the government, while there is also discontent among the top brass of the army over Pakistan's stance on Kashmir. Inamul Haq is the new foreign minister and Jehangir Asharaf Qazi the new ambassador to the US.

The army leadership is known to be very critical of the Pakistani Foreign Office. After September 11, Sattar and Lodhi briefed a joint meeting of the federal cabinet and the National Security Council as well as corps commanders separately to impress upon them that Pakistan's support of the US in its war against terror (and Afghanistan) would benefit the region. And they insisted that this policy would give Pakistan the upper hand in the region, especially with regard to Islamabad's position on Kashmir.

In the current military standoff, though, all of these pledges have meant nothing. US officials have linked the Kashmiri movement with al-Qaeda and they have placed heavy pressure on Musharraf to stop cross-border incursions, while they have not said a single word against Indian state suppression and atrocities in Indian-held Kashmir. India's diplomats, clearly, have won hands down and their Pakistan contemporaries have not even been able to muster support among the 56 members of the Organization of Islamic Conference (OIC). To add salt to the wound, Indian Prime Minister Atal Bihari Vajpayee has stated that "we won the war without firing a bullet". Not something that Pakistan's generals like to hear.

And on the domestic front, the political parties are making a mockery of Musharraf's Kashmir policy. Politicians such as Alliance for Restoration of Democracy (ARD) chief Nawabzada Nasarullah Khan; former premier and chairperson of the Pakistani People's Party, the exiled Benazir Bhutto; Qazi Hussain Ahmed, the leader of the largest Muslim party, Jamaat-e-Islami (JI); and Maulana Fazalurehman, chief of the Jamiat-i-Ulema-i-Islam, have made routine statements saying that Musharraf has sold out Kashmir. And sources say that the military leadership is keeping up the pressure on Musharraf, arguing that if Pakistan reverses its support for the militants in Kashmir in midstream, 12 years of the Kashmir struggle would go waste.

The sacking of the two top Foreign Office officials, presumably to appease hawkish elements, indicates that Musharraf is not going to change his tack on Kashmir entirely, and in coming days Kashmiri fighters will definitely carry out some big military actions and the situation will return to how it was before the easing of action a few weeks ago. And now, after a relatively long silence, Musharraf has started talking in the same tone he has used in the past when referring to the Kashmiri freedom struggle.

Musharraf has rejected suggestions that he has sold out Kashmir under US and Indian pressure, saying that he ordered a halt to the infiltration of militants for the same reason of "national interest" that he cited in ditching the Taliban in Afghanistan. "Absolutely not," he said in an interview with the UK-based Independent newspaper. "The cause of Kashmir must be resolved. Kashmir is a festering wound ... since partition; there is a United Nations Security Council resolution on Kashmir and we are demanding its implementation. We must resolve the Kashmir dispute, this is our stand even now." He said the conflict between India and Pakistan over Kashmir was "another Palestine in the making".

"I keep telling the United States and everyone: We must understand the dangers of this region. These dangers can only be averted if we resolve the Kashmir issue. We must do that. Otherwise, there is another Palestine here in the making," he said, adding, "Kashmir needs to be resolved. I also say it needs to be resolved in a peaceful manner. But if the other side does not want to resolve it, then we are stuck again."

Musharraf denied reports that Richard Armitage, the US deputy secretary of state, resorted to threats to pressure him to halt cross-border infiltration into Kashmir. In another interview to the US-based publication News Week he clarified that he had never promised the United States that he would stop incursions into Kashmir permanently. However, the US was quick to dismiss this claim.

A US spokesman asserted that the military ruler had given assurances to Armitage during his visit to Islamabad recently. "Deputy Secretary Armitage was given assurances by President Musharraf on June 6 that ending of infiltration across the Line of Control would be permanent," a US Embassy spokesman said in New Delhi.

Now, in Muzzafarabad (the capital of Pakistan-administered Kashmir), the leaders of the Kashmiri militant groups with their Islamic background as well as those Kashmiri leaders with a nationalist background have started hitting out at Musharraf. The chief of the Jammu Kashmir Liberation Front, Amanullah Khan, said Pakistani leaders had no right putting a ban on Kashmiris crossing the Line of Control that divides Kashmir as it was a divide that they had never accepted. He termed the latest Pakistani policies as stabbing the Kashmiri struggle in the back. Amanullah Khan is a nationalist Kashmiri leader who wants an independent Kashmir.

Similar sentiments were expressed by Syed Salahuddin, the chief of the United Jehad Council. He adheres to the Jamaat-i-Islami school of thought, a premier fundamentalist party that exists in India, Pakistan and both the Indian and Pakistani sections of Kashmir. Musharraf has shuffled the top ranks of the army leadership several times since September 11 to silence those opposed to his policies of siding with the US and ditching the Taliban, for example. This time, though, it will be much more difficult for him to change his position on Kashmir radically as, unlike in the past when the issues were largely related to fundamentalism, this is not the case with Kashmir - nationalism is involved.

India and Pakistan have been separate states for more than 50 years. But the fact that they are the same people divided by a border created in 1947 is continuously underscored when one examines the modalities of a number of policies that they have adopted throughout their existence as independent nations. These include their views of the superpower competition during the Cold War years, their decisions to become nuclear powers, their views of the United States' global war on terrorism, and, most important of all, implications of the war on terror for their respective positions on the obdurate Kashmir conflict. The strategic relations between the two South Asian neighbors have been anything but neighborly for most of their existence. During and after the Cold War years, but especially in the post-September 11 era, they conducted their antagonistic mutual relations on the basis of a zero-sum game, whereby they regarded gains made by one side vis-a-vis the United States as losses for the other.

The two South Asian nations fully comprehended what made the United States tick during the Cold War years. Then, the containment of global communism through alliance formation drove the engines of US foreign policy. Pakistan jumped on the US bandwagon by becoming a member of two such alliances in Asia - the Central Treaty Organization (CENTO) and the Southeast Asian Treaty Organization (SEATO). India opted for the Nonalignment Movement, and used it to disparage those military alliances, and Pakistan's membership in them.

Even though India remained supposedly a nonaligned state, it also signed a treaty of friendship with the former Soviet Union, apparently not at all concerned about the contradictions between its continued self-proclaimed status as a nonaligned country and its alliance with one of the major parties to the Cold War-related mega-conflict.

The two South Asian rivals were carrying out their own version of a regional Cold War. Pakistan viewed its alliance with the United States as a source of military assistance and even protection from any aggressive measures from India. Those aggressive tendencies from both sides raised their ugly head in the 1965 war involving Kashmir. As that war started, the United States - the supposed ally of Pakistan - immediately imposed a blockade of weapons supplies to Pakistan, while the Soviet Union continued to supply all sorts of weapons platforms to India under very generous financial agreements.

Pakistan never recovered from the disparity in conventional military strength that those policies of both superpowers created in the subcontinent. There prevails a view in the subcontinent that one of the variables that motivated Pakistan toward military action at that time was the information it received about the Soviet Union's then impending decision to become a major weapons supplier for India. The aggressive tendencies on the subcontinent became larger than life with the passage of time. When India signed that friendship treaty with the Soviet Union, it hoped to use it as a restraint against the United States and China, both of whom were viewed as friends of Pakistan. Indian premier Indira Gandhi might have been stunned at the so-called American "tilt" toward Pakistan when president Richard Nixon sent the USS Enterprise to the waters of the Bay of Bengal as a show of support for Pakistan during the East Pakistan crisis in 1971 that led to the formation of Bangladesh. A former Indian military officer narrated to me how scared the Indian top leadership became at the sight of that show of force. Within only three years of that incident, in 1974, India conducted its so-called "peaceful" nuclear explosion.

If one becomes skeptical of the linkages among that so-called US tilt of 1971, an earlier humiliating defeat of India at the hands of the Chinese in 1962, and that nuclear explosion, then one has to recall the statement of an Indian general in the aftermath of the Gulf War of 1991. The greatest lesson India learned, he is reported to have said, is "don't mess with the United States unless you possess nuclear weapons". On the US side, that statement has been recounted on a number of occasions, especially since India's nuclear tests of May 1998.

Pakistan behaved in exactly the same way. Its defeat in and the consequent loss of East Pakistan - which India euphemistically refers to as the "liberation" of Bangladesh - was the defining moment for its decision to acquire nuclear weapons of its own. Thus, India's "tit" of becoming a declared nuclear power in 1998 got a "tat" from Pakistan's own declaration along the same lines. But when the mandarins of India's foreign policy offered a "no first use" fig leaf, their Pakistani counterparts disparagingly rejected it. The two sides - the two people of the same origin - fully knew the ridiculous nature of India's offer of no first use to a country that had just acquired "strategic parity" with its neighbor. The most noteworthy irony was, of all the people in the world, the

Hindu fundamentalist Bharatiya Janata Party (BJP) was then at the helm in India. One also wonders whether by declaring itself a nuclear power in 1998 India trumped the "nuclear weapons states", or whether Pakistan trumped them all.

After becoming a declared nuclear power, Pakistan seems to have been following the perspective of former French president Charles de Gaulle on nuclear weapons. When critics berated its independent nuclear force, Force de Frappe, by saying that France would never be able to match the awesome nuclear arsenals of the two superpowers, de Gaulle in 1964 is reported to have stated, "It is obvious that the megatonnes which we could employ do not match the numbers which America and Russia could unleash.

But once a certain nuclear capacity is reached and in regard to our direct defense, the size of the respective arsenals does not have an absolute value." He went on to observe, "... since a man and a country can only die once, deterrence exists once one has the means to inflict mortal damage on a possible aggressor, the determination to use them and the confidence in one's ultimate decision". Even though the actual size of Pakistan's nuclear force is not publicly known, its leaders seem to have opted for smaller numbers of highly mobile land-based ballistic missiles. Given the current depressed nature of Pakistan's economy, that small force might be a reasonable deterrence option for now.

India, on the other hand, through its "draft" nuclear doctrine issued in 1999, proclaimed its intentions of developing a nuclear "triad". However, under the extant state of its research and development, that notion of a nuclear triad has to wait for at least a decade, if not more, before it becomes a reality. By announcing its intentions of having a nuclear triad, India had two external audiences in mind, the international community and China. To the former, India was signaling that it was ready to join the exclusive clubs of the United Nations Security Council's permanent five and the nuclear-weapons states. The same five countries - the United States, Russia, China, the United Kingdom and France - are members of both those clubs. To China, India signaled that the strategic competition between them was to acquire an entirely different framework and hue, whereby India would no longer be wary of China's strategic superiority in the nuclear realm.

But on this very point, the China-Pakistan nexus remains a major source of diversion and concern to leaders in New Delhi. Pakistan knows full well that, unlike India, it does not have realistic chances of becoming a great power. But it can stay in the competition by siding with China. That very reality is a major source of satisfaction for a relatively weaker Pakistan, and a constant irritation for India.

India has the immutable advantage of size over Pakistan; its economy seems to have acquired a steady rate of at least 5 percent annual growth. If this growth pattern is not halted by the still strong socialistic predilections of its senior leadership, which tends to get spasmodically nostalgic about the Fabian socialism that was the sine qua non of India's economic policies in previous decades, India might be well on its way of achieving the status of a great power that it deserves. India also has a very large pool of indigenous scientific knowledge, which is a vital requirement for any country to become a power of great substance. In fact, in this realm, India is considerably ahead of even China. But Pakistan must also know that it has the potential of catching up with India in all variables, except for its size. But come to think of it, size is not a vital condition for a country to become a great power. France and the UK, certainly, fill that bill, despite the disparity between their size and the size of the other three permanent five members. The greatest challenge is whether Pakistan can indeed convert its potentials into realities and become another rising power of South Asia.

The best example of how Pakistan and India use similarly competitive tactics to outbid each other is regarding transnational terrorism. When the United States was gearing up to carry out its military operations against the Taliban/al-Qaeda nexus in Afghanistan, India immediately attempted to seize the opportunity and offered its territory to carry out those operations. India also envisaged its own participation in those operations, especially against what it described as terrorist camps in Pakistan-administered Kashmir. It will be recalled that around the same time - that is, between October and December 2001 - there were public discussions inside the US on how safe the nuclear weapons in Pakistan really were, and whether al-Qaeda elements could gain access to them, or whether they might even use these weapons against the US. Thus, there has been wild speculation that the US Special Forces were practicing with Israeli forces at snatching Pakistan's nuclear weapons.

One can only speculate about what measures Pakistan took to safeguard its nuclear weapons from becoming part of legends of swashbuckling raids of the US-Israeli (or just the United States') Special Forces that posterity would see in future Hollywood movies. The issue of significance here is that in the pre-Operation

Enduring Freedom (the official name of the US military operation against Afghanistan) days, there was little doubt that India was champing at the bit to make a Nepal or even a Bangladesh out of Pakistan through a US-approved military operation.

Pakistan correctly read India's maneuvers and masterfully pulled a coup of its own by readily agreeing to join the United States in Operation Enduring Freedom. It is well nigh impossible for outsiders to comprehend the significance of that decision for Pakistan, for it is still suffering the deleterious consequences stemming from it. But perhaps the decision not to join the US would have been more detrimental, for the Bush administration would have readily lumped it in that infamous and highly contentious list of "rogue" or even "axis of evil" states. The decision to join America's war on terror might have created opportunities for Pakistan that, if they were properly exploited, would enable it to become a significant regional actor.

Finally, the way India and Pakistan exploited the war on terror regarding the Kashmir conflict also speaks volumes about the similar origin of their native talents. India knows that the opportunities stemming from the war are unique such that, if properly used, they might enable it to realize the cherished objective of converting the present Line of Control (LoC) in Kashmir into its permanent international border. Pakistan is fully aware of India's motives, and has done a very effective job of keeping the Kashmir dispute in the international limelight. Because the US has become involved in the Kashmir dispute in a significant way since the Kargil round of military clashes of 1999 between them, Pakistan wishes to see Washington become a party to the Indian-

Pakistan negotiations for a peaceful resolution of the Kashmir conflict, a la America's participation in the Palestine-Israeli peace process. India, on the contrary, does not want to see Washington acquire such a role for it is not interested in offering any territorial concessions to Pakistan in that dispute.

The Kashmir dispute might be the only international flash point in which one party has been totally intransigent about resolving it through territorial adjustments. But Pakistan has shown an equal amount of intransigence in remaining focused on resolving it. From the perspective of Pakistan, a promising development is that a number of US officials have made statements that the Kashmir dispute needs active negotiations and some sort of political solution. It will be interesting to see whether the United States' increased role in the "crisis management" aspect of the Kashmir conflict is also extended to its formal involvement in the "conflict resolution" aspects of it.

The ultimate question regarding the similarity of the Indian and Pakistani frames of reference is whether it enables them to resolve the Kashmir dispute peacefully, or whether, if left to their own predilections, they destroy each other through a nuclear exchange. Indian Prime Minister Atal Bihari Vajpayee stated on Monday that his country was "prepared for an atomic war ... but", he continued, "we were confident that our neighbor would not commit such an act of madness". Fortunately, the United States correctly read that eeriness emanating from the similarity of their orientations, and remained heavily engaged in order to avert a potential nuclear exchange. But how many more times can the United States or any other great power succeed in keeping them from blowing each other up? NRDC's nuclear experts think about the unthinkable, using state-of-the-art nuclear war simulation software to assess the crisis in South Asia. The months-long military standoff between India and Pakistan intensified several weeks ago when suspected Islamic militants killed more than 30 people at an Indian base in the disputed territory of Kashmir. As U.S. diplomatic pressure to avert war intensifies, Secretary of Defense Donald Rumsfeld is going to India and Pakistan this week to discuss with his South Asian counterparts the results of a classified Pentagon study that concludes that a nuclear war between these countries could result in 12 million deaths.

NRDC (Natural Resources Defense Council) has conducted its own analysis of the consequences of nuclear war in South Asia. Prior to this most recent crisis we calculated two nuclear scenarios. The first assumes 10 Hiroshima-sized explosions with no fallout; the second assumes 24 nuclear explosions with significant radioactive fallout. Below is a discussion of the two scenarios in detail and an exploration of several additional issues regarding nuclear war in South Asia.It is difficult to determine the actual size and composition of India's and Pakistan's nuclear arsenals, but NRDC estimates that both countries have a total of 50 to 75 weapons. Contrary to the conventional wisdom, we believe India has about 30 to 35 nuclear warheads, slightly fewer than Pakistan, which may have as many as 48.Both countries have fission weapons, similar to the early designs developed by the United States in the late 1940s and early 1950s. NRDC estimates their explosive yields are 5 to 25 kilotons (1 kiloton is equivalent to 1,000 tons of TNT). By comparison, the yield of the weapon the United States exploded over Hiroshima was 15 kilotons, while the bomb exploded over Nagasaki was 21 kilotons. According to a recent NRDC discussion with a senior Pakistani military official, Pakistan's main nuclear weapons are mounted on missiles. India's nuclear weapons are reportedly gravity bombs deployed on fighter aircraft.

NRDC's Nuclear Program initially developed the software used to calculate the consequences of a South Asian nuclear war to examine and analyze the U.S. nuclear war planning process. We combined Department of Energy and Department of Defense computer codes with meteorological and demographic data to model what would happen in various kinds of attacks using different types of weapons. For our first scenario we used casualty data from the Hiroshima bomb to estimate what would happen if bombs exploded over 10 large South Asian cities: five in India and five in Pakistan. (The results were published in "The Risks and Consequences of Nuclear War in South Asia," by NRDC physicist Matthew McKinzie and Princeton scientists Zia Mian, A. H. Nayyar and M. V. Ramana, a chapter in Smitu Kothari and Zia Mian (editors), "Out of the Nuclear Shadow" (Dehli: Lokayan and Rainbow Publishers, 2001).)

The 15-kiloton yield of the Hiroshima weapon is approximately the size of the weapons now in the Indian and Pakistani nuclear arsenals. The deaths and severe injuries experienced at Hiroshima were mainly a function of how far people were from ground zero. Other factors included whether people were in buildings or outdoors, the structural characteristics of the buildings themselves, and the age and health of the victims at the time of the attack. The closer to ground zero, the higher fatality rate. Further away there were fewer fatalities and larger numbers of injuries. The table below summarizes the first nuclear war scenario by superimposing the Hiroshima data onto five Indian and five Pakistan cities with densely concentrated populations.

As in the case of the bombs dropped on Hiroshima and Nagasaki, in this scenario the 10 bombs over Indian and Pakistani cities would be exploded in the air, which maximized blast damage and fire but creates no fallout. On August 6, 1945, the United States exploded an untested uranium-235 gun-assembly bomb, nicknamed "Little Boy," 1,900 feet above Hiroshima. The city was home to an estimated 350,000 people; about 140,000 died by the end of the year. Three days later, at 11:02 am, the United States exploded a plutonium implosion bomb nicknamed "Fat Man" 1,650 feet above Nagasaki. About 70,000 of the estimated 270,000 residents died by the end of the year.

Ten Hiroshima-size explosions over 10 major cities in India and Pakistan would kill as many as three to four times more people per bomb than in Japan because of the higher urban densities in Indian and Pakistani cities.In January, NRDC calculated the consequences of a much more severe nuclear exchange between India and Pakistan. It first appeared as a sidebar in the January 14, 2002, issue of Newsweek ("A Face-Off with Nuclear Stakes"). This scenario calculated the consequences of 24 nuclear explosions detonated on the ground—unlike the Hiroshima airburst—resulting in significant amounts of lethal radioactive fallout.

Exploding a nuclear bomb above the ground does not produce fallout. For example, the United States detonated "Little Boy" weapon above Hiroshima at an altitude of 1,900 feet. At this height, the radioactive particles produced in the explosion were small and light enough to rise into the upper atmosphere, where they were carried by the prevailing winds. Days to weeks later, after the radioactive bomb debris became less "hot," these tiny particles descended to earth as a measurable radioactive residue, but not at levels of contamination that would cause immediate radiation sickness or death.

Unfortunately, it is easier to fuse a nuclear weapon to detonate on impact than it is to detonate it in the air -- and that means fallout. If the nuclear explosion takes place at or near the surface of the earth, the nuclear fireball would gouge out material and mix it with the radioactive bomb debris, producing heavier radioactive particles. These heavier particles would begin to drift back to earth within minutes or hours after the explosion, producing potentially lethal levels of nuclear fallout out to tens or hundreds of kilometers from the ground zero. The precise levels depend on the explosive yield of the weapon and the prevailing winds.For the second scenario, we calculated the fallout patterns and casualties for a hypothetical nuclear exchange between India and Pakistan in which each country targeted major cities. We chose target cities throughout Pakistan and in northwestern India to take into account the limited range of Pakistani missiles or aircraft. The target cities, listed in the table below, include the capitals of Islamabad and New Dehli, and large cities, such as Karachi and Bombay. In this scenario, we assumed that a dozen, 25-kiloton warheads would be detonated as ground bursts in Pakistan and another dozen in India, producing substantial fallout.

The devastation that would result from fallout would exceed that of blast and fire. NRDC's second scenario would produce far more horrific results than the first scenario because there would be more weapons, higher yields, and extensive fallout. In some large cities, we assumed more than one bomb would be used.

NRDC calculated that 22.1 million people in India and Pakistan would be exposed to lethal radiation doses of 600 rem or more in the first two days after the attack. Another 8 million people would receive a radiation dose of 100 to 600 rem, causing severe radiation sickness and potentially death, especially for the very young, old or infirm. NRDC calculates that as many as 30 million people would be threatened by the fallout from the attack, roughly divided between the two countries.Besides fallout, blast and fire would cause substantial destruction within roughly a mile-and-a-half of the bomb craters. NRDC estimates that 8.1 million people live within this radius of destruction.Most Indians (99 percent of the population) and Pakistanis (93 percent of the population) would survive the second scenario. Their respective military forces would be still be intact to continue and even escalate the conflict.After India and Pakistan held nuclear tests in 1998, experts have debated whether their nuclear weapons contribute to stability in South Asia. Experts who argue that the nuclear standoff promotes stability have pointed to the U.S.-Soviet Union Cold War as an example of how deterrence ensures military restraint.

There are major differences between the Cold War and the current South Asian crisis. Unlike the U.S.-Soviet experience, these two countries have a deep-seated hatred of one another and have fought three wars since both countries became independent. At least part of the current crisis may be seen as Hindu nationalism versus

Muslim fundamentalism. A second difference is India and Pakistan's nuclear arsenals are much smaller than those of the United States and Russia. The U.S. and Russian arsenals truly represent the capability to destroy each other's society beyond recovery.

9

Future of Kashmir

Pakistan is determined to demonstrate to the world that Kashmir is the real thorn in developing friendly relations with India though this is not the reality. The fact that the Kashmir dispute is being given religious overtones exposes the real intentions of Pakistan in seeking a long term relationship with India. Further, perpetuating the 'two-nation theory', wreaking vengeance for the dismemberment of erstwhile East Pakistan to give birth to Bangladesh – all these and more are built into the Pakistani plans in Kashmir.

What is going on in J&K is not an insurgency situation; it is a regular war. It is not even a proxy war. The whole game plan of Pakistan stands exposed. The involvement of the local people, if at all it is there, is very minimal. The core elements that are fighting are from outside India and are perpetrating violent activities with the active and open support of the Pakistani Administration.

We are dealing practically with a regular, large scale, organized military action by foreign elements against us and on our soil. We have to take this to its logical end. We have to deal with it in a straightforward manner and crush it as we would in a war. We should make sure these elements are eliminated and driven out of the country without any further loss of time. Government's policies, especially its directives to the Forces that are in the field, should be very clear and consistent with our ultimate objective and the threats we are facing on the ground. One often gets the feeling that the desire of the government is not matched by its willingness to give shape to its desire by enunciating appropriate policies. We seem to be very much bothered about international opinion, which tends to hamper our style.

There is a danger of no one taking us seriously unless we act decisively and in time to safeguard our security interests. Such action should be swift and result-oriented. What directives do you feel should the government give to the security forces?

First of all, we should make sure that terrorist activities which are taking place are not fought on our soil. We should contain them on the border or across the border. To do so is logical since the threat to the country is emanating from the other side of the border – in terms of moral, physical, material and political support by the ISI, Pakistan Army and the Administration of Pakistan. So we should have a policy which would make sure that the infiltration is stopped right at the border at all costs. Further, if required, we should not hesitate to go across the border and demolish all the infrastructure and logistics that promote terrorism on our soil; after all, Pakistan is openly supporting terrorist activities within India. We know where the bases are. We have to act. We have waited and pondered for far too long – more than a decade and half. There seems to be significant change in militancy in Kashmir in terms of the weapons used and the targets chosen. The target is well chosen either to have a political or military significance.

The militancy phase in Kashmir has passed long ago. For quite some time now, it has been a proxy war. It is a war by foreigners on our soil. Therefore, political aspects should not be allowed to dilute our efforts to deal with the terrorists. Our security forces, whether army or paramilitary, should act firmly and should not bother about the political consequences. After all, there can be no politics when the territorial integrity of the country is threatened. At the same time, what is important is for the political leadership, comprising all shades of political opinion, to see reason in a consensus to act on these lines. Without such a backing it will be difficult for the security forces to act on their own. The paramilitary forces have to fight the terrorists and prevent them from disturbing the peace and order. If this is not done, the normal life of people will be affected adversely and the effectiveness of the Administration to look after the welfare of the people will be considerably weakened. In contrast, it is the responsibility of the political and other streams of the society to deal with terrorism. It is important to recognize the subtle difference between 'terrorists' and 'terrorism'.

The sources and brains, besides all kinds of support – physical, financial, logistics etc., etc., are located across the border. The Army and the Border Security Force (BSF) which man the borders with Pakistan will naturally have a major role to play. If they do not contain the intruders at the border, the local population will become, whether wittingly or unwittingly, victims. This will bring in its wake, issues of human rights and is bound to divert the attention of the security forces from their operational priorities. Everything is already there – the unified command etc. The Army, which is equipped to cater for higher capabilities, should augment the efforts of the local police and the various paramilitary forces deployed on the ground. It is perhaps necessary to highlight the fact that we have got used to clubbing all kinds of forces as 'paramilitary'. In fact, the capability, capacity, organization, training, professional skills and structure vary widely among the various non-military organizations like the BSF, ITBPF, CRPF, CISF etc.

Therefore, it is necessary that while utilizing them, each of these forces should be tasked strictly according to their inbuilt capability and capacity. These forces are not interchangeable as seems to be impression generally prevailing.

In terms of actual day to day support, there is no problem – they are being supported. But we have allowed the proxy war to prolong too long. The decision to curb and finish the proxy war should be taken at the political level. The ceasefire is basically for the benefit of the people and is not for those perpetrating activities against the country. If it has benefited the people then the ceasefire is justified. This does not mean that we will give a free run to the foreigners on our soil. There can be no debate about the need to uphold human-rights. But the rules should be the same for all, including those who are waging a war against the country. Human rights standards should be enforced not only on the security forces but also on all those anti-Indian elements who come inside and engage in killing and injuring innocent people.

The rules of the game in Kashmir should be like when you fight a war. Unfortunately, civilians are being affected – no doubt, but this is no more a civilian situation. There is a need to protect the security forces as you would protect them in a war. Any measure which discourages or impairs the security forces will tell upon their ability to counter the ongoing proxy war and therefore, their ability to protect the territorial integrity of the country. It is good to quote Lord Denning, the famous Lord Chief Justice of England: "the freedom of the individual must take second place to the security of the State".

The steps the government should take for tackling the proxy war in Kashmir should include the following:

— First, they have to be very firm in dealing with the foreign elements.

— Second, they should not allow religion to be brought in. There is an old saying – "if you do not win an argument, attack with the butt end of the gun". Here the butt end of the gun is religion. Kashmir has been secular. Any attempt to poison the Kashmiris on religious grounds should be repulsed.

— Third, we need to ensure that the government is fully responsive to public needs. We should keep the people on our side. Fourth, we should make sure that all sections of the population in Jammu and Kashmir are able to participate in the elections and the benefits of democracy are available to all.

There is nothing wrong in letting them to observe the elections whenever they are held. However, we should leave the decision on this matter to the Election Commission. They should ensure that only independent and apolitical persons and organizations are allowed to be observers.

On the various solutions suggested – trifurcation, conversion of LoC into an international border. It goes against the spirit of India. By trifurcation, we are talking about Hindu-majority, Muslim-majority and Buddhist-majority areas. It is against the secular credentials of India. We have to look at Jammu and Kashmir as one entity and deal with it on that basis. On converting the LoC into an international border, perhaps it is the most plausible and desirable way of dealing with the problem which has evaded any solution for over fifty years. But we have to create conditions which are conducive for taking such a step. We have to educate the people on both sides of the border. Pakistan's claim that Kashmir is the core issue has never been consistent. On 12 April 1999, Gen. Musharraf said that he considered India to be a hegemonic power and low intensity conflict with India would continue even if the Kashmir issue was resolved. Further, at Agra, he made it clear that Pakistani action in Kargil, which was related to its Kashmir policy, flows from its desire to avenge what happened in December 1971. So, the policy of the Pakistani Army establishment in Kashmir flows from its desire to destabilize the secular plural body politic of India. It is simply using the developments in Kashmir to achieve its larger aim stemming from its compulsive hostility towards India.

The drive for deweaponization within Pakistan has not got anything to do with the mutually reinforcing nexus between the ISI on the one hand and the terrorist organizations like the Lashkar-e-Toiba, Jaish-e-Mohammed and Harkat-ul-Mujahideen on the other. This nexus also has its own linkages with the Taliban. All these have to be viewed as a single entity. The much talked about deweaponization drive by the Musharraf regime is basically targeted against organisations involved in sectarian violence. There is naturally apprehension among the Shias in Pakistan that this will be directed more against them rather than the Sunni groups. It had therefore not met with success so far. The numbers of weapons surrendered are marginal and meaningless. A mutually reinforcing nexus exists between the ISI and these groups. There is no question whether the ISI can control these groups; they are armed and trained by the ISI. It provides them with staging areas to cross into India and operational details of how they should operate once they cross into India. It provides them with info on assets and safe houses once they are inside. If such assistance is not provided, we can eliminate them as soon as they cross the Line of Control. So there is no question of the Jehadi groups operating independently of the ISI. They are fully hand in glove with the ISI.

It is very difficult for any state to govern efficiently and carry out developmental programs in the light of persisting insurgency. This is an inevitable consequence of violence perpetrated from outside. Now that elections to panchayats have been held, we need to identify imaginative means to see that developmental funds reach the people. There needs to be enhanced interaction between the Centre, that provides the funds, the State Government, that implements it, the security forces, and the newly elected panchayat leaders at grassroots level. Agra summit was a sincere effort made by the Indian government to see whether an agreement could be reached with Pakistan on a number of issues. India did make such efforts in the past - Shimla and Lahore – to engage Pakistan. India will continue the dialogue with Pakistan. As far as Kashmir is concerned, the violence that is being witnessed is due to cross border terrorism. Pakistan is not indirectly involved in abetting the violence but directly. People of Kashmir lost faith in militancy by 1993-94, after which Pakistan started sending trained Pakistani and Afghan nationals who were called guest militants.

The first round of these guest militants was unorganized, which did not make them popular among the people. As a result militancy declined in 1995-96. Elections were held for the State Assembly of Jammu and Kashmir. After this period, Pakistan converted the militancy into a jehad. It made the Hizbul Mujahideen a front-line organization, but the Pakistani mercenaries do most of the actual fighting. Militancy in Kashmir, in terms of targets and techniques, seems to have undergone a change. How to tackle militancy effectively? What measures need to be taken at the military level? Today, the security forces are being primarily targeted. Besides, civilians who are against Pakistan, persons belonging to the Village Defence Committees, political leaders belonging to National Conference and the surrendered militants are also being targeted by the jehadis and pro-Pakistan militant groups. Most of the Kashmiris, who are aiding the militants, are doing so out of fear. This fear needs to be removed and we should take strong action, especially against the mercenaries.

The Jammu and Kashmir Police needs to be provided better training. One should remember that the police personnel are living in the towns and their families are exposed to mercenaries. We should focus primarily on development projects in Kashmir. Education in the state is free upto university level. But there are no job opportunities for them. Job opportunities should be created. If adequate opportunities cannot be created inside the State, then efforts should be made to employ them outside the State. On the administrative side – there are many dedicated young administrators in the state. A determined and sincere effort to improve the state administration, and provision for more resources would improve the situation considerably.

A number of solutions have been suggested – Regional autonomy, trifurcation, conversion of LoC into international border. What steps should the government adopt? Trifurcation of the state is not acceptable to the people of the state. But within the state there is scope for devolution, which need to be given. More autonomy for Jammu and Kashmir will psychologically help the Kashmiris; hence the government should take steps in this direction. Conversion of LoC into international border is broadly accepted, and may become inevitable.

The Pant Mission has initiated the basic framework for a dialogue with the Kashmiris. This should have been initiated much earlier. A lot of time has been lost. But it is still worthwhile to have a person at a high level dealing with political affairs in Kashmir. There are a number of groups in Kashmir that need to be engaged. The Pant mission should basically consult a wide range of groups and make recommendations on the relationship between the Union government and Kashmiris. The mission should also attempt to define who should be involved in determining the above-mentioned relationship with the Centre. The APHC is incoherent and greatly divided. It would be better if a clear leadership emerged in the APHC. But the Union Government should not do anything in this regard. That would be self-defeating. At this stage, the Union

Government should avoid showing any preference in dealing with the numerous leaders belonging to the APHC.

India should engage the APHC and resist any temptation to split or delegitimise it. The APHC should be allowed to travel to Pakistan. New Delhi should have done this a long time ago. India is a liberal country and must allow the APHC to travel to Pakistan. The APHC's going to Pakistan may result in its finding out Pakistan's actual position on Kashmir. There is also every possibility of the differences between the APHC and the militants coming out into the open. All this is necessary for the peace process to move forward. India is too strong for the APHC, and if the Indian government is afraid of this group, then the case is already lost. Allowing it to go to Pakistan would increase the prestige of India at the international level, not derogate from it.

The governance issue in Jammu and Kashmir is not worse than any other state in India. Like all other states, Jammu and Kashmir also suffers from corruption, a bad work culture, lack of leadership, etc. Obviously all these should be remedied, as anywhere else in India. The violence in Kashmir makes good governance even more difficult. Curbing the violence is therefore the core issue. Grievances in Jammu and Kashmir can be redressed only by giving the people of the state more autonomy. Regional autonomy is one part of the autonomy issue, and this needs to be worked out to the satisfaction of all people in Jammu and Kashmir. The criticism that providing regional autonomy would communalize the State is politically motivated and is not correct. All over India there have been a number of instances in which such measures have been taken.

On the question of State autonomy, Center-State relations must revert roughly to the 1950 position. The State may choose to maintain some structures such as the Chief Election Commission and jurisdiction of the national judiciary. Article 370 needs to be honoured in its original form. This would increase the confidence of the Kashmiris in the Center.

Plebiscite as a solution is difficult. Had India used the plebiscite option in 1948, it would have gone in favour of India. There are a number of problems in holding a plebiscite. What are the modalities? What would be a decisive result (e.g. fifty-one percent, sixty percent, or seventy-five percent of the verdict)? Who would vote in the plebiscite – Kashmiris, Jammuites, people in Pakistan Occupied Kashmir? Who would conduct the plebiscite? What questions need to be asked? And, can an effective plebiscite be held? Given these factors, a plebiscite is not the answer.

Index